Transforming
Big Pharma

To Diane Hélène Ansell

Transforming Big Pharma

Assessing the Strategic Alternatives

JOHN ANSELL

Routledge
Taylor & Francis Group

LONDON AND NEW YORK

First published in paperback 2024

First published 2013 by Gower Publishing

Published 2016 by Routledge
4 Park Square, Milton Park, Abingdon, Oxon OX14 4RN

and by Routledge
605 Third Avenue, New York, NY 10158

Routledge is an imprint of the Taylor & Francis Group, an informa business

British Library Cataloguing in Publication Data.
A catalogue record for this book is available from the British Library.

The Library of Congress has cataloged the printed edition as follows:
Ansell, John, 1947–
Transforming big pharma: assessing the strategic alternatives / by John Ansell.
   pages cm
Includes bibliographical references and index.
ISBN 978-1-4094-4827-3 (hardcover: alk. paper)—ISBN 978-1-4094-4828-0 (ebook)—ISBN 978-1-4724-0364-3 (epub)
1. Pharmaceutical industry—Management. 2. Strategic planning. I. Title.

HD9665.5.A574 2013
338.4'76151--dc23

               2013006115

ISBN: 978-1-4094-4827-3 (hbk)
ISBN: 978-1-03-283733-8 (pbk)
ISBN: 978-1-315-55013-8 (ebk)

DOI: 10.4324/9781315550138

Contents

List of Figures

List of Tables

List of Abbreviations

ACRO	Association of Clinical Research Organizations
AIDS	Acquired Immune Deficiency Syndrome
API	Active Pharmaceutical Ingredient
BRIC	Brazil, Russia, India and China
CEO	Chief Executive Officer
CFAST	Coalition For Accelerating Standards and Therapies
CMO	Contract Marketing Organization
CNS	Central Nervous System
CRO	Contract Research Organization
CTTI	Clinical Trials Transformation Initiative
DTC	Direct to Consumer
EMA	European Medicines Agency
EphMRA	European Pharmaceutical Market Research Association
FDA	Food and Drug Administration
FDAAA	FDA Amendment Act
FMCG	Fast-Moving Consumer Goods
GCP	Good Clinical Practice
HTS	High Throughput Screening
ICD	International Classification of Diseases
LDC	Least Developed Countries
LPLD	Lipoprotein Lipase Deficiency
M&A	Mergers & Acquisitions
NBER	National Bureau of Economic Research
NCE	New Chemical Entity
NDA	New Drug Approval
OTC	Over the Counter
PAH	Pulmonary Arterial Hypertension
PBM	Pharmacy Benefit Managing Company
PCAST	President's Council of Advisors on Science and Technology
PhRMA	Pharmaceutical Research and Manufacturers of America

PTSC　　　　Predictive Safety Testing Consortium
R&D　　　　Research & Development
REMS　　　Risk Evaluation and Mitigations Strategies
SCID　　　Severe Combined Immunodeficiency
SWOT　　　Strengths, Weaknesses, Opportunities and Threats

Acknowledgements

As you may imagine, with my surname I never object to the of use of alphabetical order. Here, I begin by thanking my wife Diane in particular for her work on the indexing and other compilation work for this book. And whilst mentioning the family, I wish to thank in particular our relatives in Belgium, Pierre Depiesse and Jacqueline Depiesse-Ausloos, for use of their house at Profondeville as a writer's retreat in the summer of 2012, and for providing an atmosphere conducive to writing.

Thanks also to my former colleague at Glaxo, Stephen Appelbee, for alerting me to what turned out to be crucial new material. Also to Dr John Arrowsmith, Scientific Director, Thomson Reuters, for bringing to my notice additional data published by his organization.

My twice ex-colleague from Glaxo as well as Fisons days, Jeremy Chancellor, kindly brought me up-to-date on his speciality, health economics, and likely developments stemming from this.

Ian Lloyd, Citeline Editorial Director, cooperated in clarifying the last elusive figure from a valuable recent published report based in the Pharmaprojects® Citeline R&D database, which allowed me to complete calculations on new product productivity. I also want to thank him here for previous collaborations on publications stretching over a dozen years.

I wish to acknowledge EphMRA for permission to show an extract from its 2012 Anatomical Classification Guidelines in Figure 1.3.

I am grateful to Jonathan Norman, editorial director, Gower Publishing, for suggesting the title of this book, and for his friendly and constructive guidance at the outset. That attitude has run through all my dealings with his colleagues at Gower in the production of this book: Chris Muddiman, Fiona Martin, Kathy Bond Borie and Maureen Lazenby, with whom it has been a pleasure to work.

I also wish to thank in particular the staff of two London libraries who have helped me to delve into the many topics I have needed to cover. They are the staff of the Business 1, Science 2 and Science 3 reading rooms at the British Library, St Pancras, and of the Information Centre of the King's Fund, Cavendish Square, all of whom have been unfailing in assisting me in tracking down sources.

I have been struck whilst writing this book by the sheer number of freely accessible, detailed and in the main good quality reports on pharmaceuticals that are now being published. The sources include industry associations and economic research bodies as well as providers of a wide variety of industry services. These include investors, data providers and consultancies. I would also single out the journal *Nature Reviews Drug Discovery* as essential reading in interpreting the commercial aspects of pharma R&D. All these sources have enabled me to explore issues to a greater extent than I had imagined possible at the outset.

Whilst I benefited from the help of all of the above, the opinions expressed in this book do of course remain my responsibility.

John Ansell
Thame, Oxfordshire
January 2013

About the Author

Since 1989 John Ansell has been a pharmaceutical industry consultant based in Thame, near Oxford, UK. He has advised over 150 clients (www.johnansell.com). He has worked with many major pharmaceutical companies and advises companies of all sizes including start-ups, as well as those providing services to the industry and those investing in it. He also has served as an expert witness in legal cases. Most of his projects are international, commercial and strategic, reflecting his previous industry experience in marketing and business development.

Ansell received an honours biochemistry degree from Liverpool University and a Master's degree in business studies from Sheffield University. He started his 20-year pharma company career in Holland with Organon. He subsequently worked for Schering AG and Fisons in the UK, and again in Holland, with Solvay. From 1985 to 1989 he worked in international marketing in the UK for Glaxo Holdings.

Since 2012 Ansell has been gaining an additional perspective on the industry as a senior partner at the contract research organization TranScrip Partners.

Ansell was a long-standing member of the Editorial Advisory Board of the US journal *Pharmaceutical Executive* (1990–2002), served on the Editorial Board of *the Journal of Biotechnology in Healthcare* (1994–98) and also was Chairman of the Advisory Board of Decision Resources Inc. (2005–06). Since 2007 he has been an honorary consultant to the University of Manchester School of Pharmacy and Pharmaceutical Sciences.

Ansell has served as chairman at well over 30 pharmaceutical conferences over the past 25 years, on a wide range of topics, including biotechnology, R&D, business development and licensing, technology transfer, due diligence, marketing, promotion, pricing, life-cycle management and corporate governance.

He also has been a frequent speaker at industry conferences in Europe, the US and Japan.

Over the past eight years Ansell has run many courses and workshops on pharma marketing and business development. He also has contributed to still-current distance learning programmes on these topics. The experience of running courses for pharma audiences has been important in formulating ideas for this book.

Ansell is married with four sons and in his leisure time he plays tennis and runs teams.

Introduction

Nearly everybody now active in the pharmaceutical industry will have spent most or all of their career in a climate of long-term decline in R&D productivity, which has been in progress now for over 30 years.

For longer than most commentators expected, that declining number of new products continued to support growth levels of the pharmaceutical industry way above those of the global economy. But it became clear several years ago that there would come a point where the trickle of new products reaching the market would no longer offset those reaching patent expiry. It is big pharma – the Top 20 global pharmaceutical companies by global sales – which stands to feel this ultimate impact most severely. It is therefore big pharma whose strategies and practices are more likely to need transforming than any other players in pharmaceuticals. Nevertheless, much of what I propose in this book to transform big pharma will also apply to medium-sized and smaller pharmaceutical companies. There are implications, too, for biotechs and start-up companies.

In anticipation of the impending peak in patent expires in 2011–13, big pharma in particular has been forced since the early years of this century to consider alternative means of bolstering sales and profits. Consequently over the past few years there has been an increase in the range of strategies pursued by big pharma. This has sharply contrasted with the previous two decades during which companies focussed down on their pharmaceutical activities, progressively discarding any activities that did not fit that description.

We have thus begun to see many big pharma companies venturing into areas outside mainstream prescription pharmaceuticals. Often this appears experimental in nature, with exploratory dabbling in a variety of directions: generics, biosimilars, developing territories, OTC and so on. It is, however, not at all clear that these various efforts to diversify are going to make a big impact in offsetting deficits in revenues – or, more to the point, on profits.

At the same time there has been a widespread perception that the existing model for operating a pharmaceutical company is broken, and a search – so far, I believe, fruitless – for 'a new business model'. If the existing model is broken then it follows, proponents believe, that everything must need changing, the more radically the better.

As Daniel Hoffman of Pharmaceutical Business Research Associates has colourfully put it: 'A wide range of advertising gurus, global consultants and self-styled wise men has offered "new paradigmatic approaches," most of which amount to hollow ambiguities. Their suggestions include admonitions to "listen to your customers" and "lose the obsessive control over messaging," as well as an array of familiar tactics under new-fangled names' (Hoffman 2011). I will elaborate on this current climate of management change extensively within this book.

But first, to set the scene, some long-term perspective. As I mentioned above, the global growth rate of the pharmaceutical industry rate is now much less than at its peak (Figure I.1). However, the pharmaceutical industry continues in most years to grow at two to three times the rate of the rest of industry.

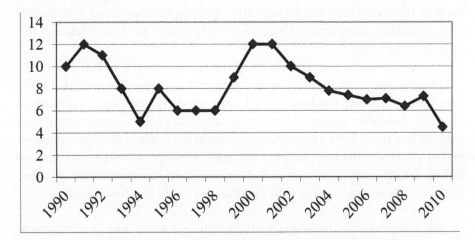

Figure I.1   Pharma industry annual global growth rates (per cent)
Source: John Ansell Consultancy based on *Scrip & Scrip Magazine* Annual Reviews (1991–2003) and IMS Pressroom data (2003–12) (*Scrip & Scrip Magazine* 1991–2003; IMS 2012d)

How bad have things become for pharmaceuticals? In December 2011 one dispassionate observer, the ratings agency Fitch, considered that the pharmaceutical industry was in relatively good shape – at least when compared with other industries: 'Despite the continued operating headwinds in 2012, global pharmaceuticals is expected to remain one of Fitch's highest-rated industries' (Grogan 2011b).

Fitch produced a whole list of positive factors to support this: 'This is due to its superior cash flow generation, large cash balances, strong liquidity and solid growth prospects', which were driven by 'high unmet medical need, favourable demographics, technological advances and the persistence of chronic diseases.'

Why should the pharmaceutical industry performance have way outstripped that of other industries for so long? There are several reasons why there has been an ever-increasing demand for healthcare treatment, and most of these will continue to apply in future:

- General population growth – in particular, strong growth in the industry's key market, the United States.

- Greater awareness of consumers of treatment – aided by the Internet in particular. Also, today's consumers are much more educated than previous generations – and much more able than previous generations to get to grips with medicine.

- More demanding consumers, related to better education and greater articulacy in arguing for their rights for healthcare than previous generations.

- An increasingly aging populations, with the elderly accounting for a very significant share of total healthcare costs (IMS 2012a).

- The often greater cost-effectiveness of pharmaceuticals in comparison with other types of healthcare cost.

- The increasing availability of new and often expensive therapies, adding to or supplanting existing cheaper therapies.

But the current global financial crisis has made even more difficult the predicament of many big pharma companies. The aim of this book is to propose how in the current state of flux, big pharma can best pilot its way through the current crisis and transform its prospects.

I believe that the search for a single new business model is naïve, and that in any case, different big pharma companies need rather different strategies. The reality is that – just like life in general – managing a company is a much more complex task than many simplistic management philosophies would have us believe.

The pharmaceutical industry is often criticized – by insiders as well as outsiders – for not being open enough to new ideas from outside the industry, or of being slow to adopt them. In this book I suggest that whilst being open to new ideas is certainly healthy, it is folly to adopt new ideas uncritically. It wastes a great deal of effort and resources when – as more often than not – a new concept is taken up by a company, to be rejected before very long as unworkable or impractical. In my view companies should therefore be devoting much more effort to assessing what is likely to work and what will not. I will also suggest several concepts and practices which should be dropped by big pharma or radically modified.

In this book I critically assess concepts from general management theory that have been widely adopted and retained by the pharmaceutical industry. I go on to assess temporary enthusiasms within the pharmaceutical industry. Remarkably, some of these enthusiasms, like the current one of big pharma for generics, are cyclical: they come round every decade or so, apparently regardless of their success. I explain why it is that companies do not necessarily learn from negative experiences and avoid the enormous cost of readopting failed strategies, sometimes more than once.

Then there are similar but actually quite different opportunities to generics, like biosimilars. How much of an opportunity for big pharma are such opportunities? Could biosimilars be more of an opportunity for other types of companies?

I go on to argue that the light at the end of the tunnel for big pharma is not that far off. As I explain, there are firm grounds to expect an upturn in new product approvals shortly, given encouraging increases in the number of advanced-stage projects in R&D. I also show how the pharmaceutical industry commonly underestimates the commercial potential of those new products which do become successes.

What are the implications of all this for big pharma? Which formerly successful strategies would it make sense to revive? And when will new ones have to be employed?

A common theme running through this book is time. The quarter century timescale for developing and exploiting a successful new product creates particular difficulties for those employed in the industry – particularly given that they may well spend only a few years in each position they hold. My own career in the pharmaceutical industry started within a few months of the end of the 1960s as an advertising copywriter in Holland with the Dutch company Organon. It continued for 20 years, mainly in international marketing and business development. In all I worked for five different pharmaceutical companies, with a second spell in the Netherlands, but otherwise in my home country of the United Kingdom.

When I began my career, it was still an era dominated by the consequences of the thalidomide disaster. In the late 1950s and early 1960s over 10,000 children whose mothers took this drug to prevent morning sickness were born with phocomelia – birth defects affecting the limbs. This led to the introduction during the 1960s and 1970s of modern regulatory requirements internationally, and a consequent increase in development time and costs for pharmaceuticals. The seeds were sown which before long led to the long-term decline in the number of new products reaching the market.

Since the end of the 1980s I have spent over 20 years working as an independent business consultant to pharmaceutical companies of all shapes and sizes, to biotech companies and to companies of many descriptions serving the pharmaceutical industry. These have included contract sales force companies, training companies and investors in the industry.

As time has gone on, the range of activities involved in the ever-more difficult task of developing new products and then marketing them has grown. For nearly a year now I have been heavily involved with one of the growing phenomena of the pharmaceutical industry – outsourcing, as a senior partner at the contract research company TranScrip Partners. This is giving me further perspectives on the industry.

I have come to believe that there are often good reasons for the needs of the pharmaceutical industry to be treated differently to industry in general. To move quickly to the point as to why the pharmaceutical industry behaves at it does, I first discuss the ways it is different to other industries.

PART I

How Pharma Differs and Why This Is Important

How Pharma Differs

What is long life for a corporation – 100 years? Two hundred years? Defined legally as a person, modern public corporations don't live very long. Most expire within 25 to 50 years. A few of the best ones survive for more than a century.

Daniel Pascheles and Christopher Bogan, Merck & Co/
Best Practices, LLC, 2012

Countless numbers of new management concepts are offered to industry each year. The majority are never adopted or are soon proven to be inadequate. Sometimes this applies regardless of industry type but this is not necessarily the case. Occasionally there are concepts which seem to apply particularly well to some industries, and there are examples which I shall mention in this book for pharmaceuticals. Far more commonly, management concepts sold across the board turn out to be particularly unworkable in some industries. Again, there are plenty of examples in pharmaceuticals which I shall also go into. But new concepts more often fall down for a particular industry because of its inherent characteristics.

Only some eight years ago, when I was first putting together courses providing a general introduction to the pharmaceutical industry, did I hit upon the importance of defining its distinctive characteristics at the outset. There was no ready reference which I could use – and so I set out to develop the material myself. As I gained more experience in giving these courses, I began to realize how many misconceptions about the industry – from insiders as well as outsiders – could be prevented if these basic characteristics of the pharmaceutical industry were explained at the outset.

Since I was to give my first course to a group of accountants at a company in Switzerland, I decided to start with a cost breakdown of the pharmaceutical industry. That proved to be a sound basis for steering the participants in the right direction and avoiding misapprehensions about the pharmaceutical industry. It has become a feature of the opening sections of this course ever since. And so I also make it my starting point in this book.

The Pharmaceutical Company Cost Structure

Dr Barrie James (2003) produced the following typical breakdown of costs for the pharmaceutical industry expressed as a percentage of sales revenue:

R&D	16.5%
Cost of goods	13.2%
Sales & marketing	35.0%
General & administrative	8.0%
Total	72.7%
Hence margin:	27.3%

Let's look at these areas of cost one by one:

R&D COSTS

In major pharmaceutical companies, R&D accounts on average for the equivalent of around 16 per cent of sales revenue. This is the highest percentage for any industry by far. It reflects two associated factors: the long duration of the pharma R&D process, which I shall address later in this chapter, (see pp. 17–19) and the complex and demanding nature of regulatory requirements.

Critics of the pharmaceutical industry sometimes urge it to spend much more of its resources on R&D (see also p. 12). Yet it spends far more as a percentage of sales than any other industry. The 2012 EU Industrial Scoreboard measures R&D expenditure across industries for the Top 1,000 companies globally. (The 2012 EU Industrial R&D Scoreboard.)

This R&D Scoreboard showed that the *Pharmaceuticals and biotechnology* industry spent the equivalent of 15.1 per cent of sales on R&D. This was more than half as much again as the second-ranked industry, *Software & computer services*, which spent 9.5 per cent. Only one other industry, *Technology hardware & equipment*, spent anywhere near as much, with 7.9 per cent. All of the 35 other industries covered spent less than 7 per cent and 30 of them spent less than 4 per cent.

Another indicator of the importance of pharmaceutical R&D is its share of total R&D expenditure conducted by all industries. The R&D Scoreboard showed that no less than 17.7 per cent of all global R&D was accounted for by the pharmaceutical industry. This was just ahead of *Technology hardware & equipment* (16.8 per cent) and *Automobiles & parts* (15.8 per cent). Also , the R&D Scoreboard report gave rankings of the Top 1,000 global companies by absolute R&D expenditure. In 2012 no less than seven pharmaceutical and biotech companies appeared in the Top 20 highest spending companies. *Automobiles and parts* accounted for another six, these two industries therefore dominating these rankings. In the upper reaches of the rankings four pharmaceutical companies, Novartis, Pfizer, Roche and Merck & Co all appeared in the Top 10 companies, more than any other industry.

MANUFACTURING COSTS

Pharmaceutical manufacturing is not labour intensive like many other industries. In pharmaceuticals manufacturing costs are typically equivalent to only 10–15 per cent of sales. For new products, which are usually relatively highly priced, the figure is often well under 10 per cent and sometimes as low as 5 per cent. This means that manufacturing is much less at the forefront of company management priorities than it is in many other manufacturing industries. It is uncommon, for example, that the director of manufacturing has a seat on the main board, or if that is the case, it is normally in combination with other responsibilities.

Traditionally, pharmaceutical companies had a rather cavalier attitude to pharmaceutical costs. This was because costs were not considered the main priority. In developing a new production process for a forthcoming product, it is far more pressing that perfection of the process be on time to avoid delaying launch. Every month's delay can cost millions of dollars in lost revenue. Before pharmaceutical companies began to become cost conscious across the board some 10–15 years ago, manufacturing cost considerations were therefore not an important issue. Concepts such as 'quality by design' and continuous manufacturing are now gradually being introduced to benefit quality as well as ultimately reducing costs.

SALES AND MARKETING COSTS

The pharmaceutical industry and in particular some industry associations have often tended to be coy in their representation of sales and marketing costs. They have presumably feared criticism if they fully stated these costs. Sometimes figures as low as 20 per cent of sales have been suggested for this cost area.

In reality the figure is much higher than this. Look at a handful of big pharma company accounts and you will find that the equivalent of about 35 per cent of sales turnover is commonly accounted for by marketing and sales costs. Some companies with a preponderance of specialist products who therefore do not have to employ mass GP sales forces may spend a smaller percentage than this.

As mentioned above, critics of the pharmaceutical industry often complain at the high percentage of sales spent on marketing, and propose that the industry should spend less on marketing and sales and more on R&D. Yet across all industries, marketing costs typically amount to 35–40 per cent of a product's selling price according to a PricewaterhouseCoopers Global Best Practices report for 2005.[1] Thus pharmaceuticals is very much in line with other industries.

GENERAL AND ADMINISTRATIVE COSTS

Dr Barrie James cited a figure of 8 per cent for general and administrative costs. Often in US company accounts, sales and general and administrative costs are combined. James gives a figure of 43 per cent for this (James 2003).

NET MARGIN

What remains is the net margin. In the pharmaceutical industry the figure is typically 25–30 per cent. This is higher than for most other industries – and far higher than for many. At one time – though not so commonly in the past 20 years – this impressive net margin level attracted companies from outside the pharmaceutical industry to enter it. But, as most of these companies found, pharmaceuticals is also a relatively high-risk industry. And the high level of risk has often proved too uncomfortable for new entrants to persist for very

---

1   The Global Best Practices report for this year is no longer freely available at: http://www.globalbestpractices.com.

long (see p. 57). Established pharma companies are more used to though not necessarily comfortable with the high risk – high gain environment.

I deal in more detail later with barriers to entry for potential newcomers to the pharmaceutical industry (see pp. 53–9).

COST CONSEQUENCES OF THE TREND TO BIOLOGICALS

The cost percentages discussed above are for traditional, small molecule products. Over the past decade there has been a trend towards biologicals, that is, large molecule products. The figures that apply to large molecules are different in several important respects.

Taking *R&D* costs first, there is no good evidence that large molecule products are any more or less expensive to develop than small molecules. Thus the standard percentage of around 16 per cent still applies.

However, the cost of goods is often considerably greater than the 10–15.2 per cent for small molecules. Large molecule biologicals are more difficult and hence more expensive to manufacture.

On the other hand, *sales and marketing* costs can be very much lower with large molecule biological products. This is because in the main biologicals are not mass-market pharmaceuticals prescribed by general practitioners (GPs); they are purely specialist or, at least, specialist-oriented products. As the numbers of each type of specialist doctor are far less than of general practitioners – for example in the United States often a few thousand rather than tens of thousands – the cost of promoting a large molecule product to a few or sometimes just one specialist target group is very much less than is the case for a mass GP product. Thus, rather than the 35 per cent of sales which is the norm for small-molecule, GP-oriented products, the figure for a large molecule specialist product can be 10 per cent or less. Another factor depressing the percentage here is that the price of specialist-oriented products tends to be far higher than for mass GP products.

Regarding the remaining cost area, *general and administrative*, there is no difference between small and large molecule.

But the costs aggregate to a much lower total percentage for large than for small molecule products. Rather than a margin of 25–30 per cent for small molecules, a figure of around 50 per cent is the norm for large molecules. Companies such as Roche were trend setters in switching their emphasis in the early years of this century from small to large molecules. With only a limited number of small products worthy of promotion, Roche was one of the first to disband its large GP sales forces and concentrate instead on promoting its growing range of hospital- and specialist-oriented products.

To focus more on large molecules products is now an aim of the majority of big pharma companies. Though still representing a minority of all products, the number of biologicals is increasing, and this is becoming possible for more companies. However, as I show later there has recently been some reversal of this trend (see pp. 42–3).

CONCLUSIONS ON COST

When an outsider without a pharmaceutical background is appointed as company doctor to sort out a pharma company in distress, the first thought is usually to cut costs. For most industries this is a not unreasonable first move. However, unfortunately the scope for reducing costs in pharmaceuticals is much less than it is in most other industries. When Jeffrey Kindler, with a background in General Electric and McDonalds, became chairman of Pfizer in 2006 this was one of his prime aims. But as was already evident, it was R&D productivity rather than costs that were the fundamental problem of Pfizer, and Kindler left the company four years later.

In the light of vastly increasing absolute levels of R&D costs over the past 15 years, various attempts by big pharma over that time to carry out 'smarter' R&D more efficiently and so reduce costs have so far been unconvincing. To cut R&D risks hampering the longer-term future of the company – although it is an option that many companies have in the past couple of years begun to take to protect their shorter-term profits. There is likely to be a longer-term penalty, as I explain later (see pp. 236–7).

With manufacturing there is often scope to reduce costs through disposal of surplus manufacturing capacity (often resulting after mergers and acquisitions) but as manufacturing is not a major cost area, it is unlikely that there will be scope to turn the company around on that basis.

How about marketing costs? It is often tempting to reduce the size of sales forces. But unless there are other factors in play, like the trends mentioned above from small to large molecule products and from GP to specialist products, then this can lead to inadequate support of products.

The sales of Lipitor began to decline several years before patents expired on atorvastatin. Whilst the availability of older, cheap, off-patent statins played its part here, Pfizer's reduction in effort on Lipitor undermined the sales of the product and also allowed a product which was then widely viewed as an unimpressive latecomer, AstraZeneca's Crestor (rosuvastatin), to make steady inroads into its sales. By the time major atorvastatin patents were expiring in 2012, Crestor sales had reached $6.622 billion dollars, it was ranked the seventh best-selling product globally and was still growing strongly, by 17 per cent in that year (see also pp. 76–7, 114).

Unfortunately sales forces remain the most effective medium for promoting products – and still account for over 60 per cent of total promotional expenditure – not much less than in their heyday several years ago. A variety of ploys to replace sales forces have over many years been ineffective. Sooner or later sales forces bounce back. In the US, where detailing by sales representatives had been declining in recent years, IMS data showed an upturn in expenditure on sales forces in 2011 to a level higher than any since 2007 (IMS 2012b). This may well reflect the increased number of new products approved in the US in 2011 (see p. 194). On another front, it is noteworthy that in China, local pharmaceutical companies are busy currently in setting up huge sales forces.

Maximizing Revenue

In pharmaceuticals the best way of pulling out of a crisis is quite different from the conventional company doctor's medicine for other industries: it is to find ways of increasing revenues rather than prioritizing cost reduction. Of course it is easier said than done to identify opportunities within or outside a company which can achieve this.

Schering-Plough was in a parlous position when Fred Hassan joined it as chairman and CEO in 2003. The team he brought in quickly identified opportunities in the late R&D pipeline which could be developed within a few years into major new products. The additional revenues from these new products completely turned the company around.

And so, crudely speaking, success in pharmaceuticals has much more to do with *maximizing revenues* than it does with reducing costs, though that does not rule out the merits of also doing the latter. In pharmaceuticals new products are truly the lifeblood of the industry. Putting a new product on the market is the best way of increasing revenues. This explains why pharmaceutical companies generally make sure that they strive to market products proficiently and adequately. And it also explains why they go to such lengths to gain commercial rights to potential new products. This means that deals – with other companies or with other types of organization party – are much more important in the pharmaceutical industry than they are in most other industries.

Now let's turn to several other features of the pharmaceutical industry which have a big impact on its distinctiveness.

Who Is the Customer?

Although the patient consumes medicines, it is the doctor who prescribes them. Thus there is a disconnect between the (physical) consumer and the prescriber/ immediate decision-maker. It also means that traditionally the primary target, although today by no means the only one for pharmaceutical marketing, is the doctor. Each doctor is primarily responsible for the prescribing of a very considerable quantity of often expensive pharmaceuticals each year.

Because the number of doctors in the general population is relatively limited, it is cost effective for pharmaceutical companies to promote their products very actively through sales forces and other promotional media targeted at doctors: the importance of detailing is a function of the market situation in which it operates.

In 2010 the US pharmaceutical market was worth $307.4 million (Source: IMS 2012b). There were in that year 850,085 licensed physicians in the US (Young et al. 2011). If we divide the first figure by the second, this means that the average expenditure on drugs per US doctor in that year was $362,000.

Thus compared with other industries, pharmaceutical companies have needed to reach only a limited number of targets, whose average expenditure on products is very high. This explains why, in comparison to other industries, it has been cost effective for pharmaceutical companies to spend so much per target.

Of course the situation is now not that simple, because the payer is an increasingly important decision maker. Pharmaceutical companies find themselves needing to devote increasing effort to reaching payers and those influencing them. The new discipline of market access is being increasingly pursued by pharmaceutical companies, as financial considerations increase in importance in the prescribing decision.

There is an increasing need to demonstrate that a product is superior to already available therapies financially as well as clinically. Before a company can begin to make a financial return on a new product, it also has to gain market access. Not only does it have to satisfy regulatory authorities that its new product should be allowed onto markets but it also has to have a strategy for market access so that it is reaching decision makers at all levels who govern use of a product. I deal with this in more detail later (see pp. 71–3).

Constraints on Marketing to the Consumer

With pharmaceuticals there are strict constraints on how and to whom an approved product may be marketed. Thus in most countries there is limited or, more often, no scope for consumer promotion. This means that many consumer product marketing channels and techniques cannot be used in the same way in marketing pharmaceuticals.

Long Development Timescales and Costs

The timescale to develop a product is much longer than applies in most other industries. PhRMA suggests that on average a new product takes 10–15 years to develop. Consumer products by contrast usually take just a few years to develop. The major consequence of such a long development process for new products is that R&D costs are very high for pharmaceuticals in comparison with other industries' products.

The classical figure from the Tufts Center for the Study of Drug Development which has been quoted widely for more than a decade, of $800 million to develop a new product, is now out of date. The equivalent figure today is probably closer to $2 billion. Tufts are shortly to update this figure. The most recent estimate has been by the Office of Health Economics (Mestre-Ferrandiz, Sussex and Towse 2012). Their study published in December

2012 estimated that the average cost of developing a new product is, at 2011 prices, $1.506 million.

Particularly expensive is the most advanced phase, Phase III, of clinical trials, which cost more than any other development phase: 27 per cent, according to a detailed analysis by Paul et al. (2010). Companies think twice about putting borderline projects through Phase III because of this high cost of development. They know that in recent years about a third of all projects which have entered Phase III have failed to reach the market (Arrowsmith 2012 and see also pp. 187–8).

The second most expensive phase is the *Preclinical phase*. This has accounted for just under a quarter of total costs in recent years. Since 2010 many companies have begun to cut their R&D budgets. It is preclinical work that has tended to be sacrificed.

A radical recent example is GlaxoSmithKline. In 2011 GlaxoSmithKline's head of R&D, Moncef Slaoui, announced that the company was reducing its total R&D budget from £3.2 billion to £2.8 billion. Whereas GlaxoSmithKline had been spending 60 per cent of its budget on discovery and 40 per cent on development, it would, Dr Slaoui announced, be reversing the emphasis, spending 38 per cent on discovery and 62 per cent on development.

As I will review in detail in Chapter 15 (see pp. 185–95) attrition rates of projects in R&D are high. From the late 1990s for about a decade, several factors contributed to a sharp deterioration in these attrition rates.

Finally, the need to continue to invest in R&D after getting a product onto the market – Phase IV studies – has become increasingly important. This is not so in, say, a consumer product company, which does not generally expect to have to spend significantly on R&D after the product has reached the market. Expenditure in recent years on Phase IV studies has in recent years accounted for just under 10 per cent of total pharma R&D expenditure.

In 2011 the Tufts Center for the Study of Drug Development found that the total number of preclinical and clinical studies globally had risen from 4,900 in 2000 to 8,600 in 2010, an increase of 75 per cent (Tufts CSDD 2011).

Outsider companies attracted by the potentially high rewards to enter pharmaceuticals have often underestimated the extent to which high risk, high investment and long development time apply. It has also not helped their resolve that the situation became increasingly adverse during the first decade of the twenty-first century as R&D costs rocketed.

In the same way, investors in the pharmaceutical industry have commonly failed to appreciate the true timescales involved in developing pharmaceuticals and this has contributed to them losing heart in further investing in the industry. Clayton Christensen, the apostle of creative disruption (see p. 95), has described hedge funds and private equity funds as the big bad actors in the system because they concentrate on shorter-term returns rather than the long term (Comer 2012a).

But pharmaceuticals will never be other than a long-term business. And if the true picture is fully realized this makes it difficult to attract these types of investors back to pharmaceuticals.

Timespan for Marketing

To explain this, I briefly need first to outline how different types of intellectual property protection apply to pharmaceuticals.

INTELLECTUAL PROPERTY PROTECTION

For pharmaceuticals, the key form of intellectual property protection in each country is patent cover. Next to this, market exclusivity is becoming an important form of intellectual property for pharmaceuticals. In Europe now as well as in the US, this may provide significant cover beyond the life of the patent. However, other types of intellectual property such as trademarking and copyright, which are of key importance for consumer products, for example, are not nearly so important with prescription pharmaceuticals.

The standard patent term from filing is 20 years, though various forms of extension are available internationally. Today, market exclusivity quite often extends beyond the term of the last effective patent, particularly in the US. This may give several years of very valuable additional cover.

Once all intellectual property protection has expired, then for most intents and purposes the life of the product as a marketed brand is over. At that point generics can enter the market. This leads to price competition, with a normally sharp fall in price levels, as well as substantial erosion of the market share of the original brand. This is quite different from other industries, where brands can often be maintained over very many years.

This means that pharmaceutical companies make great efforts to maximize revenues whilst they have the chance. They are also prepared to defend intellectual property strongly and go to considerable lengths to extend the life of a product for as long as possible. This explains why pharmaceutical companies feature so prominently in the client lists of many corporate law firms.

When it is clear that exhaustion of all intellectual property rights is imminent, a pharmaceutical company will commonly abandon any further attempts at exploiting its product as it is difficult to defend existing sales once this stage has been reached. Sales of most products decline quite sharply as generic competitors erode them, so that effectively the period of active commercial exploitation of the original brand is over.

HOW THIS AFFECTS THE COMMERCIAL LIFE OF A PRODUCT

The commercial life of a product is therefore not, as has often been simplistically stated, what remains of the patent life after it reaches the market. Since 1994 I have tracked what I term *average longevity*, that is, time to peak sales from first launch. In Figure 1.1 I show global product longevities which I have calculated for the years from 1994 to 2011. In each year I took the Top 50 best-selling global products and calculated average longevity on the basis of time to peak sales (or to current sales levels if a product's sales had yet to obviously peak). I show the detailed method I devised for calculating this in Appendix 1.

Figure 1.1 shows that longevity was around 16–17 years when I first tracked it for the 1990s. When I first presented this data there was widespread disbelief that product longevity was so long. At the time forecasters were assuming five or six years to peak sales – or sometimes even as little as three years. This is because they were focussing on base patent terms, not realizing that other types of intellectual property were increasingly applying – particularly market exclusivity periods and patents on product range extensions. Thereafter the norm for forecasting gradually became 10 years to peak sales, which it still is currently. However, outsiders dealing with forecasts across industries frequently still underestimate longevity in pharmaceuticals.

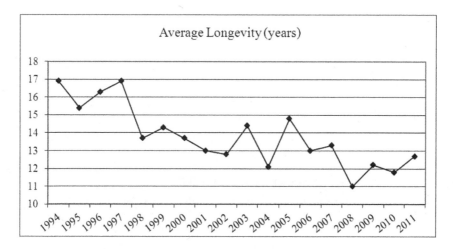

Figure 1.1   Trends in average product longevity 1994–2011
Source: John Ansell Consultancy, based on *Med Ad News* data (*Med Ad News* 1994–2011)

From 1998 for the next decade, it looked as though average longevity was stabilizing at around 13–14 years. This stability may well have prevailed because the quality of products commercially on average held up well, even if there were fewer of them. Since I last reported on longevity in 2011 (Ansell 2011) there appears to have been a slight downward trend – but it is modest. It is insufficient to put at question the standard forecasting assumption of 10 years to peak sales.

Globalization and the Rise of Blockbusters

Those products that did reach the market were from the late 1990s increasingly available across a wide range of countries. Before that time availability of new products could be much more limited. In particular, there were a substantial number of products only made available in Japan up till this time.

With the increased globalization of pharmaceuticals, the number of billion-dollar blockbusters rose sharply, as shown in Figure 1.2. Contrary to received wisdom in the pharmaceutical industry, it is only recently that growth in the numbers of blockbusters showed a downturn for the first time. This happened in 2010, when the number dropped to 118 from 126 the previous year, as widespread patent expiry amongst leading products set in. However, despite the impact of this factor, in 2011 numbers did rather remarkably recover

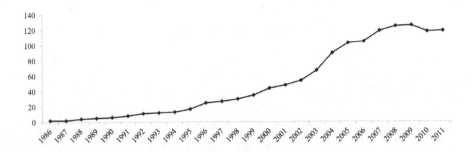

Figure 1.2   Number of blockbusters from 1986

Source: John Ansell Consultancy, based on *Med Ad News* data (*Med Ad News* 1994–2011)

to 119. Thus whatever else its problems are, the pharmaceutical industry does not appear to have lost the art of creating new blockbusters.

Some of the most successful big pharma companies are projecting increases in the number of blockbusters they will be marketing. In November 2012 Novartis, amongst the most successful pharmaceutical companies in recent years, announced that it projected the number of blockbusters in its product range to increase from seven in 2011 to 14 by 2017.

Whatever the future trend in new product productivity – and as I will show in Chapter 14 (see pp. 173–83) this now looks encouraging – it takes time for new products to make a commercial impact. My calculations over the past decade show that it takes on average six years on the market before a product becomes a blockbuster (Ansell 2006).

The Total Lifespan of a Product

Thus from discovery to exhaustion of all intellectual property spans two periods of approximately 10–15 years each, so that the total lifespan of a successful product can be 20–30 years. That is not particularly impressive when compared with other types of products – in particular consumer brands, whose life can, at best, span three centuries.

In conclusion, the onus in pharmaceuticals is therefore on:

- maximization of commercial potential over the period of commercialization;

- extending that period by whatever legal means;

- filing subsidiary patents;

- developing novel presentations (range extensions);

- gaining approval to additional indications;

- and ensuring that intellectual property is thereby extended, whether in the form of new patents or additional market exclusivity. This is termed product life-cycle management. I deal with this in Chapter 4 (see pp. 82–4).

The Role of Marketing in Pharmaceuticals

Just as in other industries, the techniques of marketing are employed in the pharmaceutical industry to satisfy the demands of the consumer. Traditionally, general marketing textbooks concentrate on examples from fast-moving consumer goods (FMCG) markets, the field where marketing was first developed. But there are many differences between FMCG and pharmaceuticals which means that marketing's role in pharmaceuticals is in many ways different. This determines that marketing techniques are applied in a distinctive way in the pharmaceutical industry.

I have already mentioned one of these (see p. 16), the fact that although the patient consumes medicines, it is the doctor who prescribes them. Formerly, pharmaceutical companies did not promote their products to the consumer, and this is still true for most parts of the world. The US is the main exception.

In the US the situation only effectively began to change in 1997, when the Food and Drug Administration (FDA) became more relaxed about the latitude it allowed pharmaceutical companies in marketing their products to the consumer. Apart from New Zealand there are no other countries where this *Direct-to-Consumer* (DTC) marketing has been legally permitted since that time. Also, even where DTC is permitted, pharmaceutical companies are still more limited in the types of information they are allowed to communicate to the patient than what they may convey to the physician.

Despite the development of DTC, the prime target for pharmaceutical marketing remains the doctor. Indeed the popularity of DTC in the US appears past its peak, with audit figures showing dipping expenditure on this medium since 2009.

Meanwhile detailing of doctors by sales representatives still accounts for over 60 per cent of pharmaceutical marketing expenditure in most countries. This medium remains subject to well-defined regulations as well as to industry codes of practice in each major market, of the FDA and PhRMA respectively in the US, and of equivalent bodies in all other developed countries.

Brand Management

Turning to another aspect of marketing, the concept of brand management was invented by Procter & Gamble in the US in 1931. At that time the company was solely active in FMCG and not at that time in prescription pharmaceuticals.

Brand management can be defined as the application of marketing techniques to a specific product, product line or brand. Procter & Gamble developed the brand management concept in marketing its range of FMCGs, for example different brands of soap such as Camay, Palmolive and Ivory. Each brand was the responsibility of a separate marketing team devoted to considering every aspect of marketing that single brand. The Procter & Gamble marketing philosophy directed that each brand should be marketed as if it were a separate business. Effectively, this decentralization of management control acted as a counterbalance to the centralized management system already operated by Procter & Gamble – and practiced by many leading US companies.

With brand management at Procter & Gamble, each brand was differentiated from competitive brands of product – including others it marketed as well as those from competitors such as Unilever. Over the years this concept of product differentiation became a key element of marketing. It included distinctive packaging to differentiate the product from its competitors, a feature that is also applied today in marketing-oriented pharmaceutical companies.

Through its success, brand management became widely adopted by US companies, not only in FMCG but gradually also outside this sector, including by the pharmaceutical industry. The marketing concept also became adopted outside the US, particularly in Europe.

From the 1960s, marketing techniques were accommodated by the majority of major pharmaceutical companies, particularly those in the US, with brand management accepted as a key concept within the marketing philosophy. It became common in the pharmaceutical industry for brand – or more commonly product – managers with genuine commercial rather than just technical responsibility to manage products.

That pharmaceutical companies tended to opt for the title 'product' rather than 'brand' manager is telling. Indeed if the title 'brand manager' was found in a pharmaceutical company, it was usually in the OTC or consumer brand department, indicating the more direct fit there of the FMCG brand concept. But job titles were not the only aspect of marketing where some adaptation of the marketing concept was necessary for prescription pharmaceuticals.

Firstly, as I have discussed above, pharmaceutical brands have a limited life. The principal form of intellectual property cover for pharmaceuticals is patents, whereas for FMCG they are not crucial in the same way. Instead, the intellectual property associated with the brand, including copyright rather than patent cover, is most important. This means that FMCG companies can create and nurture brands with the hope of creating a property with everlasting life – for well over a century so far for Coca Cola, for example.

But for prescription pharmaceuticals the situation is very different, principally because the intellectual property situation is quite different, as discussed above (see pp. 19–21). Certainly by the late 1980s, with the increasingly rapid and more severe erosion by generics following patent expiry enabled in the US by the 1984 Waxman-Hatch Act, the concept of the brand had a limited life. With luck this might be as much as 20 years but, as my longevity data discussed above shows (see pp. 20–21, 243–6), on average it was globally not much more than a dozen.

Secondly, television advertising: apart from in the US since the mid-1990s with DTC promotion (see pp. 23–4), the powerful medium of television is not permitted for the promotion of prescription pharmaceuticals.

In most parts of the world, therefore, the general public is not the key target for prescription drugs. It is a lesser priority for a pharmaceutical company to establish its name with the general public. Thus in Interbrand's list of best global brands of 2011, only one pharmaceutical company made the rankings, Johnson & Johnson, in 83rd position. Johnson & Johnson is, of course, also a consumer product company – the main reason, no doubt, that it does appear in the rankings.

In a similar survey, Superbrands (UK) Ltd listed just 10 pharmaceutical companies in its 2012 Top 500. GlaxoSmithKline, Johnson & Johnson, Pfizer, Bayer and AstraZeneca all appeared in the Top 100, Roche and Merck & Co in the next hundred, the remaining ranked companies being Novartis, Eli Lilly and Bristol-Myers Squibb (Superbrands 2012).

Lastly, the scope for building up and then managing a brand image for a product is more limited in prescription pharmaceuticals than it is for FMCGs. In particular, a pharmaceutical product may only be marketed for approved indications, limiting the claims that can be made for it. This means that they must be made in a much less subjective way than is usually possible for FMCGs. As mentioned above, national trade organizations for the pharmaceutical industry have codes of practice to which their member companies must conform, including details on what is allowable in claims. These codes help to prevent pharmaceutical companies overstepping the mark when making claims to doctors and committing legal infringements.

The divide between pharmaceuticals and FMCG increased from the 1960s onwards, as regulatory authorities became more stringent following the thalidomide disaster (see p. 5). This reduced the scope which pharmaceutical companies had for making promotional claims.

One common strategy in FMCG is product rebranding, that is, giving a brand a facelift of its image, or retargeting to different audiences. Thus Beecham's glucose solution product Lucozade was in my youth targeted for invalids. Later it was repositioned as an energy-giving sports drink. Often, as in this case, there is a radical redesign of a product's image. This revamping process can take place every few years for FMCG products if the marketer considers it worthwhile.

Whilst rebranding is possible for prescription pharmaceuticals, the scope is much more limited than it is for consumer products. This is because the attributes of a pharmaceutical product are less malleable than they are for consumer goods – only the approved indications may be promoted.

However, sometimes companies can take radical decisions on branding when the opportunity arises – for example with a new indication. Thus sildenafil was first marketed by Pfizer as Viagra for male erectile dysfunction. Several years later Pfizer gained approval to market the compound in a quite different indication: pulmonary arterial hypertension (PAH). The company decided to launch the product as Revatio. Whereas Viagra is marketed as oblong blue tablets, Revatio is marketed in a lower dosage strength as a round white tablet. Similarly, Amgen has marketed denosumab for osteoporosis as Prolia in a 60 mg subcutaneous presentation and for cancer indications as Xgeva in a 120 mg subcutaneous presentation.

In such situations where the same compound is destined for two very different therapeutic markets it can be important to market two separate brands. This is not only because the image of each product may need to be very different, with two entirely different target groups, but also sometimes to avoid confusion and use of an inappropriate strength presentation in the wrong indication. In the particular case of sildenafil, it may also have been an opportunity for Pfizer to avoid erosion of sales of Viagra by the lower – strength Revatio brand.

But the above constraints on the brand concept in pharmaceuticals do not gainsay that many of the techniques of marketing are very much applicable to prescription pharmaceuticals. It is just that pleading by consumer marketing specialists that the pharmaceutical industry is lagging other industries and should adopt consumer techniques often misses the subtleties that have to be applied in pharmaceutical marketing. This is my first example of outside experts presuming that the way they do things is superior or ahead of the pharmaceutical industry, when there are often fundamental reasons which explain why practice in pharmaceuticals inevitably has to be different.

A further, recent example is the frustration of industry outsiders as well as enthusiasts within it at the slow adoption of social media by the pharmaceutical industry. Senior pharma management are criticized for being set in their ways in their reluctance to adopt it. But there are genuine problems for the pharmaceutical industry with social media – some of which may be insoluble. Also regulatory authorities have mostly been far from helpful in giving advice on what is permissible.

Understanding the Customer

Another tenet of marketing theory is that companies or countries or any other type of organization don't buy – it is people who do the buying. Individual people make the decision, use the product, influence and validate other people's purchasing. Also according to marketing theory, customers purchase products that fulfil their needs and/or solve their problems; they do not merely buy products. Marketing theory stresses that it is critical to know about these needs, particularly those currently unsatisfied. Social and cultural factors influence the lifestyles, customs, needs and buying behaviours of consumers. Therefore, for the marketer, understanding about people and what makes them behave the way they do – for both business and consumer markets – is vital.

This may appear to be fanciful in the often life-or-death setting of medicine, but it still needs to be taken into account in marketing pharmaceuticals. Personal characteristics such as age, gender, education and profession also cause differences in buying criteria, as do psychological factors such as attitudes, perceptions and beliefs. This is important, for example, in determining whether a significant market does actually exist for an untreated indication, and the size of the commercial opportunity that might exist. And so in the apparently highly rational field of medicine these factors are still important. Therefore, pharmaceutical companies spend considerable effort in determining how these factors affect demand for their products.

But with pharmaceuticals it is not immediately obvious who the customer is (see p. 16). The actual user of a prescribed pharmaceutical product – the patient – commonly has very little say in which product is selected. Only in the case of OTC medicines do patients fully exercise their choice.

Conventionally, the prescriber is considered to be the customer. But that does not take into account that other players have power in the purchase decision. For example, a formulary board can decide to include or totally exclude certain products prescribed in a particular hospital. Thus in the case of products at risk of exclusion, they have the overriding customer power.

This means that pharmaceutical marketers and business development professionals must be aware of these different types of customer. And usually each national market is subtly different, and within each country the local situation will also differ.

Pharma Industry Concentration

Now I turn to a quite different distinctiveness metric: industry concentration. The pharmaceutical industry is a relatively unconcentrated one. This means that even a big pharma company competes against any other big pharma company only across a limited part of its range of products.

DISEASE CONCENTRATION

The low level of concentration in the pharmaceutical industry stems from the very diffuse nature of the demand for its products – far more so than is the case for most other major industries. This is a direct result of the diverse nature of disease and the consequent fragmented demand generated by treating the many different types of disease.

Most of us do not realize how diverse disease is. But when you look into it, the sheer number and variety of diseases is amazing. I analysed the World Health Organization's current International Classification of Disease, ICD-10 (ICD-10 2012). It contains some 58,000 different disease categories.

Moreover, our understanding of this diversity is ever increasing. Current estimates are that 250 new rare diseases are identified annually (Meekings 2012). Of course, some diseases are extremely rare. Also others are not treatable by pharmaceuticals (or sometimes even today by a medical measure of any kind). But the majority of disease is treated – and much of it by pharmaceuticals.

I have been interested in this impressive level of the diversity of disease for quite some years. In 2000 when I was conducting a consultancy project, I found that in the United Kingdom there were some 700 International Classification of Disease (ICD) codes which doctors used 50,000 times or more yearly in prescribing pharmaceutical products.

The European Pharmaceutical Market Research Association (EphMRA) has been modifying its Anatomical Classification system since 1971. Figure 1.3 shows a specimen page from the 2012 version, V2012.

This is the system used by audit companies, notably IMS. Sometimes categories fall out of use when drugs become redundant and are withdrawn, whereas novel drugs sooner or later require new categories. EphMRA makes modifications when this happens. In the 2010 version of this classification

---

D6 TOPICAL ANTIBACTERIALS AND ANTIVIRALS

D6A TOPICAL ANTIBACTERIALS

D6B Out of use.

D6C Out of use.

D6D TOPICAL VIRAL INFECTION PRODUCTS

D6D1 **Topical antivirals**
Includes topical forms of antivirals eg acyclovir, idoxuridine and podophyllotoxin.

D6D9 **Other topical products used in viral infections**
Includes products, eg those containing carbenoxolone, used for the symptomatic treatment of viral infections such as herpes simplex. Other products not containing podophyllotoxin used to treat external condylomata acuminata (genital warts) are classified here, eg fluorouracil injectable gel.

Figure 1.3   Specimen page – EphMRA Anatomical Classification Guidelines

Source: EphMRA Anatomical Classification Guidelines V2012, © EphMRA, 2012

system I counted 588 categories which are currently actively used to classify therapeutic pharmaceutical products.

I logged up the number of discrete disease descriptions and tallied the categories being used to classify pharmaceutical use. Thus on the page from the EphMRA Anatomical Classification Guidelines shown in Figure 1.3, the classification system for Topical Antibacterials and Antivirals, D6, appears.

Within D6 is D6A, Topical Antibacterials, which is in use. (I don't count both D6 and D6A as this would be double counting.) The next two categories, D6B and D6C, are out of use and so I don't count them. But D6D, Topical Viral Infection Products, is used. Moreover, it has two subclasses, D6D1, Topical antivirals, and D6D9, Other topical products used in viral infections. Thus I count as discrete classes currently used to classify pharmaceuticals a total here of three categories: D6A, D6D1 and D6D9.

How active are companies across active therapeutic categories? Let's take the biggest pharmaceutical company, Pfizer. As the biggest pharmaceutical company globally, Pfizer has a very long product range. This to some extent differs by country. In Germany, for example, the company has products with sales greater than €5 million per annum in 24 different therapeutic classes. By no means are all of these products going to be big enough to promote actively. Thus the products that Pfizer, the largest pharmaceutical company, markets actively, compete in probably less than two dozen of the 588 discrete therapeutic classes established by EphMRA, or 4 per cent of the total.

The modest level of competition of each pharmaceutical company against any other is an important factor in making strategic alliances particularly advantageous for the pharmaceutical industry, as I will explain in Chapter 4 (see pp. 84–6). This is something not particularly appreciated by one particular management guru, Michael Porter (see p. 95).

CONCENTRATION BY PRODUCT

As there are so many different diseases, it is not surprising that a very large number of products have been brought onto the market over the past 150 years by the pharmaceutical industry to treat them. Since many of these diseases are not that common, and several products at least are usually available to treat many of them, there are many small products by value on the market.

As Figure 1.4 shows, whilst sales of the best-selling product in 2011 globally, Lipitor (atorvastatin, Pfizer), exceeded $10 billion, sales of top-ranked products soon drop. The no. 10 product, Avastin (bevacizumab, Roche) had sales of just under $6 billion. Sales dipped below $4 billion after the first 23 products and below $3 billion after the first 35. But then the decline was less steep: by the two hundredth product, sales were still just above half a billion dollars. In 2010, the last year when *Med Ad News* produced rankings for the Top 500 products, there were 333 products with sales above a quarter of a billion dollars.

Looking at product concentration from another angle, the Top 100 products in 2011 accounted for just 31 per cent of sales. The pharmaceutical industry therefore has a long 'tail' of modest-sized products. Midsized and small companies can be perfectly viable commercially in this milieu – they can make a living just from products in that long tail. The strength of competition along that long tail tends to be moderate at most – since modest-sized products are too small to interest big pharma.

($ billion)

Figure 1.4   Sales taper for the top 200 globally best-selling products in 2011

Source: John Ansell Consultancy, based on *Med Ad News* data (*Med Ad News* 2012b)

DEGREE OF CONCENTRATION CORPORATELY

Concentration can be measured using several different parameters. The degree of concentration by corporation is much higher. I first examined concentration and mergers in detail in an article published at the time of one episode of megamerger mania (Ansell 1996).

I calculate now that the Top 30 companies accounted for 61 per cent of total global pharmaceutical sales in 2011, using *Pharmaceutical Executive* rankings (Cacciotti 2012) and online IMS data (IMS 2012b). During the 1985–95 period the Top 30 company share fluctuated between 52 and 57 per cent. Rather surprisingly perhaps, despite the many mergers over the past quarter century, this degree of corporate concentration is not that much higher than in the 1980s and 1990s.

With this level of corporate concentration there is some discrepancy with product/disease concentration. This presents something of a problem as far as exploitation of the smaller products is concerned, since those small products do not each amount to much in terms of total turnover (and profit) which they can contribute to a company.

As the majority of big pharma companies are notoriously conservative about divesting products to smaller companies, these assets remain underexploited, and their commercial potential tends to go to waste. This is an example of pharmaceutical companies growing to be too big for the good of the industry as a whole, as I first pointed out in my 1996 article (Ansell 1996).

DIVERSITY OF R&D EFFORT

The pharmaceutical industry is not only diverse in terms of product ranges each company markets. You can see this also in the differences in the therapeutic areas each company is developing. Table 1.1 indicates the therapeutic areas in which the top 19 pharmaceutical companies were, according to their websites, significantly represented in October 2012. (The twentieth-ranked company, Mylan, is a generics company not currently active in originating novel products which is why I have restricted Table 1.1 to the Top 19 companies.)

This is the latest of several such snapshots of R&D activity by company I have conducted over the past 15 years, most recently in 2009 (Ansell 2009). This is just one way of assessing company R&D activity by therapeutic area – there could be many others. It does, however, help in showing the diversity of approaches therapeutically between companies.

To qualify in a therapeutic area in this analysis, companies must have R&D projects advanced at least as far as the second phase of clinical trials: Phase II. A Phase II cut-off indicates not only the desire of a company to be active in a particular therapeutic area but also some tangible progress. Projects continue to qualify in any successive development phase including the granting of registration and when products are still in the immediate postlaunch phase.

In Table 1.1 companies appear in order of ranking by global sales. The therapeutic areas appear in order of popularity, from left to right. As Table 1.1 shows, there is one therapeutic area in which all companies are active: metabolic. In two more, cardiovascular and cancer, all but one company in the Top 19 are active. Indeed excluding the tenth-ranked company, Teva, which is essentially a generics company and has only recently been concentrating additionally on novel product R&D, cardiovascular is also a full house.

But as we go from left to right through Table 1.1, the differences between companies become increasingly marked. There are some intriguing patterns. Only six companies are active in vaccine development – all are amongst the Top 7 companies. Interest in ophthalmology is also skewed quite heavily towards the largest pharmaceutical companies.

Table 1.1 Therapeutic areas where the Top 19 pharmaceutical companies (by global sales) are active with projects at Phase II and beyond

Ranking		Metabolic	Cardiovascular	Cancer	CNS	Anti-infectives	Rheumatology	Respiratory/Allergy	Dermatology	Gastroenterology	Ophthalmology	Vaccines	Transplantation	Anaesthesia	Total
1	Pfizer	x	x	x	x	x	x	x	x	x	x	x	x		12
2	Novartis	x	x	x	x	x	x	x	x		x	x			10
3	Merck & Co	x	x	x	x	x	x	x	x	x		x			10
4	Sanofi	x	x	x	x	x	x	x	x			x			9
5	AstraZeneca	x	x	x	x	x	x	x	x	x	x			x	11
6	Roche	x	x	x	x	x	x	x	x		x		x		10
7	GlaxoSmithKline	x	x	x	x	x	x	x	x	x	x	x			11
8	Johnson & Johnson	x	x	x	x	x		x	x	x		x			9
9	Abbott	x	x	x	x	x	x	x		x					8
10	Teva	x	x		x	x									4
11	Lilly	x	x	x	x		x				x				6
12	Takeda	x	x	x	x	x	x		x		x				8
13	Bristol-Myers Squibb	x	x	x	x	x	x	x	x	x					9
14	Bayer	x	x	x	x	x					x				6
15	Amgen	x		x			x		x	x	x		x		7
16	Boehringer Ingelheim	x	x	x			x	x							5
17	Novo Nordisk	x	x	x						x					4
18	Daiichi Sankyo	x	x	x		x		x		x					6
19	Otsuka	x	x	x	x	x	x	x	x						8
Total		19	18	18	15	15	14	13	12	10	9	6	3	1	

Source: John Ansell Consultancy

Look also at the range in number of therapeutic areas in which companies are active. Teva, which to date has principally been a generics company but has recently been increasing its efforts in R&D, qualifies in just four therapeutic areas, far fewer than most Top 10 companies. The rest are active in between four and twelve areas – a considerable difference in therapeutic breadth.

However, greater therapeutic breadth does not necessarily make for a better strategy. Eli Lilly has for many years concentrated on a limited number of therapeutic areas – currently according to my criteria just six. Most observers would agree that it has over many years been one of the more successful pharmaceutical companies.

Activity in the less popular therapeutic areas ebbs and flows. Anaesthesia used to be a much more popular therapeutic area than now. In 2012, of the Top 19 companies, only AstraZeneca was active in this therapeutic area. Transplantation is another area where interest has dwindled – with Pfizer the only company currently qualifying. On the other hand, dermatology has undergone a sharp increase in interest. In 2007 only two companies were represented. By 2012 there were 12, mainly as a result of novel biologicals being brought into development.

I see this diversity in areas of R&D activity as being a strength of the pharmaceutical industry. Where the approach of companies tends towards uniformity, as in the most popular therapeutic areas, this could be associated with increased risk because of the likelihood of more intensive competition.

Cancer is the most popular therapeutic area in which to conduct R&D. By 2011 there were just under a thousand products in development for cancer. Whilst it has become by some distance the biggest therapeutic market, there can still be competition problems. In a 2002 article I wrote with Dr Brian Minter, we suggested that not every company producing a registrable product for cancer would go on to have commercial success. The sheer number of new anticancer products which were likely to reach the market meant that those with only moderately good profiles could become commercial failures (Ansell 2002). That is now indeed beginning to happen.

Early and Strong Globalization of Pharmaceuticals

In its broadest terms, globalization has been defined as the freer movement of goods, services, ideas and people around the world. The pharmaceutical industry has always been ahead of most other industries in the extent to which it is globalized. Over the past half century it has consistently forged further ahead in this respect. However, there is still much scope for further globalization. But why should pharmaceuticals have been ahead of many industries in globalizing?

THE NATURE OF DISEASE GLOBALLY

The nature of demand (from the treatment of disease) tends to be less differentiated between national markets than is the case for most other types of goods. This is particularly the case across developed markets, where most commercial potential still exists currently. Also, developing markets are growing to resemble to an increasing extent the developed markets in terms of the spectrum of diseases suffered. In the first half of the twentieth century infectious diseases were still the most important cause of disease everywhere. Then in the West and Japan, cardiometabolic diseases began to take over as the leading cause. Now cancers are becoming the leading cause of disease there.

Some of the most successful developing countries have now reached the cardiometabolic phase. Doubtless the more economically successful ones will before long go on to reach the stage where cancer becomes the most important cause of disease, whilst others meanwhile begin to transition from infectious disease to cardiometabolic disease prominence.

REGULATORY HARMONIZATION

There has been a gradual long-term trend for regulatory requirements to be harmonized for drugs, which continues; as late as the 1970s there were considerable differences in data sheets for a given product between countries. Older drugs sometimes even had different dosage levels in different countries, for example. These older drugs were steadily replaced by more recent ones registered in an era when regulatory requirements had become far more harmonized. In particular the development of the European Community has led in large part to the standardization of regulatory requirements across Western and later much of Eastern Europe. Now, it is uncommon for there to be essential differences within Europe in data sheet details for commonly used products.

Today many products can therefore be marketed across many markets with no or only minor local modifications. The types of modification still required today are typically different pack sizes or pack liveries. These are usually a function of local regulatory needs or of national market practices.

Although they have been slow to do so, national regulatory authorities are increasingly sharing information, so that their review processes are becoming more harmonized and integrated with each other.

In 2010 the European Medicines Agency (EMA) and the FDA agreed that for orphan drugs (see pp. 196–8) – that is, those treating only a limited number of patients – they would accept a single annual report from sponsors developing them, to be exchanged electronically. The idea is to accelerate access to new medicines and make it easier to take steps to protect public health. Then in 2012 the FDA and EMA started to share manufacturing inspections, thereby reducing duplication of effort. This followed two pilot projects which aimed to enhance global drug quality and safety: joint active pharmaceutical ingredient (API) inspections, and a Good Clinical Practice (GCP) initiative.

Also in 2012 the EMA reported increased interaction with the Japanese regulatory authorities; particular progress had, according to the EMA, been achieved with orphan drugs and there had been increased interaction on paediatrics, advanced therapies, pharmacogenomics and biomarkers, nanomedicines and inspections.

In 2008 the EU and Canada agreed to exchange confidential information on medicines in areas such as safety concerns and product approval assessments. But a similar initiative in 2007 along the same lines for Australia and New Zealand failed.

There is still very considerable scope for further regulatory harmonization and cooperation. The increased emphasis on cost reduction recently probably explains the increasing tempo of such harmonization between authorities over the past few years.

RELATIVELY LIMITED COST OF INTERNATIONAL DISTRIBUTION

For prescription pharmaceuticals, distribution costs are relatively low. They are not negligible, but are usually modest compared with those borne by other industries. Thus they are not commonly a critical issue in marketing products.

Pharmaceuticals are unusual amongst other categories of products in that they can routinely be flown around the world. It was noticeable during the volcanic ash crisis caused by the Eyjafjallajökull glacier in Iceland which grounded flights internationally in April 2010 that pharmaceuticals featured commonly amongst cargoes being held up. Thus for at least some types of expensive pharmaceutical product, transport costs are not critical – or at least air transportation is preferable to setting up multiple local production sites.

Thus the marginal costs of making a pharmaceutical product available in an additional country tend to be relatively modest. As I have discussed earlier, (see p. 16) the cost of developing new pharmaceuticals is so high that the onus is on maximizing sales – and therefore marketing a product as widely as possible. Indeed today the very high costs of pharmaceutical R&D means that unless a compound can be marketed across most markets, its development may not be viable.

INTERNATIONAL CLINICAL COOPERATION

Healthcare professionals regularly travel internationally to conferences and exchange ideas and information. Cross-border cooperation in research and, in turn, coauthoring of clinical publications across borders has become commonplace over the past 20 years. This all serves to stimulate more uniform treatment of disease internationally.

SIMPLIFICATION OF MARKETING NETWORKS

Factors driving globalization and the wider acceptance of universal product presentations have served to reduce the former need to appoint strong indigenous companies as partners – for example in Europe. Increasingly since the 1980s, global pharmaceutical companies have been able to successfully market products largely through their own subsidiaries. This has tended to simplify globalization of products. It means that smaller pharmaceutical companies than formerly are now capable of achieving good marketing penetration in most major markets worldwide largely without marketing partners. A good example of a start-up company essentially growing under its own steam is Celgene, which in 2012 became the no. 27 ranked company by global sales, according to *Pharmaceutical Executive* (Cacciotti 2012).

The Importance of Distinctiveness

As I have shown, the pharmaceutical industry is distinctive in many ways. This distinctiveness critically shapes how it operates. It determines in particular which types of management concepts work well and which do not in the pharmaceutical industry. Of the many companies entering the pharmaceutical industry from outside over the past 50 years, most have – sooner or later – found the experience so trying that they have exited it. The *modus operandi* needed for success is so different from their existing experience that most eventually in frustration exit the pharmaceutical industry. I deal with this in more detail in Chapter 3 (see pp. 55–9).

As I shall show throughout the rest of this book, many misconceptions arise because this distinctiveness is not well understood – inside as well as outside the pharmaceutical industry. Whilst I do not wish to encourage an ivory tower mentality and prevent good ideas from being adopted by the pharmaceutical industry, I believe that those in the industry should have a good grasp of why things are as they are and what the consequences are. They will then have a sounder basis for making decisions and will, I believe, less easily be led astray by some of the zanier concepts and ideas they are confronted with.

Before I go on to consider management concepts in the remaining two chapters of Part I, I am going to look at the consequences of the distinctiveness of the pharmaceutical industry. To start with, I consider the consequences of the extraordinarily long timescales with which it is faced.

2

The Consequences of Extended Timescales

We hope to have a vaccine [against AIDS] ready for testing in about two years.

Margaret Heckler, US Secretary of Health and Human Services,
23 April 2004, Frontline 2006

A major consequence of the extended timescales in pharmaceuticals is that things commonly take much longer than ever expected to come to fruition. The most important feature of this is the great deal of time and cost involved before a new product reaches the market.

There is also the risk that promising technology gets rejected prematurely because a company loses patience with a slowly progressing project. In this chapter I review several examples of this phenomenon, some of which are still current. I start with the whole concept of biotechnology. Of my other examples, some belong within biotechnology; others can be described as enabling technologies for drug development.

Biotechnology

I suspect that if pioneer investors in biotechnology had realized that it would take so long for products to come to fruition they might never have gone ahead with their investments! As far as pharmaceutical development is concerned, modern biotechnology began in the early 1970s when the first biotech companies were set up.[1]

---

1   By no means all 'biotech' companies are working on biological therapeutics. BIO, the US industry association for biotech companies, estimated in 2011 that only 35 per cent of companies so described conduct research into cell-derived biologic drugs, whereas 65 per cent conduct

It took until 1982 before the first product of biotechnology, human insulin (Humulin, Eli Lilly), reached the market. By 1988 only five proteins from genetically engineered cells had been approved as drugs by the FDA. It was only in the 1990s that pharmaceutical biotechnology really took off in the market. By the end of that decade the number of biotech products approved in the US exceeded 125.

According to IMS (2012a), by 2011 biologicals (which include a number of conventionally produced products such as vaccines that are not necessarily the result of modern biotechnology) accounted for 23 per cent of total pharmaceutical sales, with the remaining 77 per cent being small molecule products. A different source found a somewhat lower figure for biotech products: Evaluate Pharma showed that by 2011, biologicals accounted for just 19 per cent of the world pharmaceutical market (EvaluatePharma 2012). However, they did account for 34 per cent of sales within the Top 100 products.

IMS data for 2011 (IMS Health 2012) showed that nine of the Top 20 globally best-selling products were biologicals:

> Humira (adalimumab, Abbott)
> Enbrel (etanercept, Amgen, Pfizer)
> Remicade (infliximab, Johnson & Johnson, Merck & Co)

were all ranked in the Top 10. In addition:

> Rituxan/Mabthera (rituximab, Roche, Biogen Idec)
> Lantus (recombinant human insulin analogue, Sanofi)
> Avastin (bevacizumab, Roche)
> Herceptin (trastuzumab, Roche)
> Neulasta (pegfilgrastim, Amgen)
> Gleevec/Glivec (imatinib, Novartis)

were all biotech products appearing in the Top 20. Some 30 biotech products were blockbusters in 2011, with sales over $1 million. They accounted for just over a quarter of all blockbusters in that year.

Evaluate Pharma forecast in 2012 in the above report that by 2018 biotech products would account for 23 per cent of the world pharmaceutical market,

---

small molecule research. Here, when I refer to biotech products I am not alluding to those small molecule products emanating from biotech companies.

and 49 per cent of sales within the Top 100 products. Thus biotech products are definitely now making their mark – and much more at the top end of the market by value. With a very considerable number of biotech products in development currently there is clearly much further to go in terms of their market penetration.

However, small molecule products still feature strongly in cohorts of new products recently reaching the market. According to Pharmaprojects® Citeline, in 2011 only 7 out of 33 new products launched for the first time were biologicals (Pharmaprojects® Citeline 2011a). Perhaps this was an anomaly – the previous year there were 19.

A 2012 McKinsey & Company study (Berggren et al. 2012) based partially on Evaluate Pharma data that I will describe in further detail later (see pp. 220–21) suggested that the importance of small molecules would decline over the next few years. Small molecules launched in the 2012–16 period would account for 56 per cent of total revenues in 2016, whereas for the previous five-year period to 2011 they had accounted for 65 per cent.

In March 2012 the UK law firm Withers and Rogers found that by 2009 biologics accounted for 60 per cent of the patents filed by the Top 10 pharmaceutical companies – which may well foretell the future balance of products after 2020.

Gene Therapy

One source of potential new large molecule products of the future is gene therapy, a concept long in development that has only recently begun to fulfil any level of potential. The aim of gene therapy is to replace a mutated, disease-causing gene with a healthy copy, knocking out a faulty mutated gene which causes disease, or introducing a new gene to combat a genetic disease.

The concept of gene therapy was first proposed 40 years ago, but the exponential growth of publications did not occur until the late 1980s. Pharmaceutical companies began to get involved in developing gene therapy in the early 1990s. Glaxo, Merck & Co and Novartis all made big efforts.

However, there were a series of setbacks with gene therapy. Progress was severely affected when in 1999 an 18-year-old patient with a deficiency of the ornithine transcarbamylase enzyme, Jesse Gelsinger, died after an adenoviral vector carrying it caused a fatal immune response. Another adverse event emerged in 2000 when a vector for X-linked severe combined immunodeficiency (SCID) was found to carry a high risk of leukaemia. However, since then, with progress in developing safer vectors, further deaths have been avoided.

There are considerable problems in manufacturing pure and potent gene therapy vectors in sufficient quantities. Also quite a number of large companies were reluctant to get involved in gene therapy because most of the disorders for which it could prove useful were orphan diseases – which they considered would have inadequate commercial potential. However, some major pharmaceutical companies have become more prepared over the past few years to countenance entering apparently smaller markets. Therefore some of this reluctance is dispersing.

GlaxoSmithKline, one of the companies involved in gene therapy development for cystic fibrosis in the early 1990s that proved unsuccessful, has nevertheless ventured recently again into the area. In 2010 the company announced a deal with Fondazione Telethon and Fondazione San Raffale to develop gene therapies for nine diseases, three of which it identified: adenosine deaminase deficiency, Wiskott-Aldrich syndrome and β-thalassaemia.

By 2011 36 gene therapies were being developed as orphan drugs in the United States. Several products were by 2012 in Phase III development for a variety of cancer indications as well as for angina and SCID.

Then in November 2012 came a breakthrough: the first gene therapy product approval in any Western country was announced by the EMEA.[2] It approved uniQure's Glybera (Alipogene tiparovevec), the first-ever treatment approved for lipoprotein lipase deficiency (LPLD). The company described the approval as being the culmination of 40 years of research.

Thus there is some momentum now building behind gene cell therapy, with a renaissance in drug development activity. But progress to date has been very protracted and after close to 30 years since the pharmaceutical industry's first involvement it is still unclear how important gene therapy will become in medicine or to the pharmaceutical industry.

---

2   In 2003 one product had been approved in China. Also Epeius Biotechnologies's Rexin-G was approved for solid tumours in the Philippines in 2007.

Stem Cells

It is only recently that the first two stem cell products have reached the market. In November 2011, Hemacord, which is derived from haematopoietic stem cells was approved in the US. This product is used in haematopoietic stem cell transplantation procedures for individuals with disorders affecting the hematopoietic system. Then in May 2012 Prochymal (remestemcel-L), a treatment developed by Osiris Therapeutics for acute graft-versus-host disease in children was registered in Canada. (It was also the first ever product approved for this indication.) Prochymal had been in development for nearly two decades, according to Osiris.

But stem cells go back much farther than this. Experiments conducted in the 1950s with bone marrow established their power in enabling regeneration of some tissues. They were first introduced to the scientific community in 1981 when they were isolated from mice; this was the real trigger for increased interest in their therapeutic development.

Over a decade later in the late 1990s human embryonic cells were isolated, which for the first time appeared to offer great promise in regenerative medicine – in neurological disorders and diabetes, for example. Stem cells are also now beginning to provide valuable information on toxicity and disease profiling.

But the pace of development of stem cells has been rather slow. The initial enthusiasm of big pharma abated with the disappointing rate of progress in the early days, so that today it is smaller companies that are most active in the field. They have difficulties in financing expensive late-stage clinical trial programmes.

In October 2012 Professor Sir John Gurdon from the UK and Professor Shinya Yamanaka from Japan together won the Nobel Prize for Medicine for their work in stem cell research. This is bound to give impetus to the whole field. The amount of work in progress in the clinic is now very substantial: there are currently just over 4,000 clinical trials involving stem cells underway worldwide.

Genomics

Around the year 2000 I carried out several analyses of deals on genomics with Cambridge HealthTech Institute which led to several now outmoded articles and reports. At the time I also spoke at several genomics conferences on this theme. Most of these took place in Germany, where the government had recently begun to heavily support start-up biotech companies, including those involved with enabling technologies. At that time the term *genomics* had become applied to a variety of enabling technologies as well as just the study of the genome.

But by 2002 disillusion with most of these enabling technologies was beginning to set in. Genomics had failed as an enabling technology to produce a 'quick fix' to the perennial problem for the pharmaceutical industry of producing enough new products. It did not help that the companies providing the technology oversold its virtues. Too many compounds predicted to be active by enabling technologies eventually turned out not to be when they reached the clinic.

Hence genomics rapidly became a dirty word. Conference organizers who had been using genomics in the titles of their periodic conferences replaced it with less specific terms such as 'Life Science Technologies'. Thus in the space of some five years, genomics had moved from high fashion to disdain. Even the full mapping of the human genome in 2003 also did little to revive the term.

However, there is now a renaissance. By 2011 genomics was beginning to prove its worth in developing new products that actually reached the market. In that year Benlysta (belimumab, GlaxoSmithKline/Human Genome Sciences) was approved, the first new product for lupus in 52 years. Human Genome Sciences, which was subsequently acquired by GlaxoSmithKline, developed the product by using genetic analysis to identify proteins causing lupus.

Also in 2011 Santaris Pharma began a trial of miravirsen in hepatitis C. This compound blocks the activity of genetic material needed by the virus to grow in the liver. In the same year Daiichi Sankyo paid $935 million to acquire Plexxicon. This company's B-Raf kinase inhibitor for melanoma, Zelboraf (vemurafenib), was first approved in 2011, in the US, for metastatic melanoma. Roche maintained ownership of marketing rights. Plexxicon had mapped the genomes of melanoma cells and identified a key mutation. Zelboraf inhibits the secretion of an enzyme triggering cell division. In 2012 it won the Scrip Best New Drug Award.

In the longer term, we can expect to gain from the growing ability through association studies on the genomes of patients with particular diseases to identify new drug targets. For example, complement factor H was found to be highly associated with age-related macular degeneration, and there are now new compounds in pre-clinical development resulting from this finding.

Thus after a shaky start genomics is now beginning to generate the first products to reach the market.

High-Throughput Screening

First developed in the 1990s, in high-throughput screening (HTS), chemical technologists use robotic or other automated techniques to make very small quantities of hundreds or thousands of related chemical compounds. Promising molecules are identified, protein is added to wells in a plastic plate and interacting compounds are identified through fluorescence techniques.

Disillusion set in in recent years with HTS. Overreliance on it led to bottlenecks, and a consensus has been growing that quality is more important than the sheer number of leads this technology is capable of generating. HTS is still quite widely viewed as being a useful tool, but it is expensive to set up and run. Rather damningly, it was described in 2010 by Dr Trevor Perrior of Domainex as like searching for a needle in a haystack using a very expensive and sophisticated bulldozer.

But a particularly stout defence of HTS was made in a review of HTS (Macarron 2011). This opinion piece, coauthored by a dozen experts in the field from seven major pharmaceutical companies as well as from academia, tackled what it termed common myths that have built up about HTS. They disputed claims that it generates poor quality data, is anti-intellectual and irrational, and fails to find leads for many targets. More to the point, the authors also contested the widespread impression that HTS has not been successful in producing new products which have reached the market.

Macarron et al. pointed out that the concept of HTS is still young. The first paper citing 'HTS' in its title was published in 1991 and it was not until 1997 that 10 such papers were published in a single year. Standards facilitating supply of equipment to conduct HTS were only published in mid-1999. And as the review pointed out, drug discovery, from target identification to approval, is currently taking a very long time: the authors mentioned 13.5 years. They argued that therefore only a very few screens could have had sufficient time to lead to development of drugs reaching the market by 2011 when the paper was published.

Macarron et al. considered that the expectations in the early days of HTS were 'misplaced and naïve'. It was, they said, now understood that hits from screening were simply chemical starting points that needed to be optimized – they did not directly generate marketable compounds. The authors argued that it was unfair to blame alarming attrition rates (see Chapter 15, p. 191) on HTS, when many other aspects of R&D contributed to this.

As evidence of HTS's power, the authors cited an analysis of 58 drugs approved up to 2008 where the starting lead was known. No less than 19 were found to result from HTS. These ranged from AstraZeneca's anticancer product Iressa (gefitinib), which was approved by the FDA in 2003 and resulted from an HTS run some 10 years earlier, to GlaxoSmithKline's antithrombotic agent Promacta (eltrombopag), approved by the FDA in 2008, which resulted from an HTS run in 1997.

The authors experience was that 'HTS is the most productive technique at our disposal and the one that is more universally applicable to a diverse portfolio of targets.' They concluded that 'HTS has matured to become an integral part of pharmaceutical research and a cornerstone in the expansion of biomedical knowledge' and claimed that many side benefits had arisen from the development and implementation of HTS technologies.

The HTS saga shows how impatience with a technology risks unjustified dissatisfaction with it and its unwarranted demise. Clearly there is evidence of HTS's value in bolstering new product productivity. The technology now has to provide further evidence over the next few years that it is capable of making a solid contribution to new product productivity.

Monoclonal Antibodies

In the mid-1980s some dozen novel monoclonal antibodies were entering clinical trials each year. But rather than monoclonal antibodies, the main thrust of biological development during the 1980s was into hormones and cytokines.

I remember in 1982 meeting a US pharmaceutical business consultant in Germany at a licensing meeting between the company he was advising and my company. He strongly tipped monoclonals – they were, he said, the flavour of the month – and he urged me to invest in them.

If I had done so, I would very likely have had a long wait to get my return. It took 15 years before the first commercially successful monoclonal antibody, Rituxan/MabThera (rituximab), reached the market in 1997. Sales of this product globally had reached an astonishing $6.8 billion by 2011.

Back in 1997 the number of monoclonal antibodies entering clinical trials had still not risen that dramatically – they totalled 19 in that year. However, numbers then took off, no doubt as the first big commercial success became evident, as well as for several other reasons which a Tufts Center for the Study of Drug Development report cited: advances in antibody engineering and design, improvement in cell lines and manufacturing, and a better understanding of targets and mechanisms of action (CSDD 2011a).

By 2010 there were no less than 53 monoclonals entering clinical trials and a total of about 314 monoclonals in clinical development worldwide, according to the Tufts report. They represented by far the single largest category of biopharmaceuticals then in development. In 2011 monoclonal antibodies occupied half of the positions in the Top 10 globally best-selling products. One of the 2011 new entrants was Benlysta, the new product for lupus mentioned above (see p. 46).

Monoclonal antibodies had certainly arrived – but what a long time they took to do so! Suppose the industry had given up on monoclonals in the early 1990s. They would have exited a technology now making a very substantial contribution to current new product productivity. Are there, I wonder, similar technologies out there today which have been pursued for 10 years or more without yet yielding apparent returns which might similarly make a major contribution to new products reaching the market from 2020?

Personalized Medicine

With the growth in knowledge about genetics, and the increasing ability to develop biomarkers – cellular or molecular indicators of disease or susceptibility to disease – subtypes can be identified. This potentially allows more specific targeting of medicine to a patient with one particular genetic type of a disease.

As I will discuss in Chapter 18 (see pp. 221–2) personalized medicine has already led to some big successes. But its full impact will take longer than many observers – mainly pharma industry outsiders – thought just a few years ago.

In 2005 the UK Royal Society published the report *Personalised medicines: hopes and realities*. This perceptive landmark survey explained that the situation was much more complex than had previously been suggested. It considered that the future of personalized medicine depended on more than science. The report pointed out that most countries had individual laws, regulations and guidelines for conducting genetic research which hindered essential pharmacogenetic studies across populations and that harmonization of international regulatory, legal and clinical frameworks across different countries was needed. That situation has not been greatly improved since the report was written.

In particular, the Royal Society report considered that for personalized medicine, 'The major determinant of the rate of progress will be the clinical use and cost effectiveness of the new treatment regimes rather than development of the technology'.

The report also found that 'the pharmaceutical industry foresees a gradual rather than revolutionary movement towards implementing pharmacogenetic science, with certain therapeutic areas such as oncology taking the lead'. So at least the industry already by then had a better perception of the reality on personalized medicine than many outside observers did. The Royal Society report concluded that there was likely to be 'a gradual increase in its clinical applications; its true potential may not become apparent for 15–20 years'.

We now know from the outcome of the Human Genome Project that common diseases like diabetes and heart disease tend to be polygenic, that is, many genes have been found to be implicated in each disease. The contribution of each gene might be as low as 2 per cent. It is also evident now that in disease the interplay between genes and environmental and behavioural factors is usually complex.

Whilst there are indeed diseases, such as Tay-Sachs syndrome, where a single mutation causes disease, they are the exception rather than the rule.

Cystic fibrosis, which has often been cited as an example of a single gene disease, is so far known to be associated with over 1,200 different mutations of the cystic fibrosis transmembrane regulator (CFTR) gene. Finally, we also now know that there is far more pleiotropy – that is, where one gene expresses multiple physical traits – than was generally anticipated. Thus the first widely popularized explanations of personalized medicine linking genes with disease were much too simplistic.

Sometimes the commercial viability of a test is the critical factor which can prevent a pharmacogenetic approach being adopted for treatment. According to the Tufts Center for the Study of Drug Development, the number of personalized medicines and companion diagnostics in use in the United States has still only gradually increased, from a handful in 2001 to several dozen 10 years later (CSDD 2011b).

Certainly not all are enthusiasts. Robert Beckman, executive director of clinical development oncology at Daiichi Sankyo, interviewed in October 2011 by events company Hanson Wade, considered that 'frankly there is a lot of hype around biomarkers and everybody expects them to be spectacularly successful every time. Of course the failures don't get published in *Nature* and *Science*' (Grogan 2011a).

Many of the most promising personalized medicines are still in the early stages of research. But the Tufts report above found that biomarkers have already have had a considerable impact on drug development. Practically all pharma companies of any size are now investing in personalized medicine. Amongst treatments in preclinical development, nearly 60 per cent rely on biomarker data. But the impact on later-stage R&D was by 2011 less than this. In early clinical research that proportion then approached 50 per cent; in late clinical development about 30 per cent were using biomarkers.

Other indicators are more positive. In a 2011 report, the consulting firm Diaceutics found that about half of the companies it assessed had a personalized medicine on the market with sales of blockbuster size (Diaceutics 2011). Diaceutics estimated that 46 per cent of the projects of 10 leading pharmaceutical companies then at Phase III might benefit from a personalized medicine strategy. In 2012 Roche noted that 60 per cent of its pharmaceutical pipeline projects were coupled with the development of companion diagnostics.

In 2011 two new products reaching their first markets were registered along with companion diagnostics. These were a product already mentioned above in this chapter in the section on genomics, Zelboraf, and Pfizer's anaplastic lymphoma kinase inhibitor, Xalkori (crizotinib). The companion diagnostic for the latter, Abbott's Vysis ALK Break Apart FISH Probe Kit, was approved for certain patients with late-stage non–small cell lung cancer.

In 2012 Kalydeco (ivacaftor, Vertex) was the first product targeting one of the gene defects of cystic fibrosis to reach the market. This came no less than 23 years after the discovery of the underlying mutation. Kalydeco was described as a breakthrough by the FDA, who approved it in three and a half months. Also in 2012 Perjeta (pertuzumab, Genentech/Roche), another personalized medicine for treating Human Epidermal Growth Factor Receptor 2 (HER2-) positive breast cancer, reached the US market.

Thus despite mixed indicators on personalized medicine, it should be possible, given the initial success of products in the market and the number of projects in the pipeline, for highly personalized medicine to make a much greater impact in the market than currently. It is also now becoming clear that smaller indications including orphan drugs are capable of becoming major products commercially (see also Chapter 16, pp. 196–8).

In Pharmaceuticals Patience Can Pay Off Handsomely

The examples I have discussed in this chapter show that the industry should not summarily dismiss new technologies. It frequently takes a long time before they produce results. Because of the cost of doing so, the idea of having to wait a long time for a new technology to result in marketable new products is an uncomfortable one. But as the above examples show, it is turning out to be the reality.

Companies must therefore be careful not to kill geese before they have laid their golden eggs. I suspect that some companies not wishing to bear the torture of such lengthy development will choose to exit pharmaceuticals. But for those who are committed, the payoffs should often be worth the wait.

3

The Barriers to Getting In and Out of Pharmaceuticals

In this chapter I am going to explain how the distinctive characteristics of the pharmaceutical industry make it difficult for nonpharmaceutical companies to enter it – a barrier which is to the advantage of companies already active in pharmaceuticals. I then go on to show that these characteristics also make it difficult for companies to get out of pharmaceuticals – as some have considered doing in the recent gloomy pharmaceutical climate.

How often have nonpharmaceutical companies succeeded in breaking into the pharmaceutical industry with any major impact? Compare the leading players in pharmaceuticals now with those in 1980. Figure 3.1 shows the rankings of the Top 10 global pharmaceutical companies based on global sales as they stood in 1980 and then 30 years later in 2010.

The pharmaceutical industry is often considered to be a dynamic one. But Figure 3.1 does not really support this. In the left-hand column I show the ranked companies for 1980. I show in brackets and in bold the names of today's companies into which some of them became merged. Sometimes there has been no change – in which case I also show the name in bold.

The top 1980 company, Hoechst, has ended up as part of Sanofi. The second-ranked company, Merck & Co, has retained its name. The third-ranked company in 1980, American Home Products, changed its name to Wyeth and later became absorbed by Pfizer, as has one other company listed, no. 5: Warner-Lambert.

Six of the 1980 Top 10 changed their names at least to some extent. When we compare the 2010 ranked companies after allowing for these name changes,

```
┌─────────────────────────────────────────────────────┐
│  1980 rankings                                        │
│                                                       │
│  1.  Hoechst (Sanofi)                                 │
│                                                       │
│  2.  Merck & Co                                       │
│                                                       │
│  3.  American Home Products (i.e. Wyeth → Pfizer)     │
│                                                       │
│  4.  Bayer (Bayer Schering)                           │
│                                                       │
│  5.  Warner-Lambert (Pfizer)                          │
│                                                       │
│  6.  Bristol-Myers (Bristol-Myers Squibb)             │
│                                                       │
│  7.  Ciba-Geigy (Novartis)                            │
│                                                       │
│  8.  Pfizer                                           │
│                                                       │
│  9.  Roche                                            │
│                                                       │
│  10. Eli Lilly                                        │
│                                                       │
│  2010 rankings                                        │
│                                                       │
│  1.  Pfizer                                           │
│                                                       │
│  2.  Novartis                                         │
│                                                       │
│  3.  Sanofi                                           │
│                                                       │
│  4.  Merck & Co                                       │
│                                                       │
│  5.  Roche                                            │
│                                                       │
│  6.  GlaxoSmithKline                                  │
│                                                       │
│  7.  AstraZeneca                                      │
│                                                       │
│  8.  Johnson & Johnson                                │
│                                                       │
│  9.  Eli Lilly                                        │
│                                                       │
│  10. Abbott                                           │
└─────────────────────────────────────────────────────┘
```

Figure 3.1   Rankings by global sales of the pharmaceutical industry in 1980 and 2010

Source: John Ansell Consultancy

we can see that the extent of change over the 30-year period is rather modest. And all of the top five companies existed in some guise in 1980.

There are two UK newcomers to the 2010 rankings, GlaxoSmithKline and AstraZeneca, respectively at numbers 6 and 7. Johnson & Johnson and Abbott are also new to these rankings. In fact, though they did not make the Top 10 rankings by 1980, they were both quite sizeable pharmaceutical companies by that time.

The conclusion from all this is that there has been remarkable stability amongst the leading global pharmaceutical industry over the past 30 years. Constituents of the two UK newcomers to the 2010 rankings were already significant if not major pharmaceutical companies in 1980. Thus no complete newcomer had succeeded in reaching the Top 10 by 2010.

It is true that not much farther down the 2010 rankings, the Israeli generics company Teva and the US biotech company Amgen, ranked twelfth and thirteenth respectively, are companies which did not have significant global presences in 1980. But overall, the pharmaceutical industry turns out to have been relatively undynamic in terms of its corporate composition.

This is, I believe, a reflection of the distinctive characteristics I discussed in Chapter 1. It has probably been a deterrent to newcomers entering pharmaceuticals, or at least made life difficult for those outsiders attempting it. It has also quite commonly persuaded newcomers to sooner or later withdraw from the pharmaceutical industry. Meanwhile, the major pharmaceutical players have been remarkably resilient over the years, with sudden demise practically unheard of in the pharmaceutical industry.

Difficulty of Getting Into Pharmaceuticals

It has been particularly tough for newcomers, who have aimed at becoming traditional, mass-market pharmaceutical companies, to establish themselves. It is no accident that the successful newcomer Amgen I mentioned above is a company that targets specialists only. It has benefited in its ascendancy from the fact that a much smaller outlay in setting up specialist sales forces is required than for a traditional GP product-oriented company. The obstacle to entry of having to set up adequate sales forces is much more modest if promotion can be restricted to specialist target groups.

Barriers to entry for companies in areas other than marketing are much lower. Many hundred biotech companies have been set up over the past 35 years to develop human pharmaceuticals. They have found it possible to raise finance to develop pharmaceuticals (though this has been far easier in the United States than anywhere else). However, only a very limited number have so far been successful commercially, though this number has recently been growing. By 2012 there were six companies in the Top 50 rankings which fitted that description: Amgen, Gilead, Merck Serono, Celgene, Biogen Idec and Actelion (Cacciotti 2012).

There has been no attempt by established pharmaceutical companies to try to keep biotech companies out of the pharmaceutical market. Indeed, the former have become increasingly dependent on start-up companies as a source of new products.

Likewise, a multitude of service companies to the pharmaceutical industry – from contract marketing organizations (CMOs), to contract research organizations (CROs), to business consultancies – have been set up, many of which have been able to prosper. Existing players in pharmaceuticals competing with these organizations have not found it possible to 'close out' most of these new competitors, or have indeed made great efforts to do so. Nor does small scale of operation appear to have been a factor hampering the development of small, new service companies.

This is because all parties have been able to benefit from an expanding services market. There has been strong growth since the 1980s by the pharmaceutical industry in the use of all types of service. CROs are a prime example. They now conduct over 20 per cent of all clinical trials set up by pharmaceutical companies. But also smaller, independent organizations have tended over the past 30 years to be increasingly accepted by the pharmaceutical industry because of the usually good quality of what they can offer. This ingress of start-ups – both biotech and service companies – suggests that pharmaceuticals is relatively open to newcomers.

This is in stark contrast to the remarkable lack of success of established companies from other industries in entering pharmaceutical marketing, which I describe below. In recent years there has been little interest from outside companies in doing so. This is probably because the pharmaceutical industry has performed more poorly in comparison with other industries over the past decade than formerly. It may also reflect the earlier failure of many leading companies from outside to survive in pharmaceuticals. More specifically it may well be that potential entrants from outside the pharmaceutical industry have come to realize that a multitude of skills and experience, often quite different to those suited to other industries, are required to succeed in pharmaceuticals.

Also a deterrent to outsiders has been the very long time horizon and consequent high risk levels we have discussed in Chapter 1. Associated with this is the extent to which long-term investment is needed in pharmaceuticals, far greater than that required for many other industries.

ENTRANTS WHO DID NOT PERSIST

As mentioned above, big companies from outside pharmaceuticals were not always so reluctant to enter the pharmaceutical fray. In the 1960s and 1970s companies such as Guinness, Unilever and Shell made moves to enter pharmaceuticals. But most, including all three of these companies, did not persist for more than a few years before giving up.

Two other examples of companies which persisted much longer, until just a few years ago, were Procter & Gamble and 3M. The US fast-moving consumer goods (FMCG) company Procter & Gamble entered pharmaceuticals in 1982 with its acquisition of Morton-Norwich. It exited the prescription pharmaceutical market after 27 years in 2009. The US conglomerate 3M entered pharmaceuticals in 1970, but exited in 2007 after 37 years, when it sold off its global pharmaceutical interests. Neither of these companies had succeeded in becoming major players in pharmaceuticals.

I joined the New Business Development department of Solvay in Amsterdam in 1981 at the headquarters of Duphar, the company it had acquired a few months previously, and spent four of the happiest years of my career there. Solvay, a major Belgian chemical company, had decided a few years earlier to build up its previously modest pharmaceutical presence and the acquisition of Duphar was a major step in its strategy. But the pharmaceutical division never blossomed. Solvay sold off its pharmaceutical interests to Abbott in 2010 after attempting for over 30 years to establish a strong presence in the industry.

Lastly, an interesting example of a company that persisted for much longer than this is the German chemical concern BASF. This company became a serious player in pharmaceuticals when it acquired Knoll AG in 1975. But in 2000 it sold its pharmaceutical interests to Abbott having made only a modest impact globally in pharmaceuticals. With hindsight, this divestment can be seen as a spectacular loss of opportunity, since one of the products then in the pipeline, Humira (adalimumab), went on to become the best-selling pharmaceutical product of all in 2012, with sales in that year of $9.3 billion.

This relative lack of success of newcomers to pharmaceuticals in the past stems I believe mainly from the very different mode of operation of pharmaceuticals to any other type of industry. A nonpharmaceutical company which has developed particular management philosophies suited to its own established types of products and markets usually finds it difficult to reconcile these with the very different demands of pharmaceuticals. It is also common in my experience that companies which do not have a deep understanding of another industry and know little of its different demands tend to underestimate the importance of these differences.

In particular, the staying power of outside entrants in the pharmaceutical industry is often severely tested by the inevitable setbacks that arise in developing new pharmaceutical products. It is only when they have suffered a series of setbacks that they fully realize how risky pharmaceutical development is, how long it can take to develop new products and how much investment is going to be needed to stand a chance of achieving success.

INVESTMENT BEYOND THE NORMAL CALL OF DUTY

Companies from outside the pharmaceutical industry are used to operating in ways that require less sustained investment than is needed in pharmaceuticals. A consumer goods company like Procter & Gamble accepts the need for investment in R&D up to the time of launch of a new product because this is what it expects in the FMCG market. But Procter & Gamble is not accustomed to having to continue to invest substantially in development of a product for several years beyond launch.

In contrast to FMCG, with pharmaceuticals it is now the rule rather than the exception that the company will be involved in further clinical work well beyond first launch. For example, at the time of Lipitor's (atorvastatin, Pfizer) patent expiry in 2011–12, the product had been studied in more than 400 continuing or completed clinical trials, only a very small proportion of which were completed when it was first submitted for registration. Such trials are aimed at range extension to further support claims for an existing indication or to extend the approved claims for a product in an additional indication or for a new presentation. This is life-cycle management, a fact of life to those in pharmaceuticals. (See Chapter 4, pp. 82–4). It is crucial to the full exploitation of a new product that this work be carried out and not, as Procter & Gamble imagined, an optional extra. I argue that the sheer scale and complexity of product life-cycle management has become a significant additional barrier to new entrants to the pharmaceutical market.

Also, whilst the high margins commonly enjoyed in pharmaceuticals have been attractive to outsiders, the need for sustained investment in marketing over many years – in particular in the form of expensive sales forces – is also often underestimated by companies from other industries where this is not customary. They (and managers from outside the industry who join it) are often tempted to cut promotion prematurely – which can have disastrous results.

A growing test of resolve – of established pharmaceutical companies as well as newcomers – is that the amount which companies have needed to invest in R&D has not stayed constant. Companies that have entered pharmaceuticals over the past 30 years have found that the amount they require to spend on R&D has risen steadily in real terms. Some, like Solvay, have gone into pharmaceuticals prepared to spend 20 per cent of sales or more on R&D in an effort to boost productivity. But this level has commonly had to be maintained for more years than expected, and more often than not has not had the desired effect. This has also, I believe, been an important factor in dissuading some newcomers from persisting with pharmaceuticals.

JAPANESE EXCEPTIONS

One exception to the common attitude of outsiders – that the pharmaceutical industry has become too difficult to countenance entering – are Japanese companies. They have continued to enter the industry through acquisition of pharmaceutical companies as well as partnering. For example, Japan Tobacco has over the past 15 years formed strategic alliances with several different pharmaceutical companies to develop new products, as well acquired a development company, Akros, and the established local pharmaceutical company Torii. Another example is Kirin Brewery, which in 2007 acquired Kyowa Hakko to add to its already existing pharmaceutical division, to form Kyowa Kirin. A third is the photographic equipment company Fujifilm which in 2008 acquired the Japanese pharmaceutical company Toyama. It has subsequently acquired several other interests in pharmaceuticals.

The difficulty in getting into pharmaceuticals tells us quite a lot about the industry itself. How about getting out?

Difficulty of Getting Out of Pharmaceuticals or Diversifying Away From It

There have been many cases of companies, where pharmaceuticals is just one of several divisions, who have decided to exit pharmaceuticals. But these cases have mostly been of companies which have not had a long-standing presence in pharmaceuticals, or for whom pharmaceuticals is not a major activity.

Since around 2007 there have been increasing attempts by pharmaceutical companies to spread their interests beyond pharmaceuticals: in other words, diversification rather than a straight exit of the industry. Nearly all this diversification activity has, however, been into other areas of healthcare.

It is interesting that this desire to diversify has not often stretched beyond the bounds of healthcare. There are probably three reasons for this. Firstly, pharmaceutical companies are unfamiliar with nonhealthcare industries. Secondly, they usually have to accept much lower margins than they are accustomed to if they go outside the bounds of healthcare. Thirdly, pharmaceutical companies may well realize that the experience which they have will not necessarily be relevant to nonhealthcare markets. When it comes to diversifying merely into other areas of healthcare, some of these dissuading factors still apply. The way in which other healthcare markets operate is often markedly different to pharmaceuticals. I would never dream, for example, of advising consultancy clients on the medical devices market. I always do that in association with a specialist medical device consultant. This is because medical device markets are so different in many ways to pharmaceutical markets. If I applied my pharmaceutical experience to medical devices I would risk seriously misleading my clients.

The second nonhealthcare factor I mentioned above in respect of other industries – low margins – also often applies to other areas of healthcare. In the majority of healthcare markets outside pharmaceuticals, margins will be lower – quite often much lower. In the past few years, however, in the spirit of experimentation, many diversifying companies appear to have paid only limited heed to this factor. I forecast that in a few years' time there will be some rueful post-mortems on recent diversifications which should not have been entered into because of inadequate margins. I sense the first signs of this from recent quarterly reports.

The third nonhealthcare factor, unfamiliarity with the market, ought to be less of a problem for pharmaceutical companies when considering diversification into other areas of the healthcare market. In reality this factor varies in importance because healthcare markets themselves vary considerably, with some being more similar than others to pharmaceuticals in terms of how they operate.

I deal with diversification in more detail in Chapters 7 and 8.

PART II

Assessing Management Concepts for the Pharmaceutical Industry

Companies transforming themselves have to select from a variety of different strategies. How, then, should pharma companies decide which strategies are the right ones for them?

They can look at what other companies are doing. They can also take advice from third parties with specific expertise of many different types in the pharmaceutical industry. And they can also adopt management techniques and concepts from outside the pharmaceutical industry.

In Part II I will first consider the value or not of a whole variety of such concepts. In Chapter 4 I focus in particular on those management concepts which – for good or ill – are most frequently employed by the pharmaceutical industry today. Then in two shorter chapters I take a look at some of the pronouncements of management gurus which do not fit the pharmaceutical industry, and deal with organizational issues faced by the pharmaceutical industry.

4

Assessing the Value of Concepts from Outside the Pharmaceutical Industry

> *... our search for excessively simple explanations, our desire to find great men and excellent companies, gets in the way of the complex truth.*
> *John Kay,* Financial Times, 2007

For many years the pharmaceutical industry has – just like any other major industry – been bombarded with countless apparently new management ideas and concepts. Most of them are promoted by management consultancies or the authors of management books.[1]

To adopt a new management concept requires change – and implementing that change makes work for management consultancies and sells copies of books. A few of them, like the concept of marketing (see immediately below), get taken up and absorbed into the system of companies to the extent that they become part of the corporate infrastructure. But such concepts are in a small minority. The majority never get adopted. And of those management concepts which do become adopted, the majority are discarded within a few years, if not earlier.

This can be an enormously wasteful process. Reviewing a new management concept is usually not particularly time consuming. But if it is adopted, it commits financial support and, more importantly, substantial management time to training and follow-up.

---

1 An excellent general comprehensive description of management concepts I find useful is a guide by Tim Hindle (2008).

When a management concept is adopted that turns out to be useless, this not only means a write-off of that investment of resources and time. It may well also have a considerable opportunity cost. Tying up resources in one particular management concept can mean that a more promising one – perhaps one which is meanwhile being adopted by competitors – is passed up. Also it encourages scepticism amongst the workforce and discourages flexibility and openness to adopt to change.

It is clearly healthy that pharmaceutical companies are exposed to new ideas from outside the organization – including those from outside the pharmaceutical industry. But for the reasons stated above, there should be critical assessment of these ideas. There have been only limited attempts to comprehensively assess management concepts critically. And there have been none specifically designed for use by the pharmaceutical industry.

Of course there would be limited point to me here retrospectively assessing a lot of management concepts fairly obviously well past their sell-by date. I have therefore selected management concepts that – for better or worse – have become adopted widely by pharmaceutical companies. Some are still helpful. But others, despite their popularity, can in my view actually be dangerously misleading.

The management concepts I consider vary widely in their nature, how they are applied in the pharmaceutical industry and their value to the industry. I cover them in a sequence which aims to bring out these contrasts.

Marketing

It might surprise some readers that I am even including marketing in this series of management concept assessments. As I mentioned above, it has become so well established in pharma management practice that it is almost taken for granted. It was from the 1960s that marketing started to have an impact on the pharmaceutical industry.

There are many alternative definitions of marketing. A good working one from the UK Chartered Institute of Marketing, which I have used for years, defines it as: 'the management process responsible for identifying, anticipating and satisfying customer requirements profitably' (CIM 2012).

This seems to me to be a fundamental aspect of what any industry should be doing. It helps to explain why marketing has never gone out of fashion – nor is likely to. Indeed I will be considering some of the other management concepts below according to how marketing oriented they are.

SWOT

SWOT analysis is a management technique which is simple, straightforward and can be very useful. This acronym stands for Strengths, Weaknesses, Opportunities and Threats. SWOT's origins are poorly documented but it goes back to the 1960s; the Stanford Research Institute (SRI) appears to have had more to do with developing it than any other organization.

SWOT is used very widely across the pharmaceutical industry. It can be employed, usually as an early-stage activity, to analyse the total organization. More frequently it is used to assess a product. SWOT analysis brings particular attention to less obvious factors involved in what is under review. For example, for an organization the four parameters would cover the following ground:

STRENGTHS

Looking at your organization, what strengths do you possess in relation to your:

- corporate strategy

- organizational structure

- leadership

- people

- processes

- products

- systems

- values

- culture?

WEAKNESSES

On the other hand, what weaknesses do you have in relation to each of these factors?

OPPORTUNITIES

What opportunities do you see for your business?

THREATS

Looking externally, what threats or other challenges do you face?

Classical SWOT analysis defines rather rigidly that Strengths and Weaknesses must relate to factors *inside* an organization, whereas Threats and Opportunities relate to factors *outside* an organization. In practice SWOT analysis does not need to be performed this inflexibly. The important function of a SWOT analysis at the outset is that it identifies all factors involved.

As critics have pointed out, SWOT does not represent a strategy in itself. A SWOT analysis cannot, for example, include statements about what should be done next. But whilst this does limit its powers, a SWOT analysis provides a reasonable tool for assessing the future of an organization, project or product.

In the pharmaceutical industry SWOT analysis is most frequently used in product assessment. For example, a marketing plan first reviews the product in question across all relevant aspects – its current share of the market, sales trends, the product profile and so on. Then, towards the end of the plan, the SWOT analysis encapsulates all of these aspects. A SWOT analysis is also useful in initially assessing a product opportunity offered by a third party.

SWOT analysis is simple, requires little training, and can be quick to use. But there are limitations:

- SWOT analysis does not prioritize between points identified.

- It can lead to individual points included being considered as equivalent in weight. Are those three separate points on product benefits really separate points – or are all part of one point?

- It does not necessarily help to highlight critical, make-or-break factors for projects or products.

- There is a danger that SWOT practitioners are too relentless in insisting on a long list of factors being generated. In my experience this does not often happen: people move on instead to additional analytical methods.

- Sometimes there is a tendency to stop at description without going on to strategic analysis.

However, if the above pitfalls are avoided, SWOT analysis can be very useful, particularly as a starting point. This technique is in my experience used by a wider variety of disciplines within the pharmaceutical industry than any other. Its popularity in the pharmaceutical industry is therefore in my view largely justified. Not many techniques are inexpensive in time and resources, quickly provide initial guidance and do not tend to mislead.

Benchmarking

Benchmarking in management terms is the process of comparing one's business processes and performance metrics to an industry's best practices and/or best practices from other industries. It was first introduced in this modern sense by the Xerox Corporation in the 1980s.

Benchmarking is usually time and resource consuming as it involves detailed research within half a dozen other organizations at least, involving in-depth, one-to-one interviewing. Using the resources of the Internet can, however, reduce some costs of classical benchmarking considerably.

Companies often enter into an omnibus survey project in which they each agree to be interviewed on the understanding that they receive feedback on all participants, as well as an interpretative report. It is usually an advantage for a facilitating benchmarking organization to conduct the interviews as well as the analysis and interpretation.

There have been at least two benchmarking organizations specifically serving the pharmaceutical industry. The scope of pharmaceutical benchmarking surveys currently conducted covers quite a range of topics and issues.

In 2012 the US benchmarking organization Best Practices LLC was advertising pharma industry surveys covering a wide range of topics across many industry disciplines. These included manufacturing quality and operations, new product development and clinical operations. Commercially oriented topics included launching and marketing blockbusters, brand management, and sales performance management and measurement. Also covered were influencing external organizations and managing thought leaders and speakers.

For inexperienced companies or those that have fallen behind, benchmarking can be a means of getting up to speed. But that is as far as you should expect it to take you.

Are management concepts that take you this far good enough? The answer depends on how competitive the specific area of the pharmaceutical industry you are involved with is. As well as the obvious area of the market, competitiveness relates to R&D and other noncommercial areas.

During my career the pharmaceutical industry has become increasingly competitive. If we take the most directly competitive area – the market – until the 1970s it was quite common for pharmaceutical companies to 'aim low' – just for a piece of the action, which would, they felt confident, generate sufficient revenues for them. But the room for developing such 'me-too' products has declined considerably over the past 30 years. Consequently there are no longer dozens of companies pursuing the same approach as was the case in the days 50 years ago or more of corticosteroids and beta-blockers. Companies today make more sophisticated assessments of markets and soon come to realize that there is now only room for two or three me-too products in each at most.

In R&D, the time it takes for an original approach to be copied has progressively decreased. In 2011 DiMasi and Faden reported that the period of exclusivity for first-in-class drugs had declined progressively since the 1960s. Typically it took on average nine to ten years to happen in the 1960s and 1970s, around six years in the 1980s and early 1990s, and half of this or even less thereafter up to 2003.

John LaMattina, head of research at Pfizer between 2003 and 2007, considered that this could be a contributory factor in the decline of the number of new products produced since the 1990s, as me-toos became less economically viable (LaMattina 2011).

Because companies began to realize that the copycat approach soon became self-limiting, by the 1990s only a limited number of products in each class were being taken as far as the market. Most companies had stopped actively aiming to produce me-toos by then. I think there is a more general conclusion that can be drawn from this that applies across different disciplines – all of which have become more competitive over time – that today in pharmaceuticals techniques like benchmarking that show you how to catch up only take you so far.

Benchmarking could be useful in bringing a company up to scratch in the more routine aspects of running an R&D organization or of setting up or improving a manufacturing process. But it won't provide the creative spark to set a company off on a radically new course which could lead to a breakthrough. I would therefore argue that benchmarking is less widely applicable in pharmaceuticals than it is in other, less innovative industries and that its power particularly in the commercial area has been declining with the decreased role for me-too products.

Benchmarking also has the disadvantage that it inevitably monitors practices that are historical. It tends to emphasize best practice as it now is. In itself it does not help to project future trends. Indeed it may provide false confidence that existing best practices will suffice. You could therefore describe benchmarking as not being particularly market oriented. In pharmaceuticals, becoming one of the herd is increasingly just not good enough.

Market Access

Over the past few years marketing theory and practice has extended to a new concept: market access. This concept is being applied in pharmaceuticals in different ways and at different levels. This has caused confusion as it applies at different levels in different ways.

Firstly, the term *market access* is used to include all those strategies concerned with getting a product onto the market and also all types of postregulatory approval required. By this definition it therefore embraces the whole area of regulatory affairs as well as health economics, the latter providing evidence to satisfy all those decision makers – gatekeepers – concerned with agreeing to begin purchasing a product. Thus the whole process of what was traditionally known as gaining pricing and reimbursement is also included under market access according to this definition.

But the term is also used at a more tactical, local level. As well as stressing the need to identify the different players involved in making the sales decision, it also includes the tailoring of marketing and sales strategies and clinical and health economic evidence to the needs at this level for dealing with each.

There has been a growing awareness of the complexities involved in gaining market access in pharmaceuticals. Each potential decision maker can be playing a role at several levels. For example, one particular clinical specialist could be involved:

- in day-to-day prescribing for their patients;

- via membership of a hospital formulary committee; and

- as a member of a government drug review committee.

Determining market access strategies or tactics can involve executives belonging to several different parts of a pharmaceutical organization. Consequently these contacts need to be carefully coordinated by a pharmaceutical company if sales are to be maximized.

The concept of market access makes sense because – whether it is being used at a strategic or more tactical level – it attends to what is needed in the market. It is particularly relevant to pharmaceuticals, where gaining access is a sophisticated task because of the number of different stakeholders today playing a role. It is also a helpful concept in paying due attention to the great variation in conditions for access between markets geographically. This applies between areas and regions of a country. It also applies at the national level between markets internationally. And it applies locally too. Conditions for market access can also vary markedly in different therapeutic areas and so this also needs to be fully understood.

The concept of market access began outside the pharmaceutical industry and was popularized in particular by large general management consultancies. It is one of the rare management concepts introduced from outside the industry that has been much more successful in pharmaceuticals than most other industries. Indeed it is difficult to find other industries where it has caught on. Looking at sizeable business sections of two large Oxford bookshops at the beginning of 2012, I could not see any one title dealing with market access, and thus it seems to have gained little general management appeal.

As long as there is a balance, and market access is part of a comprehensive marketing strategy that includes other important aspects of marketing such as addressing the competition and developing counterstrategies, then it can be a valid and useful part of commercial strategy.

The Product Life-Cycle Curve

Some general management concepts become so ingrained that even though they have been repeatedly demonstrated to be flawed and misleading, they nevertheless continue to be used. For pharmaceuticals the product life-cycle curve is in my view the prime example of this.

The product life-cycle concept survives in the pharmaceutical industry as it does across all industries. It became more familiar because the completely legitimate concept of life-cycle management, which we will discuss later in this chapter (see pp. 82–4), has become so important in pharmaceuticals.

The concept of the product life-cycle curve appears simple. It comprises four phases. Rather than showing the well-known theoretical curve, here in Figure 4.1 is a real-life example, for Abbott's antibiotic Biaxin/Klaricid (clarithromycin) which conforms rather well to the classical curve.

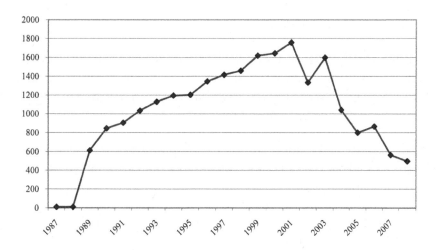

Figure 4.1   Biaxin/Klaricid sales curve ($ millions)
Source: John Ansell Consultancy

The four phases of the product life cycle are as follows:

- Introductory: In the introductory phase, there is a gradual build-up of sales.

- Growth: In this phase, sales are accelerating. A classical S-shaped curve results from these first two phases. I have found that sales curves for a minority of pharmaceutical products like Biaxin/ Klaricid actually have this S-shaped phase.

- Maturity: During this third phase, sales growth begins to slow, a peak in sales is then reached and the first signs of a downturn are evident.

- Decline: Finally, sales begin to decline more sharply, as the end of the product's life approaches.

The classical product life-cycle curve depicts four equal-length phases. Biaxin happened to have a short introductory phase and a particularly long growth phase. But in reality this is the case for many pharmaceutical products.

The product life-cycle concept is superficially persuasive. But in practice it only requires a look at a few real-life examples to undermine it. Although there are products like Biaxin whose sales do conform to the classical shape of the product life-cycle curve, they are in a minority.

See the global sales curve for one of the most famous pharmaceutical products of all: Viagra (sildenafil, Pfizer) in its first few years on the market (Figure 4.2). Viagra has an almost straight-line curve with no hint of a S-shaped kink: uptake of the product was so rapid that build up was fast.

Now look also at Lipitor (Figure 4.3). This product's curve, which was the best-selling of all between 2002 and 2011, follows a straight line for its first six years on the market.

A further leading product which describes a near-straight line is Zyprexa (Figure 4.4).

However, other, quite different types of curve are also seen. Lovenox/ Clexane (enoxaparin) (Figure 4.5) has been a major blockbuster product.

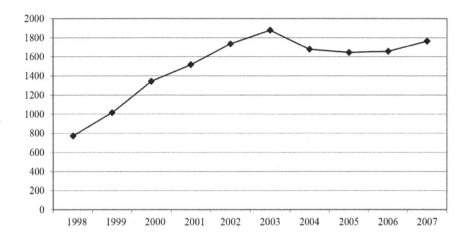

Figure 4.2   Viagra sales curve ($ millions)
Source: John Ansell Consultancy

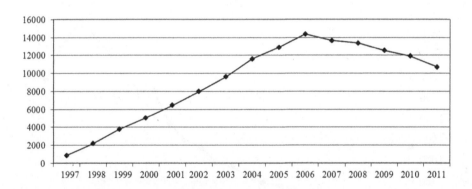

Figure 4.3   Lipitor sales curve ($ millions)
Source: John Ansell Consultancy

This product was launched in 1987 but did not enter the Top 50 best-selling global products until 1999; thereafter sales grew more rapidly. Its sales built up only gradually particularly because it was a long time before it reached the United States – the market with the greatest commercial potential.

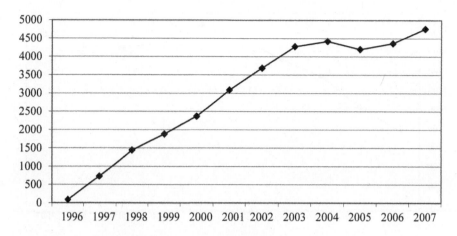

Figure 4.4   Zyprexa sales curve ($ millions)
Source: John Ansell Consultancy

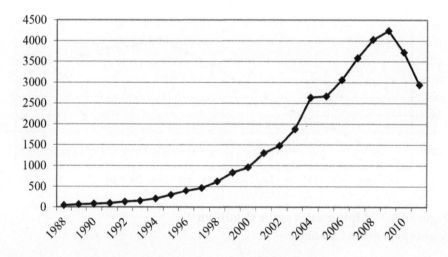

Figure 4.5   Lovenox/Clexane sales curve ($ millions)
Source: John Ansell Consultancy

Crestor (Figure 4.6), whose prospects were belittled by competitors up to the time of its launch (see pp. 15, 114), has a similar, impressive, near straight-line growth, with just a hint of an S-shaped kink at the beginning of its curve.

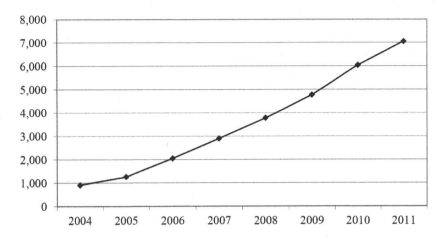

Figure 4.6   Crestor sales curve ($ millions)
Source: John Ansell Consultancy

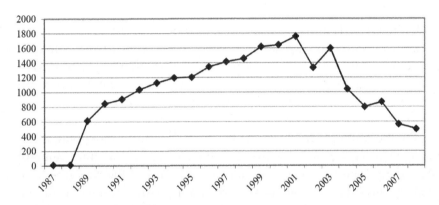

Figure 4.7   Cipro sales curve ($ millions)
Source: John Ansell Consultancy

A particular danger of the product life-cycle theory is that an apparent peak in sales can be seriously misleading. This is because products often have more than one peak in sales. Examples are not difficult to find. Sales of the antibiotic Cipro (ciprofloxacin, Bayer, Figure 4.7) looked to be levelling off towards 2000 but kicked up in 2001. This was because immediately after 9/11, it appeared that terrorists were posting anthrax spores to targets. As a precaution, enormous quantities of the antibiotic Cipro were ordered by the US government. As it turned out, it was a false alarm.

We can see that there was a consequent dip in Cipro sales in the year afterwards. But they actually recovered in 2003, before declining thereafter because of patent expiry. This illustrates how environmental factors such as 9/11 are poorly catered for by theoretical management concepts like the product life cycle. (And, by the way, the shape of the growth phase for Cipro by no means has any initial S-shape either.)

Even the classical S-shaped curves we saw above do not ultimately conform. Take Biaxin/Klaricid, for example (Figure 4.1). According to classical life-cycle curve theory, we would expect sales, which peaked in 1997, to have declined within a few years. But it turns out that there was a lengthy period of decline, with sales even picking up temporarily in 2003 and 2006.

Hence there is a danger of falsely diagnosing imminent and final decline of a product. There are often pressures within pharmaceutical companies to reduce promotional expenditure as soon as possible – to get out of the expensive launch and immediate postlaunch phases.

Later, any levelling off of sales can be eagerly seized upon by cost-conscious managers: if the beginning of the maturity phase of the product life cycle has been reached, then it must – according to life-cycle theory – be time to reduce promotion and thereby raise margins. However, in actuality it is very difficult to predict that the ultimate peak in sales is being reached.

Another example of a product that appeared to be describing a classical S-shaped curve but then went on to a higher plane is Imigran (sumatriptan, GlaxoSmithKline, Figure 4.8). By illustrating some of the background to this product's evolution in the market, we can see why considering the market environment is so much more important than adhering to any management concept.

When this first modern product for migraine reached the market it was necessary to familiarize doctors and patients with an entirely novel form of migraine therapy. Both target groups needed far more persuasion to accept Imigran than had been anticipated. It took several years of sustained promotion before its sales began to build up impressively.

Indeed, after the first two years of sales, Glaxo was disappointed that Imigran had failed to become 'another Zantac', the last big product the company had brought to the market which I had been working on in the

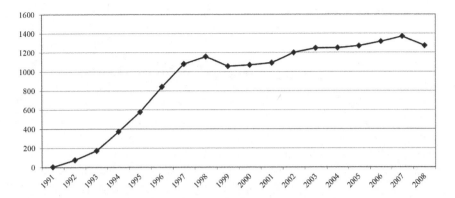

Figure 4.8   Imigran sales curve ($ millions)
Source: John Ansell Consultancy

international marketing department a few years previously. Zantac (ranitidine), an antiulcerant, was at the time of Imigran's launch not only the market leader in that market, but the globally best-selling product of all.

Sales of Imigran eventually took six years to pass the $1 billion mark. As it turned out, even with the introduction of several competitive triptan products in the late 1990s, the penetration of the potential migraine population by triptans still remained modest. However, Imigran benefited from this competition: it forced Glaxo to step up promotional expenditure on its product in its defence against the new competitors. As a consequence of the stepped-up promotion, after a couple of years Imigran sales picked up again, and Imigran continued to grow thereafter to untold new heights, well beyond the premature sales peak reached in 1998, until post–patent expiry sales erosion sales set in. Imigran thus not only saw off most of this competition but also belatedly turned into a blockbuster.

Some products have several successive peaks. The champion product in modern times as far as I am aware is Merck & Co's hospital product Primaxin (imipenem + cilastatin, Figure 4.9). This product is remarkable in that its sales have peaked no less than five times – in 1992, 1995, 2000, 2005 and 2007.

In conclusion, the Pavlovian response to apparent product maturity – cutting back on promotional expenditure – unfortunately leads normally to a more pronounced plateauing of sales and earlier-than-necessary decline.

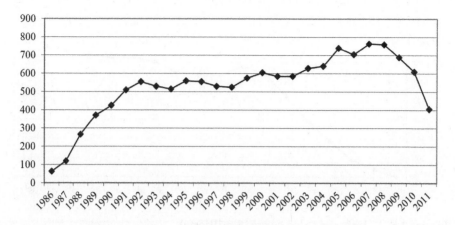

Figure 4.9   Primaxin sales curve ($ millions)
Source: John Ansell Consultancy

The entry into the final phase of the product life cycle thus becomes a self-fulfilling prophecy!

Slavish adoption of the textbook product life-cycle curve can result in premature withdrawal of promotional support from products capable in time of achieving greater success. Had misleading life-cycle theory been followed and promotion withdrawn from some of the products described above, they would never have gone on to reach greater heights.

Generally, the pharmaceutical industry has come to realize over the past 20 years that life cycles for pharmaceuticals are much actually longer than was formerly believed (see pp. 20–21, 243–6). Product sales often continue to increase right up to the time when all intellectual property rights have been exhausted. I cover this later in this chapter (see pp. 82–4). Pharmaceutical companies have therefore increasingly been ready to nurture products for longer, in order to ensure that they maximize the returns from their products.

Weak Management Concepts Can Still Survive

You might imagine that management concepts found wanting would lose credibility and go out of use. This is often the case but unfortunately some like the product life cycle seem indestructible. Within a few years of the product life cycle being proposed in the late 1950s, it was being criticized. I myself wrote an article entitled *Dispelling the Myth of the Product Life Cycle* some 25 years ago (Ansell 1988).

That the product life cycle is a simple, memorable concept has, I think, something to do with this. Simplicity seems to trump validity. That simplicity is attractive. It seems to avoid the need to make undue effort: don't bother to study the market in any detail, it persuades – just follow the curve. The product life cycle is an example of a concept which in modern parlance dumbs down marketing.

Pharmaceutical markets are not necessarily highly complex. But they are usually too sophisticated for many simple management concepts to have much useful application. The product life-cycle concept is certainly one of them.

The examples I gave above indicate the tremendous range of trajectories a successful product's sales can take. These trajectories depend upon several factors – more than half a dozen at least in my forecasting experience – even for a fairly simple market without many different products and players.

Take a rather simple example. Imagine that your company is close to marketing the second modern product which will reach the market for lupus erythematosus – after Benlysta (belimumab) from GlaxoSmithKline/ Human Genome Sciences, which as I described was first launched in 2011 (see pp. 46, 49). You have a year or so of sales data for that product in the markets where it has been launched. You believe that your product, though different to Benlysta, will appeal to the same types of prescribers. You know that GlaxoSmithKline has not performed uniformly in each market. (The product has not been launched simultaneously, for a start.) You find that – reputable company though GlaxoSmithKline is – there are deficiencies in the marketing of the product in some countries which you ought to be able to capitalize upon. But in others GlaxoSmithKline has done an excellent job. And so the market penetrations which you are projecting for each market will have to take this into account.

Whilst, like GlaxoSmithKline, you have a consistent global pricing policy, you know that in some countries neither GlaxoSmithKline nor your company will receive approval of Benlysta at the prices it wants to achieve. You consider that in a few countries you can take advantage of your only competitor by setting your price at a 15 per cent price discount to Benlysta. You therefore expect to capture a larger market share for your product – albeit with a rather lower margin – in those countries.

Meanwhile, coming up in the rear mirror are at least a couple of potentially strong competitors. You have done extensive role playing of their likely strategies and projected what you consider to be the likely market shares for each of these likely future competitors. That – along with your projections for Benlysta – guides you towards determining the shares you are likely to get with your product.

This is only a simplified example. But already we can see that the complexity of the market situation overwhelms a simplistic concept like the product life cycle. It explains why, as we have seen above, products in reality describe such a range of different sales curves. This means also that no simple concept or computer model can encapsulate such situations. Much of the skill of forecasting lies instead in a deep understanding of the market, in particular identifying the key factors which will govern market progress, and imaginative projection of its likely development.

Finally, the progress of a product is by no means passive, as the product life-cycle concept suggests, with each of the four phases inevitably following on from the previous one. The theory can engender a fatalistic complacency amongst marketers. It can lead to underpromotion of products. Quite commonly in my experience alert competitors go on to take advantage through stepping up their own promotion. I have done so personally for my companies and clients on several occasions!

I have used the product life-cycle concept as one example of what is bad about classical management concepts. However, this particular concept has led to one important offshoot: product life-cycle management.

The Product Life-Cycle Management Concept and Its Basis

Product life-cycle management is the planned development of a product throughout its active commercial life in order to maximize the commercial return from it. With the dearth of novel products, the launch of additional indications and presentations – range extensions – has become increasingly important in managing a product.

Life-cycle management can be aimed at directly increasing sales of a product. Or it can enhance intellectual property protection – sometimes pejoratively termed 'evergreening'.

Because in pharmaceuticals range extensions cannot be developed at short notice, long-term planning is essential. In this sense, the range extension philosophy is a more important aspect of pharmaceutical marketing than it is in consumer marketing, where it is usually a much shorter-term, reactive activity.

In the past, *additional presentations* featured most strongly in the total portfolio of possible range extensions for a pharmaceutical product. The main presentation of a product, typically a tablet or a capsule, would be marketed first, and then would follow a variety of other lesser presentations: injectable formulations, oral solutions and syrups, pessaries and suppositories. Usually the initially launched presentation remained the greatest contributor to sales.

This meant that range extensions received little fanfare and featured temporarily in the product sales detail. But from the 1970s drug delivery technologies began to make advances. The once-daily dosage form was shown in a number of therapeutic markets – particularly cardiovascular (for example beta-blockers and calcium antagonists) – to be a powerful marketing tool for rejuvenating aging products. Sometimes the once-daily forms not only defended the previously launched conventional presentations – they succeeded in outselling them.

Such extended-release formulations continue to rejuvenate old products. But companies commonly now have to have their once-daily formulations ready to market at first launch if they are to succeed against the competition. Hence drug delivery devices have become incorporated much more into the mainstream of development rather than being an afterthought for range extension.

Over the past 20 years there has been a marked change of emphasis in life-cycle management. *Additional indications* have become much more important. Since a new indication normally involves an extensive clinical trial programme, indication extension is usually a much more time-consuming and expensive activity than presentation extension. This trend has sharply increased life-cycle management budgets. Today the indication extension budget usually accounts for the lion's share of a company's budget for range extension and life-cycle management.

When a company can combine two range extension features in one range extension project – typically a novel indication claim together with a novel presentation, this can be particularly powerful, even if each feature is in itself of modest benefit. The impact of any range extension can also lead to a more generalized improvement in a product's sales across different presentations and/or indications because it provides a new opportunity to promote the product.

Paradoxically, pharmaceutical companies now tend to spend much more post-launch on R&D than a consumer goods company such as Procter & Gamble – the classic proponent of marketing – would ever be comfortable to invest after launching one of its consumer products. Consequently in pharmaceuticals life-cycle management has become an area of much greater scope than in most industries. This means that the level of sophistication involved and the expertise built up in pharmaceutical life-cycle management is also much greater now than in traditional FMCG companies. Perhaps for once other industries should be learning from pharmaceuticals about a classical management concept rather than the other way round.

Strategic Alliances

I first came across the term *strategic alliance* in 1988, in Zurich at the first major pharmaceutical conference I ever chaired. The keynote speaker who covered strategic alliances was Jan Leschly, then president and chief operating officer of Squibb Corporation.

Actually I had by that time already quite some experience of product-level alliances: that is, co-marketing and co-promotion, first for a couple of years in business development with Solvay in Amsterdam and then at Glaxo in international marketing. In the 1980s both of these types of strategic alliances spearheaded the success of Bristol-Myers Squibb and Glaxo in marketing major products globally. The foremost examples from these two companies were, respectively, Capoten (captopril) and Zantac (ranitidine). These two types of product-level deal both quickly became included within the term *strategic alliance* in the late 1980s.

In contrast to these alliance success stories, another company I worked for in the 1970s, Fisons Pharmaceuticals, had their fingers burnt with one early US co-marketing deal for their major product for asthma Intal (sodium cromoglycate). After this failure the company refused from then onwards right through into the early 1990s to set up product-level strategic alliances. Unfortunately the other source of new products, the company pipeline, produced little. Fisons became starved of new products with substantial potential and the commercial part of this company was absorbed into Rhône-Poulenc Rorer in 1995.

The term *strategic alliance* also embraces deals done at the corporate as well as product level. It includes joint ventures. The term was rapidly adopted by the pharmaceutical industry because it was a useful umbrella term to cover many types of cooperative deal. It has remained in use as deals has become more complex and multifaceted. Cooperation has been key to the continued globalization of pharmaceuticals. This is in my view particularly appropriate for an industry like pharmaceuticals which is not heavily concentrated.

In the 1980s pharmaceuticals was even less concentrated than now (see Chapter 1 (see p. 32). As companies have merged with each other and also increased their global footprint, their need for the conventional product-level strategic alliances – co-marketing and co-promotion – has diminished. For the past 20 years GlaxoSmithKline (and its predecessor companies) have not needed partners very often to market their products. The company has been able to do this very adequately with the extensive network of marketing subsidiaries it built up in the 1980s and 1990s. However, for GlaxoSmithKline as for all other big pharma companies, alliances remain important in doing corporate deals of all types, particularly those at R&D stages. I describe one particularly novel example of a GlaxoSmithKline strategic alliance in Chapter 6 (see p. 105).

A poll in 2012 of CEOs by PricewaterhouseCoopers found that 15 per cent of pharmaceutical and life sciences CEOs considered new joint ventures and/or strategic alliances would be the main opportunity for growth of their businesses over the subsequent 12 months (PwC 2012a). This compared with 10 per cent of CEOs from all industries, showing the particular importance of strategic alliances to the pharmaceutical industry.

In the past few years alliances between multiple companies and other organizations have become common. One particular recent aim has been to reduce costs and increase the efficiency of conducting R&D through what is termed *open innovation*. Recent alliances set up include the Coalition for Accelerating Standards and Therapies (CFAST), the Predictive Safety Testing Consortium (PTSC), the Clinical Trials Transformation Initiative (CTTI), the Biomarkers Consortium and the Serious Adverse Effect Consortium. In 2012 10 big pharma companies formed TransCelerate BioPharma, a nonprofit organization with the aim of cooperating to solve common drug development problems.

Within the pharmaceutical industry there is no disagreement now about the importance of strategic alliances to its future.

The Boston Matrix

As I have discussed above (see p. 81), even in a relatively simple pharmaceutical market there are at least six or seven key variables that need to be considered in understanding its dynamics. It doesn't take much experience with our next management concept, the Boston Matrix, which depends on just two variables, to begin to realize that this is another example of a concept that can be seriously misleading. But just like the product life cycle, it has by no means been abandoned, perhaps because it is fairly easy to understand.

The Boston Matrix was developed by the Boston Consulting Group in the early 1960s. From that time it became particularly popular, as companies sought to determine which products in their range they should concentrate on through portfolio management. Portfolio management is a challenging and time-consuming process. Simple evaluations like the Boston Matrix appear to ease the heavy workload involved.[2] Despite sometimes fierce criticism of its limitations, the Boston Matrix survives widely – I believe because no other management concept of such temptingly convincing simplicity has ever been able to supplant it.

The Boston Matrix involves companies plotting values for each of their products' *relative market share* against the *market growth rate* by means of circles on a matrix. Only these two parameters are therefore represented: a remarkably

---

2   I do not propose to go into portfolio management in any detail. As the academic and consultant Brian Smith has recently said in *The Future of Pharma*: 'In most cases, pharmaceutical companies applying portfolio management tools in the context of this single fragmented and turbulent market find that they provide little practical guidance' (Smith 2011).

simplistic representation of the multiple factors involved in the dynamics of any market. The aim of this process is to thereby determine each product's sales prospects. How companies were persuaded that this was all that mattered I find difficult to imagine.

The matrix is divided into four quadrants. Products are categorized according to which quadrant they fall into. Those quadrants are: *Star, Cash Cow, Question Mark* and *Dog*.

High market share products in *high-growth* markets are not surprisingly considered to be *stars*. They are therefore regarded as meriting concentrated support to stimulate future sales and profits.

Products with *small shares* of *high growth* markets receive the soubriquet of *question mark* because they usually generate insufficient cash flow to support growth and maintain market share. Consequently, a company then has to decide whether it should take the risk of supporting such a product any further.

Cash cows have *high market share* but are in *slow growth* markets, in which the cost of gaining market share generally will not pay off. Companies often focus on just maintaining the existing share; they then extract the extra profits produced by cash cow products to support the more promising ones – hence their name.

The *low share, low growth* market qualities of *dogs* usually means that they generate little profit and will not produce a satisfactory return on investment.

This categorization is supposed to act as a guide to future strategy but, as historical data plotted on a matrix are insufficient to predict future prospects, this aspect is then dealt with using the product life-cycle curve we discussed earlier in this chapter. As I have shown, this can also be thoroughly misleading.

Once a company has decided rightly or wrongly that a product is a cash cow or even a dog, it will go on to withdraw support from that product. Naturally, when the skids are put under a product, its sales will begin to slide, regardless of whether it really does have further potential or not.

The product life cycle is in my view a particularly egregious example of a seductively simple management technique that obscures the need for sensible investigation of, and thinking about, precisely how much support a product deserves. For pharmaceuticals at least, more intelligent thought should guide decisions about product support, innovation and life-cycle management. Instead of using such 'painting by numbers' techniques managers need to be considering more than just two parameters and also assessing qualitative factors, as well as using their imaginations and plain common sense to reach the correct decisions in allocating company resources to their products.

Only three years after the Boston Matrix appeared, its shortcomings began to be reported. Critics queried, for example, why competitive strength and product/industry attractiveness were the only parameters that should be taken into consideration rather than any others. Therefore in the early 1980s Boston Consulting Group attempted to build a model along the same lines which coped with these criticisms. It came up with a more sophisticated system relying on a battery of matrices. But it proved so complex to use in practice that this Mark 2 system was never widely adopted. And it did not supplant the original Boston Matrix, which continues to be used.[3]

Over the past decade I have noticed a decline in the popularity of matrices, particularly in general management consultants' reports and presentations. Fortunately the tendency for managers to be overimpressed by matrix systems, and to avoid fully assessing the real underlying issues in a market, has been fading. Now there is more effort to get to grips with each product in depth in each market and to really understand the factors involved.

Yet authors of new management books still feel the need to include the Boston Matrix. One example is Max McKeown's *The Strategy Book* (2012). In this little book the author includes the Boston Matrix in a personalized selection of strategy tools. Yet he states: 'There are some major problems with this matrix. Markets are not generally clearly defined, market share is not the same as profitability (or desirability), and specific opportunities and threats may completely change investment criteria. Far better to look at revenue growth and profit in general.'

---

3   The Boston Matrix spawned further matrix-oriented approaches to portfolio analysis which attempted to overcome its increasingly evident shortcomings. The General Electric Company (GEC) Grid, developed by McKinsey and Company in conjunction with GEC in the US, was one such example that did become quite widely adopted. The matrix could be used to assess constituent companies within a conglomerate company, strategic business units (SBUs) within a company and the product range of a company. Some 20 parameters were scored according to market attractiveness and competitive strength. But then a weighting system needed to be devised – which was fraught with difficulties in practice. Also, the GEC matrix was not capable of taking into account any synergies between different products or businesses that might exist.

I agree with him. But if the Boston Matrix has so many pitfalls, why include it in the book? I suspect that this is because today's management books and courses frequently satisfy the demand for management toolkits – a set of apparently practical management concepts. The Boston Matrix is one of the concepts you are most likely to find in any such toolkit. Perhaps McKeown felt that critics might consider his little book on strategy incomplete if he failed to cover the Boston Matrix within the toolkit section of his book.

In pharmaceuticals we need to aim rather higher than this! If you assume that your major pharma company competitors make their strategic decisions at this low level of sophistication then you are likely to be underestimating them. Using a matrix like this risks before long being overtaken by your more sophisticated competitors.

Core Competence

Core competence (or core competency as it is sometimes known) was first proposed by the management gurus Gary Hamel and C.K. Prahalad in 1990. They defined core competences as: 'the collective learning in organizations – especially how to coordinate diverse production skills and integrate multiple streams of technology'. They proposed that companies should focus on what they do better than others.

This can make particular sense in pharmaceuticals, most obviously in terms of therapeutic area expertise. The Danish company Novo Nordisk has since the mid-1990s concentrated on diabetes and hormones, and disposed of activities in other areas, for example, the central nervous system (CNS). On this basis it continues to do well and has become since a Top 20 company on the basis of global sales. Lundbeck, like Novo Nordisk based in Copenhagen, swapped several projects with Novo Nordisk at the same time, to further focus on the CNS area. Over the past 20 years Lundbeck has been a successful company – its main problem being, as for other companies, the difficulty of developing itself or acquiring good new products. Several promising CNS products in development by Lundbeck in recent years have fallen down at an advanced stage of development.

My belief is that it makes sense for companies to capitalize on existing core therapeutic expertise, or other expertise in manufacturing or R&D – for example with vaccines or monoclonal antibodies. There can be an advantage also in concentrating in areas difficult to imitate.

It is perhaps easier for pharmaceutical companies to define what a core competence is than is the case for other industries because diseases are classified by therapeutic area or indication. This probably explains why core competence has endured in many pharmaceutical companies as a concept. A combination of therapeutic and other technological expertise can be particularly powerful. If the company has been in a therapeutic area for some years already, it will have also built up commercial as well as R&D expertise in that area.

But companies need to review their areas of core competence from time to time. Over the past few years several of the very largest pharmaceutical companies including AstraZeneca, GlaxoSmithKline and Pfizer, have got out of or deemphasized their presence in CNS R&D, because they have come to regard it as an area too difficult to make progress in.

If a company like Lundbeck puts all its eggs in this one CNS basket, this implies focussing everything in what is therefore now becoming considered in some quarters of the industry as a high-risk area. A company like Lundbeck, trying to supplement its own pipeline by licensing, may well find that the quality of much of what is available is unimpressive. But the alternative for Lundbeck would probably be worse – to go into other therapeutic areas it has little or no expertise in, where it will frequently tend to come up against bigger competitors with at least some and often a great deal of relevant therapeutic expertise already.

Roche is a notable exception to the trend away from CNS. The company is now stressing its focus on neurodegenerative and psychiatric disorders. Eisai is another company that has been strongly increasing its presence in the CNS area. This diversity of opinion on CNS is healthy for the industry.

Though I favour nurturing core competences that a company has built up, just as with other management concepts I have analysed previously, it is too superficial merely to identify a core competence, however admirable, without examining in detail where that expertise area is heading. Did Lundbeck realize how difficult life in CNS would become when it endorsed its focus on that area in the 1990s?

Fortunately few big pharma companies are polarized in so few areas as Lundbeck or Novo Nordisk. Most major pharmaceutical companies therefore have much more scope to augment what they are already good at, periodically adding new and experimental areas to the company over time, either organically or as part of a plan to extend within an existing core therapeutic area. I described how big pharma companies differ in their active therapeutic areas in R&D in Chapter 1 (see pp. 33–5).

How Useful Can Outside Management Concepts Be?

It is evident by now that with pharmaceuticals we are dealing with a rather complex industry with a sophisticated level of competition that is hardly likely to respond to simple concepts that operate on just one level or aspect. Examples like the recently in vogue Tipping Point, Black Swans and Anti-Fragility concepts, none of which I want to dwell on, might illuminate some aspects of a particular issue. But they are hardly likely to contribute very seriously to any comprehensive strategy.

Some management concepts can be useful in pointing out that a company needs to consider a particular issue or aspect of management. In some cases the concept is used only to alert – it does not then get become built into the way the company operates.

For example, in 1960 E. Jerome McCarthy introduced a new concept, the four Ps of marketing: product, price, place and promotion. This concept is included in marketing courses, including those specifically for the pharmaceutical industry. Virtually everyone working in pharmaceutical marketing will be familiar with this concept. Unlike many management concepts, the four Ps has stood the test of time. It is difficult to argue against the concept.

But on the other hand, knowing about this concept does not obviously translate into an ability or desire to do anything with the four Ps. At worst, if that is all such concepts do then they also stand to do less damage either!

Another example is the concept of barriers to entry and barriers to exit which we considered earlier (see Chapter 3, pp. 53–61). Use of such concepts can lead to valuable insights into how markets are operating. Companies might modify what they are doing to an extent after considering them. But that is as far as many of them commonly go.

I am not aware of gurus out there today promoting these concepts or applying novel twists to them. After their initial impact, they are unlikely to further impact how a company operates. But this is not necessarily the case with some management concepts.

In his book *Strategic Intelligence* Jay Liebowitz pointed out that analytical tools such as SWOT, Michael Porter's five competitive forces and Value Chain Analysis are not sufficient as a replacement for creative thinking (Liebowitz 2006). Whilst they provide a decision-making construct – 'You need your own brains in interpreting the results and how they can apply towards improving original decisions' – Liebowitz might have expressed this better, but I feel that he is making a very important point!

Most management concepts do demand in some way to be integrated into an organization. Often they are radical and require abandoning existing corporate practices or at least modifying several of them. The astute company needs to consider:

- Is the new management concept in question effectively asking you to drop management concepts you already use?

- To what extent have those management concepts in question worked well for your company to date?

In this chapter I have shown that the extent to which management concepts adapted from outside the pharmaceutical industry are valid varies enormously. Some are essential. Others are plain misleading or even dangerous. And those in a third, common category have some good points but should not be treated as panaceas.

I sense that the number of new management concepts that have caught on in general and in pharmaceuticals specifically has in recent years been less than formerly. Perhaps this is due to disillusion with some concepts that were adopted and then misfired. But on the other hand I also sense that companies remain open to receiving a steady stream of ideas and trying some of them out.

When a few big pharma companies are seen to adopt a new management concept, this begins to place the rest under pressure. The less-ready adopters begin to be concerned about missing a trick and some become trend followers, more because of this than that they necessarily expect the new management concept to work for their companies. Management may feel that going ahead regardless will protect it against the accusation that it is resistant to change. I would cite the move of major pharmaceutical companies into generics in the mid-1990s as a particularly disastrous example of this. I describe this in Chapter 8 (see pp. 119–21).

If within three years of the adoption of a new management concept by a company it is often difficult to discern any trace of its impact in an organization, why accept this situation? Management commonly appears to accept that bringing on board fashionable management concepts is all part of running a company. But why not stop instead and evaluate a new management concept properly before adopting it?

In the next chapter I show that even the most eminent gurus can get in wrong when it comes to pharmaceuticals.

5

When Gurus Get It Wrong

Porter on Strategic Alliances

Michael Porter, one of the most famous management gurus and the inventor of the concept of competitive advantage, has set himself strongly against strategic alliances. As the apostle of the importance of competition Porter regards strategic alliances as being anticompetitive.

This may be the case in many industries. But it has not been so in pharmaceuticals, where, as I explained in Chapter 1 (see pp. 29–31) the diffuse nature of disease makes it difficult for big companies to achieve a dominant position. Porter's attitude appears eccentric to those in the industry for whom alliances have long been a part of the everyday pharmaceutical scenery. I would argue that strategic alliances have resulted in *increased* competition in the pharmaceutical industry.

Unfortunately this is not the sole example of an eminent management guru getting it wrong in my view as far as pharmaceuticals are concerned. Management gurus concentrate on concepts that will be convincing to as many industries as possible. They do not often have the time or patience to understand the different facets of each industry. That can make some of their advice irrelevant or positively dangerous for some industries.

Outsourcing Is a Sin

The apostle of disruptive technologies is Clayton Christensen (see also pp. 19, 217, 221). He has shown through dramatic examples the consequences of new technologies taking over from old, such as the wiping out of Kodak by digital photography.

But Christensen has a bee in his bonnet about outsourcing. He believes that when companies outsource, they risk teaching future potential competitors how to enter the market. This risks companies letting know-how out of their grasp and fosters future competition, according to Christensen.

Clayton Christensen has broad experience across many industries including in the healthcare sector. Whilst his first, highly popular publications in the US took examples from a variety of industries, he subsequently wrote a book specifically on healthcare. It was in *The Innovator's Prescription*, which he coauthored in 2009, that Christensen came out against outsourcing. He based this advice on evidence from industries including pharmaceuticals: 'Pharma will find a decade on that they have outsourced their core competencies.'

Perhaps Christensen was influenced by some big companies such as Pfizer. During the early days of outsourcing 20 years ago Pfizer took a corporate-wide decision not to outsource any work in drug discovery. The company was then indeed concerned about loss of intellectual property and considered that core competences should be developed in house.

In 2012 Christensen returned to his theme (Comer 2012a): 'We now understand that managing clinical trials is an indispensable element of drug discovery. And so if you outsource that, then you're outsourcing the activities that in the future will be the critical capabilities.'

Outsourcing has been going on for many years, and at a significant level since the early 1980s at least, when the first contract research organizations were set up – for example Kendle in 1981, Parexel and Quintiles in 1982 and PPD in 1985. By 2010, outsourcing accounted for over a quarter of all pharma R&D expenditure. PricewaterhouseCoopers found in 2012 that 43 per cent of all pharma and life sciences CEOs had outsourced a business process or function in the previous 12 months (PwC 2012a).

Yet what progress have pharma CROs made in the past 30 years to make inroads into the pharmaceutical industry? The answer is rather little: none have made very great progress in developing their own intellectual property. None are close to becoming anywhere near fully fledged pharmaceutical companies. And I doubt whether many of them even have the ambition now to do so.

Generally CROs have only stood a chance of acquiring intellectual property when the bargaining power of the partner has been weak. They have sometimes been able to offer a means of financing projects which start-up companies have had difficulty in otherwise financing. It is hardly surprising that none of these deals have so far led to CROs developing products with major commercial potential.

To avoid this potential problem that Christensen is so concerned about, pharma companies outsourcing to CROs or any other type of contract organization only have to ensure they retain their intellectual property. Also, contrary to the situation between start-up companies and CROs, pharma companies have sufficiently strong bargaining power relative to any CRO not to need to concede intellectual property rights. Most pharmaceutical companies are also experienced and efficient in putting effective contracts in place and are unlikely to slip up on intellectual property matters. And so the dangers which Christensen is imagining, in an industry which he has recently rather refreshingly admitted he does not fully understand, are in my view illusory.

Pfizer eventually began outsourcing certain R&D functions in the late 1990s. Now they are firm enthusiasts. For example, since 2000 the company has been steadily increasing a variety of preclinical activities it has been setting up with the Chinese company WuXi. Christensen has failed to understand that in pharmaceuticals outsourcing not only works but it is favoured increasingly by pharmaceutical companies who have seen over three decades now how it can work for them. It does not lead to the problem he raises because intellectual property rights for pharmaceuticals under active development will be strong – and pharmaceutical companies will continue to ensure that they keep hold of those rights.

The Japanese Are Coming

My third example comes from personal experience at the hands of one particular guru. I have already mentioned in the previous chapter the value I consider Hamel and Prahalad's concept of core competency has for the pharmaceutical industry. But I certainly would not take as carte blanche any other concept that the surviving of these two gurus, Gary Hamel, might have.

In 1988, a few years before Hamel's core competency breakthrough, Glaxo sent a score or so of my colleagues and I on a residential training week at the London Business School. Gary Hamel was then on the staff there. We were addressed by him one morning at their elegant Regency site. The topic of his lecture – for that is was what it turned out to be – was Japan. Hamel's message was that the Japanese were coming – and that if we pharmaceutical types did not cater for this, our goose would be cooked.

At no stage did Hamel bring in any pharmaceutical element or example to his lecture. As far as we could tell, he did not appear the slightest bit interested in the then not particularly fashionable pharmaceutical industry. For when it came to question time ... there *was* no question time! Hamel simply turned on his heels and departed smartly from the lecture theatre. That left some of us, including me, feeling a little thwarted. We would have liked to point out that actually pharmaceuticals was far from being a star market for Japanese companies – and did not look to us like becoming one in the near future.

Of course, the Japanese pharmaceutical industry has had its successes outside Japan. But it has not improved its position a great deal since then. Indeed you can argue that it has gone backwards, Japan being one of the very few markets that has become distinctly unfashionable, its thunder stolen by Brazil, Russia, India and China (BRIC) and many other fast-growing developing countries. Within a couple of years of our lecture from Hamel, the Japanese economy had imploded, and 20 years later it is still far from healthy. I consider Japan in more detail in Chapter 11 (see pp. 149–55).

In conclusion, however eminent management gurus from outside the industry are, and however applicable many of their ideas may be, they are prone to slip up from time to time when they turn to pharmaceuticals. Pharmaceutical companies must therefore be particularly careful in assessing new management concepts from outside the pharmaceutical industry – however eminent their source. Some concepts prove universally useless. But in some cases what might work in other industries could be disastrous for pharmaceuticals because of its distinctive inherent characteristics.

6

In Search of the Perfect Organization

Commonly in big pharma companies, management is constantly seeking the perfect solution to a problem – when in reality no perfect solution exists. When I worked for Glaxo in the late 1980s, the development function was, as is conventional, part of the R&D organization. But not long after I left the company in the 1990s there was a reorganization aimed at reducing the gap between the commercial function and development functions. The commercial function was combined with development, leaving research as a separate part of the organization.

Within a few years, as was becoming clear within other companies which had similarly reorganized, it was found that this set-up also had significant disadvantages. Consequently there was then a swing back to putting R&D together again, leaving the commercial function as a separate part of the organization.

Similarly, companies must decide whether to place the licensing function within the commercial area or in R&D. Some companies have tended to oscillate from one solution to the other and back again. In the mid-1990s I carried out a consultancy project for a US pharmaceutical company to review how major pharmaceutical companies organized their licensing functions within the organization.

A majority of companies were in favour of the licensing function belonging to the commercial area. However, a sizeable minority opted to place it within R&D. No consensus had at that time developed – because there was no ideal solution to this organizational issue which did not have some drawback or other. And so after a few years' experience with one particular set-up, companies began to feel that the organizational grass must be greener on the other side, tempting a switch to whatever solution the company was not then currently pursuing.

One company, Merck & Co, solved this problem by having different types of licensing people – some specialized in early-stage licensing reporting to R&D and others reporting to the licensing function. Today most pharmaceutical companies would at least have some part of its licensing activity belonging to the commercial function.

Centralization Versus Decentralization

Centralization versus decentralization is a further example of a management conundrum where companies can fall into the trap of successive pendulum swings from one extreme to the other.

No consensus has developed on this in pharmaceuticals to date. Until recently the majority of companies – particularly indigenous US pharma companies – tended to favour a relatively centralized organization. Only a few pharma companies such as GlaxoSmithKline have consistently pursued a more decentralized approach.

Two companies which can be regarded as polar opposites on this score have recently travelled in opposite directions!

JOHNSON & JOHNSON

Until 2010 Johnson & Johnson had the reputation of being a decentralized company. In the 1930s Robert Wood Johnson II transformed the company into a global, decentralized family of companies.

When Johnson & Johnson acquired the Belgian company Janssen in 1961, it allowed its prolific founder, Paul Janssen, to continue to head the company and the Janssen name was retained. It continued for over two decades to produce many new products that proved crucial to the performance of Johnson & Johnson.

After Centocor was acquired by Johnson & Johnson in 1999, that company was also allowed to operate as a decentralized company within the corporate organization – that is, until very recently. Several breakthrough biological products came out of this organization, including the current biggest product of Johnson & Johnson, the anti-inflammatory monoclonal antibody Remicade (infliximab). Its sales reached $8.963 billion in 2011.

The decentralized policy was also in evidence after the acquisition of Tibotec in 2002. This company kept its own name and website within the Johnson & Johnson organization. There were, however, occasional exceptions. After the drug delivery company Alza was acquired by Johnson & Johnson in 2001 it was soon absorbed into the organization, and the Alza name soon disappeared.

Much more recently, in 2011 both Centocor and Tibotec, which had had separate websites and organizations since they were acquired, along with a much earlier acquisition, the Swiss company Cilag, were all consolidated under the Janssen Pharmaceuticals banner within the Johnson & Johnson organization. However, Johnson & Johnson did announce at that time that all Tibotec brands and organizational structure would remain in place unchanged. But centralization had begun to set in at Johnson & Johnson by this time.

During 2012 Johnson & Johnson shareholders began to blame decentralization for the numerous product quality deficiencies that had been arising in different divisions of the company. By then Johnson & Johnson was putting more centralized reporting processes in place for certain functions including manufacturing and quality control where repeated serious issues had arisen. Some observers considered that it was not decentralization but excessively zealous cost cutting that was the chief reason for these problems within Johnson & Johnson.

This move towards centralization is not without disadvantages. It may make it more difficult for Johnson & Johnson to acquire further biotech companies like Centocor, if those companies believe they will no longer be allowed to operate in a relatively autonomous manner within the Johnson & Johnson organization.

By late 2012 there was a state of some schizophrenia within Johnson & Johnson on the centralization/decentralization score. The corporate website still claimed that the company followed a decentralized management approach: 'Each of our operating companies functions as its own small business. They are strongly entrepreneurial in character ... While our people operate in a small-company setting, they also have access to the know-how and resources of a Fortune 50 company.'

ELI LILLY

Eli Lilly has long had the reputation of being a centralized pharmaceutical company. Indeed up until 2011 for management courses I gave, I used a Eli Lilly diagram to exemplify the centralized approach. But in 2011 came a switch at the company to decentralization.

S. Michael Harrill, Eli Lilly's global brand director for neuroscience, was reported by *Pharmaceutical Executive* as explaining, 'We're now in decentralized mode, which is a big difference from five years ago' (Harrill 2011). He admitted that this represented a corporate rethinking, 'although the pendulum tends to swing from centralized to decentralized (and back) over time'.

He explained that global headquarters at Eli Lilly was now in the role of 'coach for the affiliate'. According to Harrill, global headquarters and affiliates do their own market research prior to launch, but the former does not necessarily guide the latter: 'Allowing affiliates a degree of independence lets them adapt to the situation more quickly.'

One example of this move to decentralization at Eli Lilly was that after it acquired the biotech company ImClone, the developer of the successful anticancer product Erbitux (cetuximab) in 2008, it left it as a standalone business.

According to the tenets of marketing, decentralization ought to be superior to centralization because it allows strategy to be more closely tailored to the needs of the local market. Recent advances in technology and electronic communication are also making it easier to decentralize than was formerly the case. The current emphasis on market access (see pp. 71–3) may be leading companies to consider decentralization more seriously. But it may be more costly – and this can limit the extent to which companies are prepared to go in this direction.

In conclusion, these mirror image examples of Eli Lilly and Johnson & Johnson reflect again the refreshing diversity of approach of the pharmaceutical industry. As Michael Harrill of Eli Lilly says above, centralization versus decentralization illustrates oscillation of a management policy between two poles. Constant oscillation can have its dangers as well as being expensive in terms of its disruptive impact.

If your company culture can bear it, I would recommend decentralization. I believe it is closer to the optimum because it is more possible in a decentralized organization for the local decisions in subsidiaries to be more marketing oriented.

When working at the corporate headquarters of Glaxo in the late 1980s, I found one particular advantage of being decentralized. At the time, the product I was working on, Zantac (ranitidine), was competing only against products from three big, centralized US pharma companies. I found that we could be faster on our feet at Glaxo than were our competitors.

There was one particular strategic advantage. When a competitor launched its new product in a first territory, we at Glaxo immediately had a very good idea of what the strategy would be for its product globally. In contrast the Glaxo promotional strategies for Zantac varied to quite some extent by territory, since subsidiaries were permitted to tailor market needs to a much greater extent than were their local competitors. That made it much more difficult for our competitors to predict our promotional strategies at Glaxo than we could theirs.

Regionalization

Analogous to these centralization-decentralization oscillations is regionalization – versus other types of organization geographically. Regionalization, as an apparently halfway house between national and local organization, has been in vogue several times over the past 30 years. However, it never seems to persist for very long – probably because it is not a very happy medium.

Naturally, regionalization in a large country such as the United States means something rather different from regionalization within a European country, because of the sheer difference in scale. Often sold by international consultancies as a global solution, I could never work out why an organizational concept that would work well for a company the size of the US should be suitable for, say, the United Kingdom.

My experience is that pharma organizations which adopt a strongly regional type of organization tend to switch away from it again within a few years. And so companies impressed with arguments to bring in this particular type of organization should in my view take time to consult those who have worked in different types of geographical set-ups to identify the pros and cons.

Conclusions on Organizational Oscillations

I believe companies should avoid getting into resource-consuming oscillations between one extreme of organization and the other. When presented with an apparently novel organizational concept which appears to have advantages, they should always assess what they stand to lose by abandoning their existing *modus operandi* and the sheer cost of implementing a radical change.

Conclusions for Part II

A more general conclusion from the management concepts I have reviewed in Part II is that adoption of management fashions and fads can inhibit companies from analyzing the real-life situations they are faced with – and which they ought to be addressing.

Some management concepts such as the Boston Matrix are dangerous in that they attempt to reduce dealing with a complex situation to considering just a couple of factors. Other management concepts are less pernicious.

But why cling on to a management concept? Why not instead analyse the situation in question? To do this does not necessarily have to be a difficult process. The pharmaceutical industry is one of the best provided with audit and other data. I am frequently amazed at the way big pharma companies do not more widely apply data that they have often expensively purchased.

Whilst I believe it is healthy for pharmaceutical companies to go outside the industry to access new or different ideas, the distinctive characteristics of pharmaceuticals mean that it is highly unlikely that most such concepts will prove to be panaceas. Proponents of these management concepts are generally uninterested in the exigencies of specific industries but nevertheless try to encourage their adoption as widely as possible. In most cases it should not take very much probing to raise serious questions about their applicability to pharmaceuticals.

On the other hand, whilst any new management concept is most unlikely to provide *the* one big fix, especially in a complex industry like pharmaceuticals, there may be useful points which can be applied. I believe that some major pharmaceutical companies are becoming rather more realistic in sizing up such concepts. For example, instead of hoping that benchmarking the best companies will identify the best strategies – which can then simply be taken on board en bloc – companies are setting up initiatives with less comprehensive aims.

In 2011 GlaxoSmithKline set up an 'innovative strategic partnership' with McLaren Group, which is a Formula 1 motor racing organization. This partnership is described in the two companies' announcement of this as ground breaking and game changing: 'the distillation, communication and application of 45 years' worth of winning Formula 1 expertise' will be 'meticulously adapted and tailored to the needs of a new McLaren Group partner, GlaxoSmithKline'.

That will be manifested in a variety of ways including:

- The development of more efficient planning processes;

- The development of data modelling tools to inform strategic decision making;

- The development of better real-time monitoring, scenario planning and forecasting;

- The inspiration and development of GSK's managers and the preparation of its managers to be able to make better and more informed business choices while remaining agile and adaptable to ever-changing circumstances.

There is no assumption here that a leading company in motor racing is going to provide ready-made strategies for GlaxoSmithKline. The company is rather, as its CEO Sir Andrew Witty explained, 'looking outside its sector for inspiration and fresh perspectives'.

This seems to me a much more healthy approach than searching for all-embracing panaceas. There clearly has to be questioning about the applicability of each potential benefit GlaxoSmithKline could gain from McLaren Group. Existing strategies are unlikely to be adopted lock, stock and barrel without thought about the sense of doing this.

As it happened, the first fruits were relatively down to earth: the partners announced that the then McLaren team drivers Jenson Button and Lewis Hamilton would wear the logo of GlaxoSmithKline's health drink Lucozade on their helmets!

PART III

Big Pharma's Strategic Options

In Parts III, IV and V I am going to consider in detail a variety of strategic options that a big pharma company can take to secure its future. Should pharmaceutical companies – as most have over the past 30 years – focus down increasingly to prescription pharmaceuticals, gradually jettisoning the rest? Or should they move in the opposite direction and diversify? Perhaps surprisingly, quite a number of pharmaceutical companies have begun to do both in recent years!

How successful is a company likely to become through diversifying into areas of healthcare outside pharmaceuticals? What about going further and diversifying outside healthcare? Or even exiting pharmaceuticals completely – as a few companies also active in other, nonpharmaceutical markets have done over the past decade?

There are further strategic options; a whole gamut of deals of various types. There are the ostensibly friendly ones – most of which can be included in the useful umbrella term *strategic alliances* we considered in Chapter 4. Then there is the sometimes much less friendly pursuit of mergers and acquisitions.

Further, there is the option of geographical expansion – in recent years the emphasis on building up the corporate presence in emerging territories. To what extent can that compensate for increasingly adverse factors in the developed world? I deal with this in Part IV.

Perhaps big pharma should pursue all or most of the above? But then resources are limited for perhaps all but the very largest pharma companies, and so for most this is not feasible. In which case, what emphasis should big pharma be devoting to each strategic option?

Last but certainly not least, in Part V I deal with the crucial option of bringing new products to market.

To start with in Part III, I first consider in Chapter 7 long-term trends in focussing down and diversification and the extent to which the latter should be a future strategic option.

7

Focussing Down and Diversification

Focussing Down

The majority of pharmaceutical companies which up until the 1980s were active in other healthcare (or life science) markets or quite other industries subsequently divested or shut down those interests.

In 2011 Roy Vagelos, chairman emeritus of Merck & Co and CEO from 1985 to 1994, recollected the range of activities the company was involved in at the time he joined it in 1975: 'People forget that when I arrived at Merck it was selling activated charcoal, chickens, toothpaste, and face creams, a mission totally at odds with the vastly more rarefied culture of medicine' (Looney 2011).

Another US company, Bristol-Myers Squibb, was formerly active in both orthopaedics and beauty products. And I can recall at least four major pharma companies which once had agrochemical divisions: Aventis, Pharmacia, Novartis and AstraZeneca.

Historically, nonhealthcare interests like cosmetics tended to be divested first. For decades Pfizer owned the cosmetics company Charles of the Ritz but eventually sold it in 1992. Nonhealthcare life science interests such as agrochemicals also tended to be divested by pharmaceutical companies in the 1980s and 1990s. Also, in the 1990s particularly, areas of healthcare less adjacent to mainstream prescription pharmaceuticals such as wholesaling, veterinary, dental and over-the-counter (OTC) products were spun off. Generics were also sometimes divested – at least until the early 1990s.

When I joined Glaxo Holdings in 1985 the company was vertically integrated in that it owned a UK wholesaling business, Vestric; Evans, the biggest generics company in the United Kingdom; a veterinary division, Glaxovet; a fine chemical company, Macfarlan Smith; and a health food company, Farley Health. It had just sold a surgical instrument company, Eschmann. The extent of this variety of interests was not unusual for larger companies operating in the pharmaceutical industry at the time.

But within a few years most of these activities had been divested by Glaxo, so that it became focussed almost exclusively on prescription pharmaceuticals. This had become the conventional industry wisdom – with the majority of companies in pharmaceuticals focussing down further to prescription pharmaceuticals – the most profitable activity. This focussing down is still to an extent continuing, for example in Sanofi's sale of its minority share in 2012 in the cosmetics company Yves Rocher.

The process is particularly apparent postmerger; for example following its acquisition of Wyeth in 2009, Pfizer sold off both the clinical nutrition activities formerly known as Wyeth Nutrition to Nestlé in 2012 as well as renaming Pfizer Animal Health as Zoetis in preparation for its divestment. OTC is another area frequently divested postmerger.

Meanwhile most of the remaining life science companies and broader conglomerates with an interest in pharmaceuticals sold them off – in each case to companies already in pharmaceuticals. Examples of this in recent years are the reduction in the scope of the activities of the European conglomerate Akzo Nobel, through the sale in 2007 of its Organon Biosciences (pharmaceutical and veterinary) activity to Schering-Plough. (The latter was not long afterwards in turn acquired by Merck & Co.)

FOCUSSING OF CONGLOMERATES AWAY FROM PHARMACEUTICALS

In recent years several conglomerates have focussed down – but away from pharmaceuticals (see also pp. 57–8). In 2007 the American conglomerate 3M sold off its pharmaceutical interests. And in 2009 the Belgian chemical concern Solvay and the American consumer products company Procter & Gamble both sold off their pharmaceuticals divisions.

In 2010 Nestlé sold off its share in the ophthalmics company Alcon to Novartis. On the other hand, Nestlé continued to add functional foods and other borderline pharmaceutical products in advancing its core business, foods, thereby increasing its market share in infant nutrition (see also p. 110).

THE RESULT

Thus the result of all this divestment activity has been a very long-term trend over some 30 years of aggregation of pharmaceutical activities within dedicated pharmaceutical companies. Most companies active in pharmaceuticals are now additionally active in few other areas. That the trend has continued for so long reflects that by and large it worked – companies now represented have been able to concentrate on the most profitable area: prescription pharmaceuticals.

Avoiding distraction has also been a major motivation for pharmaceuticals companies to divest other, very often much less profitable businesses. Rarely have nonpharmaceutical activities within pharmaceutical companies emerged which could match pharmaceuticals in their performance. Merck KGaA's liquid crystals activity would be one of the few exceptions; the Performance Materials division to which this belongs has over recent years at times had higher profit margins than the company's pharmaceuticals activity.

This consensus for focussing down by pharmaceutical companies undoubtedly helped to stimulate the impressive growth I described earlier (see pp. 1–2). Because it continued for so long, focussing down dramatically changed the nature of the companies making up the pharmaceutical industry.

With nonpharmaceutical activities pared back to the bone, there is not much left which is not mainstream for potential future divestment by pharmaceutical companies. It is only through mergers and acquisitions that pharmaceutical companies have accumulated further nonpharma activities, which they have normally gone on to divest within a few years.

Having described this strong trend to focussing down, there have been past efforts of pharmaceutical companies to diversify. This became an unfashionable strategy, but with failing new product pipelines and the need to look for alternatives, there was a renewed interest in diversification from around 2005.

Diversification in General

Until the 1980s it was not uncommon for pharmaceutical companies to follow a diversification strategy, more commonly into other areas of healthcare, and sometimes more broadly, into life sciences industries or even beyond. In the late 1960s SmithKline & French in the US entered the generics market with its SK Line range, which failed after a few years.

Other areas of healthcare pharmaceutical companies entered included diagnostics, hospital products, as well as the veterinary and dental markets. The consensus view which developed over the course of the 1980s was that this diversification strategy did not often work.

At the same time, the enthusiasm in industry generally for conglomerates, where an often very diverse range of different types of industry were managed by one company, went out of fashion because its apparently impressive initial successes were followed by high-profile failures. This effectively inoculated most companies against believing that if they could be highly successful in one area of healthcare they could be just as successful in adjacent areas.

It is hardly surprising that these often naïve initiatives did in the main fail. Firstly, profit margins are almost invariably lower in other healthcare industries than in pharmaceuticals – commonly much lower. This means that it is difficult for nonpharmaceutical activities to make a significant contribution to total company profit. It also means that when it comes to allocating resources to different divisions of the company it is difficult not to favour pharmaceuticals at the expense of lower-margin activities.

Secondly, the scale of other areas, whether within healthcare or not, is often much smaller than pharmaceuticals. Measured purely in terms of sales they are commonly smaller scale. And in terms of profit the difference is usually even starker.

A few years ago I was asked by a pharmaceutical company client to investigate the possibility of buying a medical device company or companies in the field of gastroenterology to complement the limited presence it already had in pharmaceuticals in that therapeutic area. After several months we abandoned the project. All the medical device companies we looked at which might be acquired were too small to make any significant impact on my client's sales or profits.

Here is another example. Sigma-Aldrich is a leading life science and high technology company. Traditionally active in fine chemicals, it is a leading supplier globally of chemicals and biochemicals and equipment used by the pharmaceutical and other industries in research and manufacturing. The company has just under 8,000 employees. It has over a million individual customers worldwide in just under 100,000 different accounts. Sales in 2010 amounted to $2.271 billion. Net profit was $384 million. Both continued a fairly steady pattern of growth over the previous five years.

Now $300–400 million is approximately half of the profit one might expect to make from selling one basic-sized pharmaceutical blockbuster. Thus a big pharma company looking to diversify is hardly likely to be excited by a company such as Sigma-Aldrich – even though it has long been a leader in the sectors in which it operates. The scale of its sales and profits are just not big enough to attract pharma company interest.

Thirdly, there are big differences in the nature of different healthcare markets and how they operate. Trying to manage a hospital supply product operation, for example, with the quite different skills, experience and expectations developed specifically within the pharmaceutical industry, is unlikely to prove a sound basis for success.

As I describe in this and the next chapter, the pharmaceutical industry has over the past 50 years blown hot and cold in its desire to diversify into other areas of healthcare.

Diversifying into OTC

In the late 1980s major pharmaceutical companies showed considerable interest in diversifying into OTC products. There were expectations at the time that the OTC market would grow faster than prescription products.

I remember in the mid-1980s finding in the basement archives of the pharmaceutical company I was working for in Amsterdam some IMS sales audit books for the UK going back to the early 1960s. At that time the size of the audited OTC market was roughly the same as that of the prescription market. But by the mid-1980s when I was in that basement, the ratio of sales was already roughly 10:1 in favour of prescription products! The rapid growth of prescription products over two decades meant that it dwarfed the much more sedate OTC market. Since then the ratio has stayed about the same. In recent years in Europe the share of the OTC market has been around 12 per cent of the total – a modest share but still significant.

In the mid-1980s the majority of major pharmaceutical companies had in their range some OTC products, but these usually made up a modest percentage of total sales. Half of the Top 20 pharma companies today are active in OTCs: Pfizer, Novartis, Sanofi, Bayer, Johnson & Johnson, GlaxoSmithKline, Teva, Boehringer Ingelheim, Bristol-Myers Squibb and Takeda.

As it turned out, from the late 1980s when the interest of major pharma grew, the growth rate for the OTC market continued for a number of years to be *less* than that of prescription pharmaceuticals. It did not prove to be the opportunity that big pharma as well as many commentators had expected.

However, it is true that in some areas of the world the situation has been a little more favourable for OTCs. In Europe, since 2009 the OTC market growth rate has been higher than that of prescription pharmaceuticals, though not spectacularly so. Globally the $78 billion OTC market grew by a total of just 3.5 per cent in the three years to 2011, little different to prescription pharmaceuticals growth.

One disappointment has been the lack of a good supply of genuinely new OTC products. You might imagine that it would be in the interest of national governments to encourage this, as it could reduce costs by leaving patients to pay for drugs previously paid for by governments. But this requires governments to facilitate this through legislation and encouragement. Only a minority of countries have set up an effective regulatory system for switching prescription products to OTC (Rx-to-OTC). The number of switched products in recent years has been rather modest. This means that the OTC sector has to make do largely with old drugs or new formulations of existing ones.

Some of the apparently promising drug categories where switching has been possible have proven disappointing. Oral contraceptives have been one success, though only in the US. Modern products for allergic rhinitis have also been successful. Other newcomers such as acid suppressants – both H2-antagonists and proton pump inhibitors – Alli (orlistat, GlaxoSmithKline) for obesity, triptans for migraine and statins have made modest or disappointing impacts.

Despite their current straightened circumstances it is difficult to see governments taking the often radical measures that would be needed to significantly stimulate the OTC sector – even though they would stand to reduce their costs considerably by doing so. Also switching of additional product categories might not prove much more successful than those permitted over the past 20 years.

The OTC market thus remains something of a disappointment. Nevertheless it can still make a significant contribution to a major pharmaceutical company's profits, though not often more than a modest one.

The New Vogue for Diversification

As mentioned above, the chief problem for the pharmaceutical industry is coping with the growing impact over the last decade or so of the lack of new pharmaceutical products. This has led to pharma companies over the past half-dozen years to seek alternatives avenues. They can step up globalization (see Chapter 10, pp. 141–7). They can diversify. But there are still a limited number of options that they can sensibly consider pursuing.

Countless case histories demonstrate diversifications over the past 40 years that went wrong, and I describe several in this book (see in particular Chapter 8, pp. 117–21). However, after such a long run of the stronger trend to focussing down, current pharmaceutical management has little direct experience or memory of diversification. Thus *cause celebres* – even those occurring as recently as the 1990s – may well not impinge on the consciousness of those currently determining the direction of corporate strategy.

In some respects we now appear to be seeing a repeat of some of the failed initiatives of the past. We discuss one particular example of this in detail – generics – in Chapter 8.

8

Diversification: Ebbs and Flows in Enthusiasms

In the pharmaceutical industry there are plenty of examples of strategies that have come into favour and then gone out again – some, as I shall explain, more than once. Particularly remarkable is the example of the ebb and flow of interest in generics, which I shall go into after describing one other particularly spectacular example.

The PBM Debacle

In the United States during the late 1980s, decision-making powers in the selection of pharmaceuticals began to shift from doctors to pharmacy benefit managers (PBMs). By then cheap, off-patent generic drugs were widely available. PBMs had by then established themselves. They enabled corporate health plans of managed care companies to ensure that their members received the lowest-priced effective drugs.

Pharmaceutical companies became interested in acquiring PBMs, with the aim of increasing their ability to integrate patient claim information with pharmaceutical data. This would enable better design of disease management programmes and the chance to work more closely with providers on drug compliance and utilization.

Merck & Co acquired Medco, one of the largest PBMs, in 1993 for $6.6 billion. Merck considered that its existing model of selling to doctors did not take account of then changing decision-making powers, and it wished to control its channels of distribution. Soon all three of the biggest and most powerful PBMs had been acquired by leading US pharmaceutical companies. In 1994 SmithKline Beecham acquired Diversified Pharmaceutical Services (DPS) for

$2.3 billion and Eli Lilly acquired PCS Health Systems for $4.1 billion. Also several other pharmaceutical companies made more modest moves to acquire pharmacy benefit management expertise.

However, none of these deals proved successful. After Merck acquired Medco, the latter accounted for over half of the combined company's total revenue. However, because its margins were so small, the Medco activity contributed only very modestly to Merck's bottom line. Also, it turned out that often a Merck product was not the choice of the PBM. Hence there was a conflict of interest between Merck and the clients of Medco.

This increasingly concerned the US authorities and eventually led to charges that the PBMs boosted sales of the products of their parent companies at the expense of other drugs. The US Federal Trade Commission eventually forced pharmaceutical companies to introduce restrictions, which in particular included building firewalls around their PBMs.

By 1997 only three to four years after the initial wave of interest, big pharma began to sell off its PBMs – in each case making catastrophic losses. Eli Lilly persisted for only three years before selling off PCS for $1.5 billion in 1997. SmithKline Beecham sold off DPS in 1999 for just $0.7 billion.

The divestiture of Medco by Merck in 2003 ended the foray of the pharmaceutical industry into pharmacy benefit management. Merck made the biggest loss of all on any of the PBM purchases. It received $2 billion for Medco, $4.6 billion less than it had paid 10 years before. Medco then operated independently for nine more years before being acquired by its rival Express Scripts in 2012.

The pharmaceutical companies thus lost 60–70 per cent of what they had paid when they sold off their PBMs. This is a good example of the difficulties big pharma runs into when it attempts diversification. In this case there were potential conflict of interest issues. But these were already out in the open and widely discussed at the time Merck announced it was to buy Medco.

Like many potential areas big pharma might consider diversifying into, margins were very much lower – described in this case by one commentator as 'paper thin'. Yet Merck went ahead. And when it made its move, that created pressures for other major US pharmaceutical companies to do the same. They preferred to become trend followers rather than risk being left out of the party.

Neither Eli Lilly nor SmithKline Beecham felt able to resist following Merck, headlong into disastrous acquisitions. Some of the biggest pharmaceutical companies operating in the US at that time were unable to size up a very different type of operation objectively.

Blowing Hot and Cold on Generics

In 2007 the German company Merck KGaA sold off its generics division to the US generics company Mylan. Merck had been marketing generics in Asia since the 1930s. In the 1990s it was particularly active in strengthening its position in the field. The company created Merck Generics in 1994 and acquired a majority holding in the US generics company Amerpharm in that year. In 1996 it set up Merck Generiques in France, a country then widely considered to have strong potential for future growth in generics. It then went on to acquire the German generics company Durachemie in 1997.

Many then leading pharmaceutical companies were also buying into generics at that time. Marion Merrell Dow, Rhône-Poulenc Rorer, Sanofi, Hoechst, Bayer, Synthélabo and Bristol-Myers Squibb all acquired generics companies in the 1990s.

As the pharma monthly magazine *In Vivo* recalled in 1997: '… in the early 1990s, most everyone in the drug industry believed that generics would become a dominant force, with unstoppable growth. Everyone was wrong'.

This disappointing outcome was reflected by the late 1990s in the revised attitude to generics within former big pharma company enthusiasts. Amongst the companies closing down or selling off their generics activities towards the end of the 1990s were Warner-Lambert, Hoechst Marion Roussel, BASF, Merck & Co, Bristol-Myers Squibb, Astra and Fujisawa. In doing so they often made a considerable loss.

For example Hoechst paid $546 million in 1993 to acquire the US generics company Copley. It was sold off again only six years later in 1999 to the generics company Teva for $220 million. Aventis, the company which had meanwhile absorbed Hoechst, cited a drive to focus its healthcare business on prescription business.

Merck KGaA was amongst a small minority of pharma companies that maintained its presence in generics for longer. But its 2007 divestment of generics mentioned above was not unexpected. Eight months previously Merck had signalled its intention to focus further on prescription pharmaceuticals by acquiring the leading Swiss biopharmaceutical company Serono. Selling its generics division went almost halfway to paying for that company.

With hindsight, this represented a low point of the prescription pharmaceutical industry's interest in generics. After 2007 only one leading pharmaceutical company remained active in generics: Novartis. This company has been consistent in maintaining for many years a strong presence in generics and is a leading company in the area: one of the constituent companies of Novartis, CIBA, acquired the US generics company Geneva Pharmaceuticals as early as 1979.

ANALYZING THE GENERICS DEBACLE

How did the 1990s generics debacle happen? One source of the stirring up of interest in generics at the time was consultants. One then prominent US industry consultant who shall remain nameless opined: 'Doing nothing with regard to the generic drug market could be a major mistake and missed opportunity.'

At the same time, major pharma companies were sizing up the imminent impact of patent expiry on their own products. Many were persuaded by the argument that 'if you couldn't beat them, why not join them?' And so, rather than carrying out a rational review of what the opportunity of getting into generics really amounted to, they decided to dive in as an immediate defence of their own products.

When pharma companies are relatively ignorant of another market sector, often the grass appears to be greener in that sector. Pharma companies also tend to assume that what applies in prescription pharmaceuticals will also work perfectly well in that sector too.

In 1997, when I gave a presentation to the annual IBC Generics conference in Amsterdam, I cited four reasons for the 1990s generics debacle. It was a failure to assess:

- The limited duration of the opportunity – often no more than 18 months post–patent expiry, and sometimes much less than this;

- How rapidly prices declined – during the 1990s they were tending to decline more rapidly than previously, and this has continued ever since;

- How many other companies – big and small, from whatever continent – would also get into global generics markets , thereby increasing competition; and

- The lack of uniformity of the generics opportunity internationally; as far as generics were concerned, undeveloped countries would not necessarily prove suddenly to be good prospects.

With hindsight, it would have been more profitable for big pharma in the face of pressures to enter generics to 'do nothing'. But usually this strategy does not go down well with pharmaceutical company top management or their investors when it is proposed.

RENEWED INTEREST OF BIG PHARMA IN GENERICS

Notwithstanding this debacle, from around 2007, only a decade after the mass exodus by big pharma from generics, a number of big pharma companies including the majority of the very biggest decided to reenter generics. They included Pfizer (which already had some generics presence in the US), Sanofi, Merck & Co, GlaxoSmithKline, AstraZeneca, Abbott and Daiichi Sankyo.

Do they all have short memories – or are there now good reasons for generics to come back into favour with big pharma? To what extent is the situation this time round different from how it was in the 1990s?

Some pharma companies have recently been claiming that the key to success is branded generics. But their particular contribution to growth has been declining. In the US, branded generics' contribution to growth declined from 12 per cent in 2007 to 10 per cent of growth in 2011 (IMS 2012c). Over the same period the contribution of *unbranded* generics rose from 16 per cent to 47 per cent. Also US patients appeared to favour unbranded generics by far when it came to having to pay themselves. In 2011 branded generics accounted for just 14 per cent of total insured patients' retail out of pocket costs, as opposed to 42 per cent for unbranded generics – three times as much.

There is one new justification for generics entry that did not feature in the 1990s: the desire of companies to get established in emerging countries. GlaxoSmithKline is one of a number of big pharma companies pursuing this strategy.

But most of the conditions applying in the 1990s still apply – and sometimes more strongly than formerly. I would maintain that all of the four points I cited in 1997 still apply at least to the same extent. The duration of the opportunity is still limited. Prices of generics are declining ever more rapidly than they were post–patent expiry in the 1990s, as leading brands from Lipitor down are now showing.

On my third point, the number of players in generics has been increasing since the 1990s, not only entrants from big pharma but also many Asian generics companies. This is increasing competition and contributing to faster and greater price erosion.

On my fourth point, whilst penetration of generics has increased practically everywhere, it has progressed more slowly than widely expected in the 1990s in key countries like France. Bayer, like Merck KgaA, made a particular play of setting up Bayer Generics in the 1990s in several countries, notably France. But growth there and elsewhere proved much weaker than expected and Bayer soon exited generics. Not surprisingly Bayer has not forgotten its 1990s foray into generics and has not been amongst the major pharmaceutical companies reentering recently.

We are currently at a peak in patent expiries. This has had a remarkable impact on big pharma sales. In 2011, sales of the Top 200 globally best-selling products declined by 10 per cent (Med Ad News 2012b). This unprecedented decline results from the sales decline of large numbers of leading products following patent expiry and the parlous economic situation in many countries.

Whilst that situation lasts, an unprecedented number of new opportunities are available for generics companies. But from 2014 the patent peak will be past and the number of generics opportunities therefore drops. This means that an inflated number of generics companies will be chasing fewer opportunities – a recipe for even more intensive competition, and more rapid erosion of prices.

I therefore still see rather strong parallels between the 1990s trend and the current wave of enthusiasm from big pharma currently in the generics market.

I expect therefore that whilst we will see a few successes, the latest attempt by big pharma to get into generics will again prove to be poor strategy. If I am right, all this will go to show that a thorough assessment of all relevant factors – and not just fear of the consequences of post–patent expiry – is still crucial in sizing up diversification strategies such as entry into generics.

Biosimilar Products – How Much of an Opportunity?

Biosimilars is another example of ebbs and flows in enthusiasms over the past dozen years. But how much of an opportunity is it really for big pharma?

The term *biogeneric* was formerly used to define a generic form of a biological product that is patent expired. However, because exact copying of a biological is almost impossible, another term – *biosimilar* – is now term most commonly used to describe a product developed to compete with an original biological product after that product's patents have expired. (A third term, *follow-on product*, is sometimes also used, most often in the United States.)

Since the early years of this century, major generics companies have blown hot and cold on biosimilars. At the moment they are in relatively 'hot' mode and as I will go on to explain, I believe they stand most to gain from this opportunity. Quite a number of big pharma companies have also made moves to enter biosimilars in recent years. How much of an opportunity does it represent for them?

A key consideration for biosimilars is that, given the relatively complex nature of large-molecule generics compared with conventional small-molecule generics, substantially more data is required in the US and Europe to obtain regulatory approval. Safety of biosimilar versions of complex large molecules is one issue. Their interchangeability with the original product is another. In major countries the rules on interchangeability mean that biosimilars cannot adopt the same generic name, as is acceptable with a small molecule product. This means that for a biosimilar a new generic name as well as a brand name have to be promoted – entailing significant marketing costs. So far, doctor resistance to interchangeability has been high, particularly in the US.

Manufacturing of biologicals reproducibly within specification is not easy. In a bioprocess, the composition varies from batch to batch; this is quite different to small-molecule manufacture.

The only way to tell whether a biosimilar is acceptable in terms of efficacy as well as safety is to conduct clinical trials – which adds considerably to the time and expense of developing them compared with small-molecule generics. Hence since in most parts of the developed world some clinical evidence is required to obtain regulatory approval, the development time for biogenerics is at least twice as long as for small-molecule generics.

Also, for biosimilars the nature and extent of the data needed depends very much on the product involved, so that general regulatory guidelines only go so far. They have to be defined product by product. The FDA has been particularly tardy in addressing this.

The cost of development for biosimilars has been estimated at between $50 million and $375 million, or from eight to a hundred times more than needed to develop small-molecule generics. The cost in developing markets, where regulatory requirements are far less stringent, is far lower. In India it is of the order of $10 million–$20 million. But this is still four to ten times the cost of developing a small-molecule generic there.

This means that the scope for price reduction with biosimilars compared with the original products is much less than is the case with conventional, small-molecule generics. Ultimately discounts on some biosimilars may reach 40 per cent, but at the moment the standard entry discount level for both biosimilars and biologic me-toos is 20 to 30 per cent.

All these challenging factors deterred quite a number of companies of various shapes and sizes interested in biosimilars around 2000 from persisting in their efforts to enter the field over the next few years. Already an ebb and flow of interest was evident. But from 2007 interest began to increase again – particularly from major generics companies.

A number of major pharmaceutical companies are currently also active in the field: Pfizer, Merck & Co, AstraZeneca, Sanofi, Amgen and Daiichi Sankyo. Also a number of big companies from other industries are active, such as Samsung and Fujifilm.

For some time until about 2010 it did seem possible that the number of eventual competitors in the market for most types of biosimilar product was likely to be more modest than was the case with small-molecule generics. This would mean at least that price erosion could be more gradual than with conventional generics. This seems to have been the case with the first half-dozen or so products launched in Europe – most of which did not actually make any great impression in any case.

But from 2012 the biosimilar bandwagon was really rolling. Quintiles estimated in August of that year that 277 companies were then developing biosimilars worldwide. The company surmised that there might be 20–30 biosimilars for each biologic rather than the three or four previously anticipated (Apothecurry 2012). If this proves to be the case, as looks most likely with monoclonal antibodies, this will dramatically reduce margins.

Moreover there is an additional pricing factor: the often greater gulf in price between biologicals and alternative available therapies. In many until recently moribund therapeutic markets where biologics compete, there have been few advances for many years. This means that standard therapies are now very cheap in comparison with much less moribund markets where there has been more innovation. Moribund markets include those for numerous autoimmune diseases, such as arthritis, the dermatological indications psoriasis as well as eczema and dermatitis, and the inflammatory bowel disorders Crohn's disease and ulcerative colitis. It also applies currently to most cancer markets. The impact of this is two-fold.

Firstly, biosimilars are likely in such moribund markets to attract much less switch business from original brands than in more dynamic, small-molecule-dominated markets with conventional, deep price erosion. The price differential between original brands and biosimilars will usually be modest and therefore switching to biosimilars will not lead to very substantial savings. Added to this, since biosimilars are not necessarily going to be accepted as truly equivalent and interchangeable, this will also reduce the propensity to switch.

Secondly, the other way in which latter-day products might make inroads – expansion of the market – is also going to be particularly difficult in moribund markets. Thus the expansion of such markets through the replacement of cheap, traditional, small-molecule products will be much less likely than would be the case in conventional markets. To put it bluntly, how much more attractive to payers is a product that costs 800 per cent of the traditional product price than one that costs 1,000 per cent?

The first biotech product whose patents expired was Eli Lilly's Humulin (human insulin). However, in developed markets competition from biosimilars has not emerged. Humulin's sales remain buoyant, edging up to an new peak of $1.089 billion in 2011, even though patents for it began to expire as long ago as 2001.

Sales from the Top 10 biosimilars companies are growing but still modest. By 2011 they totalled $693 million (IMS 2012c). But this represented only 0.4 per cent of total global expenditure on biologics. IMS considers that this will rise to about 2 per cent of the total market by 2016 – still a very modest share. Novartis accounts for almost three quarters of the market.

It now appears likely that biosimilars will start to make a real impact only when monoclonal antibody products lose their patents. Some of these products have very substantial sales. But by 2012 general guidelines for biosimilar monoclonal antibodies in the US, by far the most important market, were still at an early stage. And after that, product-specific guidelines are still needed.

But for big pharma, are even the monoclonal antibodies big enough to warrant companies' involvement? For the very largest products, sales for biosimilars could be of the order of perhaps high hundreds of millions of dollars – but still less than a billion. We can expect that at the very least two to three companies will share these sales – and given the recent inrush of so many companies into biosimilars recently, probably far more. For example, the number of rituximab and trastuzumab biosimilars in development by early 2012 were both in the teens.

Perhaps the first couple of companies entering each monoclonal market could achieve sales of a few hundred million dollars for their products. This is not a very attractive level for a big pharma company. On the other hand, it is an attractive scale of sales for generics companies or more modest-sized pharmaceutical companies. I believe the largest generic companies are best placed to exploit this opportunity.

For the long term, we can expect an increasing proportion of new products reaching the market to be biologicals. Eventually, therefore, the proportion of all products whose patents will be expiring that will be biologicals will also increase. In turn, biosimilar opportunities will also then increase beyond the commercial potential levels for the first few major monoclonal antibody products estimated above.

The biggest opportunity geographically for biosimilars ultimately is probably the US market. In March 2012 IMS projected it to grow modestly up to 2015, projecting sales of only between $1.9 billion and $2.6 billion sales globally. But thereafter up to 2020 IMS projects biosimilars' sales to rise more sharply up to between $11 billion and $25 billion. That would then represent 4–10 per cent of the total biologics market – significant but hardly a major share (IMS 2012c).

In the next chapter I turn to a quite different strategic option: mergers and acquisitions.

9

Mergers and Demergers

Mergers and acquisitions (M&A) have at times obsessed the pharmaceutical industry. Currently this is far from being the case. But every few years there is a spate of pharma megamerger mania – yet another example of the ebb and flow of a strategy in the pharma industry.

In this chapter I assess how successful or not M&A has been for the pharmaceutical industry. I consider the role of megamergers and more modest-scale mergers, and review the various rationales given for going ahead with mergers in the pharma industry. Finally, I look at the possible role of demergers.

Megamergers

In 2012 PricewaterhouseCoopers found that only 7 per cent of pharmaceutical and life science CEOs considered that mergers and acquisitions would be the main opportunity to grow their business over the subsequent 12 months (PwC 2012a). This was well below average for respondents across all industries, where 15 per cent of CEOs considered M&A to be the prime opportunity for growth. It is remarkable how limited the interest in mergers in the pharmaceutical industry today is, when we recall the past periods of pharma megamerger mania.

M&A in pharma is no new phenomenon. It was a feature in the development of the pharmaceutical industry in the late nineteenth and first half of the twentieth century. By means of mergers, prominent companies in mid-twentieth century like Merck Sharpe & Dohme, Warner-Lambert and Smith, Kline & French were formed. Towards the end of the twentieth century, pharmaceutical M&A activity intensified to an unprecedented peak, as the table below shows. Between 1994 and 2000 there were some 17 major mergers, an average of fewer than three per year.

Table 9.1 Major pharmaceutical company mergers/acquisitions since 1994

Year	Company Acquiring	Company Acquired
1994	*Sanofi*	*Sterling*
	Roche	*Syntex*
	American Home Products (later renamed Wyeth)	American Cyanamid (Lederle)
1995	*BASF*	*Boots*
	Hoechst	*Marion Merrell Dow*
	Glaxo	Wellcome
	Pharmacia	*Upjohn*
	Rhône-Poulenc Rorer	*Fisons*
1996	Novartis created from	Ciba-Geigy and Sandoz
1997	*Roche*	*Corange (Boehringer Mannheim)*
1999	*AstraZeneca*	*Astra and Zeneca*
	Sanofi	Synthélabo
	Aventis created from	*Hoechst and Rhône-Poulenc Rorer*
2000	*Pharmacia & Upjohn*	*Monsanto (Searle)*
	Pfizer	Warner-Lambert
	Glaxo Wellcome	SmithKline Beecham
	Abbott	*Knoll*
2001	Johnson & Johnson	Alza
	Bristol-Myers Squibb	DuPont
	Roche	*Chugai*
2002	Amgen	Immunex
2003	*Pfizer*	*Pharmacia*
2004	Sanofi Aventis created from	Sanofi-Synthélabo and Aventis
2005	Astellas created from	Yamanouchi and Fujisawa
2006	Daiichi Sankyo created from	Daiichi and Sankyo
	Bayer Schering created from	Bayer and Schering AG
	Merck Serono created from	*Merck KGaA and Serono*
2007	*Schering-Plough*	*Organon (Akzo Nobel)*
	Nycomed	*Altana*
	AstraZeneca	*Medimmune*
2009	*Roche*	*Genentech*
	Pfizer	Wyeth
	Merck & Co	Schering-Plough
	Abbott	*Solvay Pharmaceuticals*
2010	Novartis	Alcon
2011	*Sanofi*	*Genzyme*
	Takeda	*Nycomed*

Note: Transnational mergers are shown in italics.

Source: John Ansell Consultancy

Pharmaceutical M&A has been driven by forces that apply across all industries, such as stock market pressure and speculation. These forces can be expected to have some influence in stimulating major mergers and acquisitions in future, even when pharma industry interest is at a low ebb as currently.

The generally more subdued tempo of major M&A activity in the pharmaceutical sector over the past few years no doubt reflects dissatisfaction with the outcome of the really big megamergers in particular, stemming from their perceived lack of effectiveness. Now let's consider some of the main reasons that have been cited for going ahead with M&A.

Improving R&D Productivity

Over the past 15 years the decline in the pharmaceutical industry's new product productivity, leading to concerns over gaps in product pipelines – current and future – has commonly been advanced by enthusiasts as a key justification for going ahead with M&A. Until the early years of this century, providing critical mass for conducting R&D effectively was the most prominent of the various rationales advanced for mergers.

Naturally since the process is so protracted, it takes time for evidence to emerge that a merger has been effective in improving R&D productivity. In fact even today good evidence is still lacking that they have such a beneficial impact. As Grabowski and Kyle recently concluded in a review of mergers and acquisitions, 'There is little evidence from existing studies that M&A advances drug innovation' (Grabowski and Kyle 2012). Indeed they concluded from a review of published data that M&A has a weakly *negative* effect on R&D productivity.

Several industry commentators also believe that the sheer scale created through mergers actually hinders creativity. In 2011 the CEO of Eli Lilly, John Lechleiter, said about his company: 'We fail to see a connection between size and innovativeness' (Timmerman 2011).

The CEO of GlaxoSmithKline, Sir Andrew Witty, also believes that large scale and R&D productivity do not go together. Consequently GlaxoSmithKline R&D has gradually been reorganized into ever smaller operational units, in the hope of emulating the scale of successful start-up companies.

Some commentators have been much more forceful in their criticism of mergers. In 2011 John LaMattina, the former head of research at Pfizer, argued that industry consolidation had resulted in less competition and less investment in R&D and that 'their impact on the R&D of the organisations involved has been devastating … At a time when there is a major need for new treatments for conditions such as Alzheimer's disease, drug-resistant infections and diabetes, such a trend is alarming'. LaMattina argued that an underlying factor contributing to the good productivity observed in the 1990s was the large number of pharmaceutical companies in existence at that time (LaMattina 2011).

A further criticism of megamergers has been that they are disruptive of the general running and performance of companies. Thus whilst two companies occupy themselves with postmerger integration their rivals, free of such disruption, can, for example, focus on doing deals to acquire the most promising products available from start-up companies.

Whilst it takes time to prove whether a strategy positively influences R&D, negative evidence can emerge much more quickly. For example after years of inactivity on mergers, Pfizer became very active from the early years of this century, as Table 9.1 shows. But the number of Phase III NCEs in Pfizer's R&D pipeline actually halved between 2004 and 2006, from 12 to 6 projects. This was a period over which the company was aiming as a priority to increase the number of advanced projects in its pipeline. However, by January 2010 after Wyeth had been taken over, the number of Phase III projects was still only 13. Several of those products have subsequently gone on to reach the market. But the latest Pfizer pipeline I examined that was issued in August 2012 showed – by my calculation – that the number of NCEs at Phase III yet to be launched for any indication was back down to six again.

It certainly looks as though economies of scale do not benefit research in pharmaceuticals. Small-scale, entrepreneurial biotech companies are potentially more productive. They continue to increase their share of successful new products reaching the pharmaceutical market.

The jury has long been out on the impact on R&D productivity of the merger of Glaxo Wellcome and SmithKline Beecham in 2000. In 2011 Moncef Slaoui, Head of R&D at GlaxoSmithKline, effectively conceded that it had not worked (Stovall 2011). But perhaps this was being a little unfair: eleven new GlaxoSmithKline products were approved by the FDA between 2008 and 2011, more than from any other company.

But unless positive evidence does emerge – and with the long R&D timescale, getting proof is particularly difficult, with successive mergers quite often intervening and obfuscating the outcome of the first merger – then the R&D scale factor will not regain credibility as a rationale for future mergers.

Finally, as one small saving grace, Grabowski and Kyle did cite evidence from Danzon, Nicholson and Pereira (2003) that M&A which follows strategic alliances already existing between two companies is somewhat more successful than M&A that does not.

Saving Manufacturing Costs

Saving manufacturing costs is a rationale of relatively modest importance in pharmaceuticals. This is because as explained in Chapter 1 (see p. 11) manufacturing is not normally a major cost area for pharmaceutical companies, and so the scope for cost cutting is not great. Over the past decade this rationale has not often been advanced as a prime reason for a pharmaceutical merger.

Companies involved in earlier mergers found that cost economies achieved were much more modest than they had expected. However, some pharmaceutical mergers have been a trigger for overdue divestment of surplus manufacturing facilities and in this way significant cost savings have sometimes been made.

Broadening Geographical Coverage

Over the past few years, with the realization that they need to strengthen their position in emerging countries, pharma companies have acquired stakes in or bought outright local companies in such countries. This is a fast route to increasing local presence. None of these deals have been megamergers because the scale of companies in these countries is much less than in Western markets.

Marketing Rationales

The goal of building up much bigger sales forces is not usually a major rationale advanced to justify a pharmaceutical merger. This is because pharma sales forces can usually be expanded fairly easily if necessary, either through direct recruitment or by means of contract sales forces. Likewise, savings on marketing expenditure do not necessitate M&A – they can be achieved by cutting sales forces.

One valid reason for a merger is when both companies lack sufficient products to justify their existing sales force strengths. For example, in 1985 Rorer (later to become successively part of Rhône-Poulenc Rorer, Aventis, Sanofi Aventis and then Sanofi) acquired the pharmaceutical division of Revlon; neither company had a convincing R&D pipeline of any size and existing products were aging. After the merger Rorer was able to promote the combined product pipeline with a single sales force, thereby reducing costs considerably.

With the growing dearth of new products, more recently there have been further mergers along these lines of companies lacking sufficient products to survive and prosper. Pfizer's acquisition of Wyeth in 2009 could be described in these terms.

Mergers and Rankings

Another disappointment which became clear in the early years of this century was that most megamerged pharmaceutical companies failed to hold the global sales ranking secured immediately postmerger. This might of course have been because the component companies tended to merge when they anticipated difficult times ahead – for example, when major patent expiries on their leading products were looming. Thus mergers cannot necessarily be blamed for subsequent poor performance. However, they do not seem to be a very effective way of avoiding impending problems and can actually compound them.

Pfizer held a 4.1 per cent share of the global pharmaceutical market in 1999. After mergers this rose to 9.8 per cent in 2004. But Pfizer's share had dropped back to 7.6 per cent by 2009 just prior to the acquisition of Wyeth. This latter company held a 2.7 per cent share just before its acquisition by Pfizer. And so at merger the combined share was 10.3 per cent. But by 2011 the share for the combined company was down to 6.6 per cent, a dramatic collapse.

Likewise Glaxo Wellcome and SmithKline Beecham held respectively 4.1 per cent and 2.8 per cent shares of the global market in 1999, the year before GlaxoSmithKline was formed. Thus the aggregate share at merger was 6.9 per cent. By 2004 the merged GlaxoSmithKline held only 6.3 per cent, by 2009 4.7 per cent and in 2011 only 4.1 per cent.

However, Novartis is something of an exception, with a share of 4.0 per cent in 1999 three years after its formation through the merger with Ciba-Geigy. Novartis's share rose steadily to 6.1 per cent by 2011. Of course, as with the other examples, there were additional, smaller acquisitions as well as some modest divestments affecting Novartis's market share.

Megamergers and Problems of Product Scale

I first suggested that megamerged companies were becoming too big for their own good in a 1996 article (Ansell 1996). I will explain my concerns using recent figures.

Pfizer in 2011 had global sales of $56 billion. A basic blockbuster selling $1 billion per annum would therefore account for not much more than 2 per cent of its total turnover. Pfizer really needs products over double that size which can contribute, say, 4 per cent of its total turnover, or $2.24 billion.

In 2011 there were only 48 products with global sales of $2.6 billion or more. Let's say in order not to overcomplicate things, that this is the scale of products that will be available in the future too. Now most companies including Pfizer do not attempt to cover all therapeutic fields (see pp. 33–5) and so some of these 48 will be in the wrong therapeutic areas for Pfizer. Also Pfizer will never realistically have access to a good proportion of potential blockbusters because rights to them will never be made available whenever they belong to the major competitors developing them. Also, where the rights still belong to smaller companies, Pfizer's will have to compete with other pharma companies to acquire rights – and sometimes they will not succeed.

Hence the target number of products that might be available to Pfizer is much less than 48 products in today's terms. I argue that the number of products likely to be available is far too limited to provide Pfizer with enough new products for it to survive and prosper. It is one reason, though I would not claim it to be the only one, that explains how Pfizer ends up today after all its acquisitions and other types of deals with by my count only six NCEs at Phase III.

This scale factor suggests that there could be some merits in demerger (see later in this chapter). This is because, as discussed in Chapter 1, product concentration is low in pharmaceuticals and there is a long tail of smaller products available that can make a significant contribution to smaller companies than Pfizer.

The Pfizer Acquisition That Did Pay Off

The Pfizer corporate acquisition that most dramatically paid off was of Warner-Lambert in 2000. In doing so it captured the lipid-lowering product Lipitor (atorvastatin), to which it already had alliance rights. Judging by its abandonment of nearly all of the remainder of Warner-Lambert's R&D pipeline projects and the selling off of its consumer product interests, acquiring full rights to Lipitor was essentially Pfizer's only goal for this deal. Since the sales of Lipitor rose from $5.0 billion at the time of the acquisition to $14.3 billion in 2006, the product by itself certainly amply justified this corporate acquisition. Pfizer's acquisitions of Pharmacia in 2003 and of Wyeth in 2009 continued this process, though with much less obviously beneficial results.

But it proved impossible for Pfizer to overcome the consequences of post–patent expiry of Lipitor and other major products. In January 2012 its chief executive Ian Read, speaking at the JP Morgan Global Healthcare Conference in San Francisco, said that he was 'very disinclined to be looking at the possibility of another mega-acquisition'. That the current CEO of this formerly enthusiastic megamerging company, which succeeded in becoming the no. 1 pharma company largely through successive acquisitions, should say this, may well serve to snuff out any residual enthusiasm of pharmaceutical companies for megamergers.

Smaller Acquisitions

In certain circumstances smaller acquisitions can make more sense. Acquisitions of start-ups by pharma companies have been quite popular in recent years. This is often a means whereby a pharmaceutical company rapidly acquires novel products with attractive commercial prospects.

An early example with implications still today was Johnson & Johnson's acquisition of the US biotech company Centocor in 1999 which I mentioned earlier (see pp. 100–101). This had in 1979 been the first biotech company ever established. The now highly successful product Remicade (infliximab), which achieved sales of $8.963 billion in 2011, as well as ReoPro (abciximab) for restenosis, are the two major successes for Johnson & Johnson so far from this acquisition.

Major pharma has also been increasingly active in using smaller acquisitions to gain enabling technologies or other know-how. Although there are far more strategic alliances than mergers facilitating this, mergers are one useful channel for transfer of technology to a commercial partner. Both types of deal can increase the chances that this happens effectively, thereby helping sooner or later to bring new products to the market.

Concentration

Despite continuing merger activity, the total number of companies active in developing or marketing pharmaceuticals, including start-ups has, rather remarkably given the poor economic situation since 2008, continued to increase. According to Citeline, the total number of companies active in R&D increased by 13 per cent, to 2,705 in 2012 (Pharmaprojects® Citeline 2012). As Figure 9.1 shows, there has been an increase in the number of companies for many years, from just under a thousand in 1998 to over 2,705 in 2012.

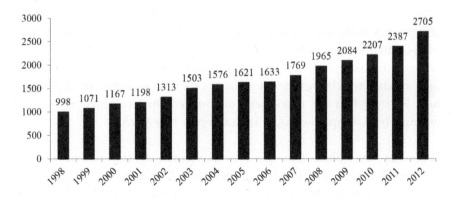

Figure 9.1   Total number of companies with active R&D
Source: Based on Data from Pharmaprojects® Citeline 2012

In 2012 just over a third of these companies (953) had one product in their pipeline and a further 17 per cent (459) had just two (Pharmaprojects® Citeline 2012). In aggregate, therefore, just over half of all companies (52 per cent) had only one or two products in their pipeline.

The Pharmaprojects® Citeline figures show that this high level of dispersion of products in development across many companies is on the increase and that the global market share accounted for by Top 10 pharma companies is slipping. Thus despite all attempts to increase the concentration of the pharmaceutical industry to what I have firmly believed for some time have been unhealthy levels (Ansell 2006), forces in the form of small start-up companies are bringing concentration back down again.

Are Demergers a Practical Alternative?

If increasing concentration has disadvantages in terms of reduced R&D effectiveness, what about the alternative: demerger?

I see the main practical problem militating against demergers as the unlikelihood that a demerged or spun-off entity would for very long remain independent. The quality of what is available for acquisition-hungry companies to purchase at any given time has in recent years been mixed to say the least. Therefore in today's environment, no sooner would most demerged entities have been formed than they would be snapped up by one of any number of acquisition-hungry companies.

In 2011 Abbott announced that it would split into two companies, a device and diagnostics company retaining the name Abbott, and a pharmaceutical company with the new name of AbbVie. The size of Abbott Pharma was, according to the company, threatening imbalance to the group's diversified business model, which includes a variety of different types of healthcare product. Scarcely had the news been announced than commentators were suggesting which companies might in due course buy AbbVie.

In my view the Abbott demerger is unlikely to be the start of a new trend. Even though it might make very good sense to split companies up and make it easier for them to operate in the relatively unconcentrated pharmaceutical market, corporate predators are unlikely to become less active as long as the dearth of new products continues.

PART IV

Where Will New Products Come From?

Over the past decade the most noticeable development in pharmaceuticals geographically has been the emergence of a number of developing territories. The size of many national markets in developing countries has grown very considerably since the beginning of this century. (Some should indeed no longer be categorized as 'developing' or 'emerging' countries.) With the slowing of growth in the majority of developed territories, big pharma has at least gained some compensation from increasing its presence in developing countries, even if lower margins have often had to be accepted.

Eventually when some of these developing countries do become wealthier, their disease profiles will come much more closely to resemble those of developed countries. At that point they will then become significant markets for the relatively expensive and highly profitable products from which big pharma already obtains most of its profits.

Thus it makes sense for this reason alone for big pharma to continue to develop its presence in developing countries in order to benefit eventually from the growth of national markets. And in the interim there are lesser opportunities in developing countries that big pharma can usefully pursue. I am therefore going to dwell only briefly in the next chapter on this aspect of big pharma and developing countries because I regard this strategy to be uncontroversial.

A quite different question is whether the pharmaceutical industry can expect novel new products to emerge from local companies in developing countries. In Part IV I want examine this in detail and suggest where new products are likely to come from.

10

Emerging Countries – Opportunities in Perspective

The foundational elements required to encourage innovative activity are clear: a well-educated population with a strong science base, sound intellectual property rules and supportive infrastructure encouraging collaboration between public and private companies.

Wilsdon 2012

Much of pharma's remaining capacity will also be targeted for building their presence in higher-growing emerging markets, rather than supporting innovation in mature ones.

Ernst & Young 2012

Emerging countries are undeniably an opportunity for major pharmaceutical companies. The pharmaceutical industry has stepped up its efforts over the past decade to seek growth in these countries. This has been at a time of the increasing impact of a shortage of new products as well as stagnant or even negative growth in developed countries.

Many emerging countries have been growing much faster than developed countries. The majority of them have been much less affected by the global financial crisis, since they did not become indebted in the way that developed countries did. However, the impact from depressed developed country economies is now beginning to make more of a negative impact on emerging country growth also.

The emerging countries by definition are growing from a low base in value terms. This means that in absolute terms pharma sales growth has been modest in many of them.

Furthermore, some sizeable emerging countries, notably China, have been wielding the considerable power they possess through their size, to limit the scale of the opportunity open to outsiders. They have clamped down on the scope of profits that Western companies eager to take advantage of new growth are able to make. There are other resultant pressures from the larger emerging countries. For example, Russia has been applying heavy pressure for foreign companies to manufacture locally.

Increased Interest in Emerging Countries

At the start of interest in emerging countries they were grouped together. But even the BRIC countries – Brazil, Russia, India and China, first defined as such in 2001 by Jim O'Neill, head of Goldman Sachs Global Economic Research – are different in many ways. Now, most pharmaceutical companies realize that it is not particularly sensible to group countries in this way. It is readily apparent now that they have widely different potential for sales growth, whether this is considered generally or for pharmaceuticals specifically. And even less is it the case that they have similar potential for profit growth.

Emerging countries may not be very profitable – because prices applying there are often much lower than in developed countries. IMS has projected that most growth from emerging countries over the next few years will come from generics rather than novel products, with unbranded rather than branded generics contributing most (see also p. 121).

Chris Viehbacher, CEO of Sanofi, has claimed that emerging territories can be profitable. However, his company has as yet provided no profit figures to show whether this is the case. Meanwhile, the company for which he worked before he joined Sanofi, GlaxoSmithKline, perhaps not coincidentally is also a strong enthusiast for emerging countries.

After his appointment as CEO of GlaxoSmithKline in 2007, one of the first major strategic moves Sir Andrew Witty made was to increase his company's presence in emerging markets. In 2010 GlaxoSmithKline set up a least developed country (LDC) unit. This was explicitly charged with a dual role – to focus 50 per cent on business and 50 per cent on reputation, across 40 countries in Africa and 10 more in Asia.

GlaxoSmithKline has since invested quite heavily in emerging countries through a variety of deals including acquisitions. In 2011 Witty stressed that in the long term he remained 'an extreme bull' on emerging markets, pointing to positive economic growth in these countries (Cooper 2011).

GlaxoSmithKline, unlike Sanofi, has supplied breakdowns of profits from 2009 showing its progress on this score. The contribution of emerging markets did indeed rise. In 2011 they contributed turnover of £3.680 billion, which I calculate was then 17 per cent of total GlaxoSmithKline turnover.

But the profit margin on this business is not much more than half of GlaxoSmithKline's business in developed countries. The nature of emerging market business is that it is heavily generics oriented, and naturally margins are far lower on generics than they are for on-patent products. That may, of course, still be acceptable to GlaxoSmithKline, because the company is trying to increase its reputation rather than just make a quick profit. But it is interesting that in 2012 GlaxoSmithKline combined emerging markets with its Europe business, which means that the difference in margins is no longer transparent.

To put the importance of emerging markets in some perspective, in 2011, when PricewaterhouseCoopers interviewed 82 pharma and life science CEOs in 29 countries, only a sixth of respondents considered that new geographic markets were the main opportunity for growth in the following year. This was far outweighed by the 43 per cent who saw new product or service development as being the main opportunity.

A More Selective Approach?

As companies come to realize that some developing countries are better prospects than others, I expect their efforts to be more selective, with prioritization of investment country by country. Developing countries represent different propositions. The BRIC concept was useful in highlighting the growing opportunity for companies that developing countries could represent. Subsequently there have been attempts, by IMS for example, to categorize developing countries into several groups according to their commercial potential in pharmaceuticals. But if companies want to do a professional job, they need to address each country as a separate proposition. This then raises the question of the criteria which should be used to judge this.

There are many country reviews published – in pharmaceutical magazines as well as in full pharma industry reports that can be purchased. However, these reports tend to focus mainly on purely pharmaceutical and healthcare aspects of countries. This is of course very necessary. But, for this whole issue I consider that there is often inadequate consideration of general, nonpharmaceutical factors applying to each country. In my view these factors need to be given more attention in assessing how much of an opportunity the local pharmaceutical markets are going to prove. But it is also necessary to fathom whether these countries will become significant sources of novel products.

Why Do Countries Perform So Differently?

In general rather than specifically pharmaceutical terms, there has never been any shortage of new ideas on why countries perform differently. When a new idea emerges, then it is only natural that the proponent focuses on that one idea. But unfortunately life is more complex than that. And so to focus on just one cause is usually misleading.

Jared Diamond is a polymath and the author of books on a wide variety of subjects. Originally a physiologist, he developed interests in ornithology, ecology and environmental history. His final academic position was as a professor of geography. He is most famous for the ground-breaking *Guns, Germs, and Steel: A Short History of Everybody for the Last 17,000 Years*. Published in 1997, this book won Pulitzer and Aventis prizes. *Guns, Germs and Steel* is a wonderful illustration of how to use a multidisciplinary approach to address a particularly complex issue. Pharmaceuticals is also complex and itself demands a another whole range of different expertises and therefore, I would maintain, a multidisciplinary approach.

Those working in the pharmaceutical industry learn to be adaptable during their career:

- Many staff with a clinical background end up in commercial or general management positions.

- Health economics was a discipline new to the pharmaceutical industry until the 1980s. Many of the first wave of health economists in the industry have science backgrounds.

- It is quite common for staff with a clinical background to convert themselves into successful marketing, business development and general managers.

- To give one celebrated example, Fred Hassan, who after senior management positions in the United States with Sandoz and Wyeth headed up Pharmacia, Schering-Plough and currently Bausch & Lomb, started out with a degree in chemical engineering.[1]

Despite this evident versatility, it is difficult for any manager regardless of background to master more than a couple of different disciplines. But to gain a balanced judgment of many issues in the pharmaceutical industry demands mastery of several. It requires tapping into expert advice often from a whole range of able staff with different areas of expertise. Failing that, outsiders can be brought in. Judging the merits of their advice can be challenging for a pharma company.

Very often a pharmaceutical issue is a multifactorial one. But much advice from outsiders pushes only one particular line. A 'single factor' response is particularly unhelpful when a sophisticated assessment is required covering multiple disciplines. But it seems to be a human characteristic to seek single causes and sometimes a strong, simple argument prevails when a more multifaceted approach is needed.

Let's return to the polymathic Jared Diamond for an example from outside the industry – but one which is directly relevant to the question I pose above. In 2012 in the *New York Review of Books*, in an extensive review entitled 'What Makes Countries Rich or Poor?' he reviewed Daron Acemoglu and James Robinson's book *Why Nations Fail*.

In that book, Acemoglu and Robinson argued that the critical factor determining whether nations succeed or not is what they term 'inclusive institutions'. This means good economic institutions which motivate people to become productive, including protection of their private property rights, predictable enforcement of contracts, opportunities to invest and retain control of their money, control of inflation and open exchange of currency.

---

1   In his recently published book 'reinvent', Fred Hassan says: 'Engineering had given me an understanding of how to get things done, and a mental discipline to help me analyze, organize and execute. Additionally, I knew that an understanding of chemistry, physics and math would later give me the ability to trust my gut on decisions that would come my way in the later career I was planning – pharmaceuticals' (Hassan 2013).

Where these conditions exist, people are motivated to work hard when they have opportunities to invest their earnings profitably. They are not so motivated when they cannot do so, or when their earnings or profits could be confiscated.

Though he praised the book and a positive quote from it appears prominently on its cover, Jared Diamond pointed out in his review why this explanation is simplistic. He argued that several other factors (including those he covered in *Guns, Germs, and Steel*, in particular the influence of geography on societies and cultures) must also be playing a role. Whilst Diamond believed there was no doubt that 'inclusive institutions' were important in determining a country's wealth, he believed that this element provided perhaps only 50 per cent of the explanation for national differences in prosperity. Disease, agricultural productivity, geographical latitude, whether a country is landlocked, and the extent of environmental damage, all played a part in whether countries were today rich or poor, according to Diamond.

Thus in assessing which emerging markets are likely to prosper in future, a more subtle, multifactorial approach along the lines of Diamond's is, I believe, necessary. A pharmaceutical company has the power to change countries to an extent. It would be possible, for example, for a pharmaceutical company bringing an effective malaria vaccine to a market to have an impact. The resulting improvement in the health status of the population could in this case significantly benefit the workforce and the chances of improving the economy. But in the main, whether a pharma company succeeds or not will depend overwhelmingly on the conditions that exist in each country.

Assessing emerging countries in this way could give some surprising results. Acemoglu and Robinson in particular provide some convincing arguments according to their criteria above as to why they consider that China's growth 'is likely to run out of steam', which I consider further in Chapter 12. I agree with these authors that companies should heed in particular how democratic the systems of emerging countries are now and the extent to which they are likely to become more democratic. This is no simple task for a country like China.

Companies need to take into account the intensity of corruption that exists. Can they recruit able employees to take the company forward locally, or will they have to settle for employees who are less than ideal but who have the necessary contacts within the country to conform with the local systems?

The conclusion for the pharmaceutical industry from all this is that, as I have suggested above, big pharma should be paying much more attention to the individual factors existing in each emerging country rather than adopting a single, across-the-board approach.

A Source of New Products?

Emerging countries are potential developers of new products. Sometimes this is seen as an opportunity, sometimes as a threat. In September 2012 John Castellani, president and CEO of the Pharmaceutical Research and Manufacturers of America (PhRMA) suggested that the important role which he argued the biopharmaceutical industry played in the US economy was very well known to competitors in the global economy. He claimed that 'they are coming after this American engine of innovation and growth ... The Chinese government has identified biotechnology as one of the keys to its future economic growth and to creating over a million new jobs. India and Russia have publicly declared their goal of strengthening their biopharmaceutical research sectors. And Singapore's vision is to be the "biopolis" of Asia, an international science cluster aimed at advancing human health'.

If these countries are capable of all this, is it an opportunity for big pharma, or, as John Castellani suggests, a threat? In Chapter 12 I will review this. But before that, an interlude. Let's see what the story of a one-time economic star which lost its lustre can tell us: Japan.

11

What Can We Learn from Japan?

Until the 1990s Japan was so successful economically that Western countries strove to imitate it as a role model. But Japan has since been through two decades of economic difficulties. And of all the major national pharmaceutical markets, Japan is now the most unfashionable.

Japan's Rise

The rise of Japan was dramatic. As late as the 1960s, Japan still had the status of a developing country. But as I have mentioned already in Chapter 5 (see p. 98), pharmaceuticals was never a star industry for Japan, even when the country was going through its era of great success up to 1990. The Japanese pharmaceutical market, with a population base rising past 100 million, has for many years been the second biggest in the world, and even its weak progress since 1990 still leaves it in second position for the moment at least. That is also the case for pharmaceuticals specifically. At its peak towards the end of the twentieth century the global market share of the Japanese pharma industry approached 15 per cent.

It took Western pharmaceutical companies many years to gain a strong foothold in Japan. Japanese government control of foreign investments made it very difficult for any Western company to set up its own local subsidiaries there until the mid-1970s. For long, the Japanese market was relatively self-contained, with most sales coming from indigenous pharmaceutical companies. The Japanese industry contained many relatively small domestic companies. In 1997, there were still 1,500 Japanese pharmaceutical manufacturers of which 1,400 were classified as small to medium-sized companies.

Since Western companies were essentially prevented until the late 1970s from marketing their own products in Japan, they licensed out their products to local companies to market. Whilst Western products made inroads in Japan, their performance still tended to be more modest than in Western markets.

Meanwhile, the framework of local regulation encouraged Japanese companies to focus on developing improvements on existing drugs rather than investing in higher-risk new chemical entity projects. Their forte was manufacturing rather than research. Also within R&D there was more emphasis on development rather than research. There were some areas where the Japanese pharmaceutical industry was strong: its expertise in fermentation technology put it at the forefront of novel antibiotic and chemotherapy R&D.

The Japanese pharmaceutical industry was very productive in the sheer number of new products launched. This reached a peak in 1994 when half of all products launched globally were Japanese. However, few of them were global products. They were designed predominantly to meet the needs of the local market. A majority of the products Japanese companies produced could be described as me-too products.

Problems with Globalization

The Japanese pharmaceutical industry came late to embrace globalization. It was handicapped because most new products developed for the domestic market offered little or no advance over what was already available in the West. Often Japanese companies did not even attempt to find partners to globalize products. In any case, the data generated to obtain registration in Japan was quite often inadequate to meet the needs of Western regulatory authorities. Japanese companies were able to trade profitably on the basis of the local market and were often not ambitious about expanding outside Japan. They tended to license out products with global potential to Western companies who then carried out the majority of the necessary further development for Western and other markets. From the 1990s, Western companies were able and willing to take back rights to their own products from Japanese partners and market them in Japan solely through their own subsidiaries.

By the early years of this century Japanese companies were coming under immense pressure. Firstly, their main source of new products had been cut off, as Western pharma companies increasingly launched their products via their own Japanese subsidiaries rather than through the joint ventures with Japanese companies that had been necessary formerly. This often also created strong competition to the many me-too-oriented products Japanese companies had successfully marketed till then in Japan.

Secondly, few Japanese companies had come anywhere near to developing the ability to match Western pharma companies in producing new products with global commercial potential. Just a few global blockbusters emerged from Japanese companies to be marketed outside Japan. To do so they relied at least partly on Western partners. This meant that Japan helped only to a modest extent to offset the growing lack of new products with global potential.

Before 2005 the idea of mergers between Japanese pharmaceutical companies had been anathema in Japan. This meant that they lagged behind the more merger-minded Western companies in their scale and power. However, from around that time several Japanese megamergers did take place, with the creation of:

- Astellas from the merger of Fujisawa with Yamanouchi in 2005;

- Daiichi Sankyo from Daiichi and Sankyo in 2006;

- Mitsubishi Tanabe Pharma from the merger of Mitsubishi Pharma and Tanabe Seiyaku in 2007;

- Kyowa Hakko Kirin when Kirin Brewery acquired a majority stake in Kyowa Hakko in 2008.

However, this proved to be a temporary phenomenon. It left the scale of the top Japanese pharma companies well behind those in the West. The largest Japanese company by 2012 was Takeda, no. 14 in the rankings by global sales of all pharmaceutical companies worldwide. Daiichi Sankyo (no. 17), Astellas (no. 19) and Otsuka (no. 21) are the other Japanese companies ranking in the Top 25 (Cacciotti 2012).

A consequence of this lesser scale has been that when Japanese pharmaceutical companies have tried to bolster their position outside Japan, they have only been able to do so on a relatively modest scale. In recent years:

- Takeda acquired the US companies Millennium in 2008, IDM Pharma in 2009, Nycomed in 2011 and Ligocyte in 2012;

- Daiichi Sankyo acquired the Indian company Ranbaxy as well as the German company U3 Pharma in 2008;

- Astellas acquired the US company OSI in 2010;

- Eisai acquired the US company MGI Pharma in 2007.

In this way several of the leading Japanese pharmaceutical companies increased their global presence but in a relatively modest way. These acquisitions were, however, sometimes valuable in boosting their R&D capabilities.

The difficulty Japanese companies have had in accessing products with global potential has also been compounded by their very poor progress in capitalizing upon biotechnology. In the late 1980s it was widely expected that the Japanese pharmaceutical industry would do well in biotechnology. I remember when chairing Management Centre Europe's major annual pharmaceutical conference in Paris in 1988 being asked by a questioner from the hall whether I considered that Japan would become successful in biotechnology. I answered that I thought this was unlikely. You could almost hear the gasps of surprise from the audience – which consisted largely of senior Western pharmaceutical executives.

Local Handicaps

One big drawback that fledgling biotech companies have had to contend with in Japan is the almost total absence of venture capital finance. This remains today at a negligible level.

The result of all this is that the majority of Japanese pharmaceutical companies find themselves with ageing product ranges. They are commonly dependent on a very few sizeable products. Further undermined over the past 20 years by the long-standing problems of the national economy, the Japanese pharmaceutical industry has been unable to maintain – let alone consolidate – its position over that time. Consequently, whilst global sales of Japanese pharmaceutical companies more than doubled between 1998 and 2008 from $306 million to $773 million, by my calculations the global market share of the Japanese industry fell from 14 per cent to 10 per cent over the same period. With the rise in the yen in recent years there has been some recovery, with the

Japanese pharmaceutical market worth $111.2 billion by 2011 and accounting for 11.6 per cent of the global pharmaceutical market in that year (IMS 2012c).

The Future

IMS believes that by 2016 there will have been no essential change in this Japan's global market share. Of most concern for the Japanese pharmaceutical industry's future is its faltering R&D productivity. Citeline found that in 2011 the Asia/Pacific region accounted for 19 per cent all companies active in pharma R&D (Pharmaprojects® Citeline 2011a). However, Japanese companies contributed only 4 per cent of that figure.

The Japanese pharmaceutical industry has never been a top industry in its home country. And this is reflected in the amount it currently spends on R&D. It accounts for just 11 per cent of total R&D expenditure by all industries in Japan (The 2012 EU Industrial R&D Scoreboard). According to Innovation.org data the number of compounds in clinical trials or awaiting registration in Japan has actually declined slightly since 1997 (Innovation.org 2012a). Given the rise in general attrition rates over the period (see Chapter 15, pp. 185–93) this can only presage lower numbers of new products developed in Japan reaching the market for several years hence.

This all goes to demonstrate, I believe, that it takes expertise across a wide range of disciplines to succeed in pharmaceuticals. Japan is deficient in several areas. And it is difficult to see these deficiencies being remedied soon.

Meanwhile, several Western pharmaceutical companies have been deemphasizing their R&D presence in Japan and have preferred to step up investment elsewhere in Asia. Some of these companies have had laboratories in Japan for many years but they appear sufficiently unimpressed by the capabilities of these facilities to move away from Japan.

It may be that a conducive atmosphere for high-quality R&D is difficult to create in Japan. This does not, of course, mean that other more favoured Asian countries are necessarily going to succeed to a greater extent. But Western companies are tending to believe that the chances of success in R&D are more likely elsewhere in Asia.

Sooner or later I think that the pressures will become too much for some major Japanese companies. There will then be another wave of consolidation of the sort we saw a few years ago. Japanese companies could also become targets for acquisition by Western pharma companies. Unable to compete effectively in the crucial art of producing new products, they are likely to be acquired on the basis of their strength in the national market – that is, for their local know-how, contacts and infrastructure.

Finally, on a more general note, it should not be forgotten that the parlous state of the Japanese economy in general has snuffed out interest in the management concepts so enthusiastically taken up by Western companies and gurus up till 1990.

In conclusion, Japan still has a local market that accounts for just under 12 per cent of the global pharmaceutical market. With the second biggest national pharmaceutical market, Japan will remain a force in world pharmaceuticals, though it is likely to be overtaken by China by 2016 (IMS 2012c). But the Japanese pharma industry's powers of innovation are likely to remain limited. Also pharma companies have only a modest local biotech industry to support them with novel products and enabling technologies.

That has not and will not in the future stop Japanese companies from acquiring rights to products and intellectual property from Western companies and institutions. This could indeed prove to be their salvation in the search for new products. A good example of success through this means is the launch of the antiepileptic drug Fycompa (perampanel) by Eisai in 2012. In this case research was conducted in the United Kingdom. A few months later Eisai set up what they termed a major drug discovery and development collaboration with University College, London, focusing on neurological diseases such as Alzheimer's and Parkinson's diseases and related disorders.

Wider Conclusions

A major conclusion I take from assessing Japan is that however big the home market for pharmaceuticals, unless a country's pharmaceutical industry develops the know-how to develop significant new products, it is unlikely to make substantial headway globally. You can become as good as any country in pharmaceutical manufacturing, for example – one of Japan's greatest strengths –

but that does not help you sufficiently if you want to build a global presence in pharmaceuticals.

Japan is by no means the only developed country to find it difficult to make further headway in pharmaceuticals. Close to my own experience is Holland. For the past half-century, Holland has tried to boost its pharmaceutical industry. It has had the right international mentality of a trading nation. And it has infrastructure and many of the conditions that Acemoglu and Robinson would consider ideal for doing business.

But despite considerable efforts it has been only modestly successful over that time in producing new products. All three leading Dutch pharmaceutical companies up to the beginning of the 1980s, Organon, Duphar and Brocades, ended up in foreign ownership. That foreign ownership has been largely unsuccessful in generating new products. Meanwhile despite efforts, no Dutch biotech company has established itself as a significant player in pharmaceuticals. This just goes to show how difficult it is to develop new products – even when a country appears to have most of the necessary capabilities.

I believe all this needs to be borne in mind in assessing whether BRIC and other emerging countries will really make their mark in pharmaceutical innovation.

12

Prospects for Emerging Countries

Not all authorities are convinced that the future will continue to be favourable for emerging countries. For example Ruchir Sharma, head of emerging markets at Morgan Stanley and author of *Breakout Nations*, questions the idea that the BRIC economies are guaranteed rosy economic futures (Sharma 2012). I think this needs bearing in mind in considering pharmaceutical prospects specifically.

I frequently see industry reviews in pharmaceutical journals and magazines providing interesting information and views on prospects for emerging countries. I feel there is a tendency in these reports to fail to take into consideration broader, nonpharmaceutical factors. Also these reports – whether they are on Brazil or biosimilars – often tend to gild the lily in order to attract business. Therefore it is worth looking at some of these nonpharmaceutical factors in a little detail before going on to specifically pharmaceutical factors.

Because of its potential importance I first consider China in some detail. Then by way of introducing other emerging territories, I consider a recent detailed report from Charles River Associates which compares prospects across several emerging territories. Finally I consider several of the emerging countries individually in further detail.

China

The Chinese pharmaceutical market was worth $66.7 billion in 2011 and it was by then the third biggest in the world. As mentioned in the previous chapter, it is forecast to overtake Japan to become second biggest market by 2016 (IMS 2012c). However, currently all but 2 per cent of over 5,000 pharmaceutical companies existing in China are generics manufacturers. Now China wants to move up the value chain, but it is not clear that it has the skills to do so.

RECENT OPINION ON CHINA

I will now review what recent authors have to say on the prospects for China, both generally and specifically as it relates to pharmaceuticals.

Currently public expenditure on healthcare is low: some 2.7 per cent of GDP is spent on healthcare. Many less wealthy countries than China currently spend a far higher proportion of their GDP on healthcare. But in 2009 a programme to institute a decent healthcare system began to be instituted. However, it will be years before it comes into full effect according to Jonathan Fenby, author of several books on China, including the recent *Tiger Head, Snake Tails*, in which he assesses the country's prospects (Fenby 2012).

Fenby points out that political corruption is endemic, there is a lack of accountability and weak rule of law in China. There are recurrent food scandals; cartons of UHT milk from New Zealand sell for several times the price of domestic milk in China because people think it is safe. In pharmaceuticals, medicines are often counterfeit, and a heparin scandal in 2007 did serious damage to China's reputation internationally.

Complicating matters is the lack of coordination between regulatory bodies within China; this means that decision making is also poorly coordinated. However, awareness and understanding about quality is on the rise. As the sophistication of the Chinese market grows, the public is less willing to take medication of inferior quality. Fenby considers that China is not going to collapse because it is far too resilient. Its growth has made people materially better off in a shorter period of time than ever before in human history and this has bred loyalty to the system.

Acemoglu and Robinson (see also pp. 145–6) consider that because China remains authoritarian to the core, its growth is likely to run out of steam eventually. By throttling the incentives for technological progress, creativity and innovation, this will choke off sustained, long-term growth and prosperity. Chinese growth, they argue, has been based on the adoption of existing technologies and rapid investment, rather than what they term 'the anxiety-inducing process of creative destruction' that produces lasting innovation and growth. Acemoglu and Robinson believe that China is unlikely to transform its political institutions sufficiently rapidly to prevent an end to growth. Whilst China is playing a spirited game of catch-up, they consider that it does not have the right framework for innovative development.

Another recent author, Gerard Lemos, in *The End of the Chinese Dream*, does not see the situation on freedom in China changing: 'Nothing about the Communist Party's behaviour however suggests that they will cultivate an appetite for freedom; quite the opposite in fact' (Lemos 2012).

China has been very vocal in advertising its intentions to become a rule-of-law society and has strengthened intellectual property protection, according to Chatterjee and Kwan of Pharmatech Associates (2012). But in reality the gap between Chinese law and governance remains wide. This, the authors believe, should be a central consideration for any business decision and risk assessment when contemplating business in China.

China is already a leading country in the amount of pharma R&D expenditure being conducted. One very positive point is the huge number of Chinese scientists working now or with past experience of working in Western pharmaceutical companies. Some have already brought their experience back to their home countries and there is a large reservoir who potentially could return in the future.

China also has some advantages over, say, Japan in the 1960s, in terms of government prioritization of the industry and in terms of the availability of financing.

In November 2012, in the Charles River report I cited at the opening of Part IV, Tim Wilsdon, Jim Attridge, Eva Fiz and Satomi Ginoza produced the most detailed report of its type to date (Wilsdon et al. 2012). This reviewed prospects for pharmaceutical innovation in seven 'middle-income' countries, which included China, India, Brazil and Russia.

The report found that the number of compounds in development from emerging countries is increasing. It mentioned a significant number of products in Phases II and III in the countries they studied. (That included other countries I do not mention in this chapter including Colombia and South Africa.) However, the report also noted that no blockbuster drugs had emerged so far from any of these countries. Also, rather than being new products with global potential, the products in development were much more linked to incremental improvements and local needs. I conclude this section with several additional points from the Charles River report.

China scored the highest of all the BRIC countries by some way in the report, across a number of innovation indicators selected by Charles River Associates. According to the report, it already has a good performance compared with other 'middle income' countries in conducting clinical trials, employment across pharma R&D and in the number of patents filed. It was also rated as excellent on the number of pharmaceutical publications, which have risen dramatically over the past few years. It was given a medium rating for biopharmaceutical R&D expenditure and in generating novel medicines. However, it needs stressing that this is medium in relation to the benchmark country South Korea – not of the major countries established in pharmaceuticals. South Korea was ranked just fourteenth by global sales in 2011 (IMS 2012c). Whilst it has made great progress, it is still far behind many other developed countries in its ability to produce new products.

An advantage for China is that it has had product patenting since 1985 and its intellectual property regime was strengthened further in 2009. This helps to explain why there has been much more collaboration between international and domestic companies in China than is the case for other developing countries and that investment by foreign companies is more than 50 per cent higher than in India over the past decade. But on the other hand, as Chatterjee and Kwan (2012) point out, changes to intellectual property law have allowed local companies to obtain compulsory licences and make cheap copies of products still under patent protection.

The Charles River Associates report also mentioned the focus on building academic excellence in China as part of its innovation plan. It also reported that in 2012 no less than 12 R&D centres belonging to international pharmaceutical companies existed in China – but this compared with 70 for the United States and 61 for Europe. However, China was a long way ahead of any of the other middle-income countries in this respect: India had three, and Brazil and Russia one each. The report found some evidence of switching of R&D activities from India to China: in 2012 there was a sharp downturn in the number of clinical trials conducted in India.

In conclusion China is doing much that is right to develop new products but several critical areas are deficient, some of which may not change. The last chapter, on Japan, showed that a country only has to have a few critical deficiencies and new drug development can be thwarted. I believe that the lack in China of the necessary freedoms upon which good science depends is particularly important here. Freedom to enquire, openness to novel ideas, the concept of peer review as well as the generation of reputable statistics are all foreign to the Chinese system and likely to remain so.

China is therefore likely to be restricted to the more routine and less creative activities within R&D. It is still likely to play a significant role in pharmaceuticals, particularly in servicing its own market. Also it is likely to develop further as a centre for pharmaceutical sourcing from the West, particularly in the regulatory field and some areas of R&D. But in those areas which need greater creativity, including the development of novel pharmaceuticals with global potential, I believe China is likely to find progress difficult.

India

India has an even bigger population than China. But so far the national pharmaceutical market has reached only thirteenth rank; in 2011 it was worth some $14.3 billion (IMS 2012c). In 2012 India announced the introduction of a policy of free drugs for all. It will be made mandatory for all doctors in the public sector to prescribe generically. To date only 22 per cent of the population received free healthcare from the public sector. This is projected to rise to 52 per cent by 2017.

According to Simon Denyer of the *Washington Post* (Denyer 2012) India's ailing and overburdened infrastructure, intermittent power supplies, clogged ports and pothole-ridden roads have long added to the costs of manufacturing. Archaic land acquisition and labour laws act as a major drag on the manufacturing industry's investment and employment planes. Indian employment growth has struggled to keep up with a rapidly expanding population. Denyer considers that the same drive does not exist in India to overcome these problems and improve infrastructure as exists in China.

India has gained a strong reputation for the development and manufacture of active pharmaceutical ingredients (API). It already supplies more than 40 per cent of the APIs used to manufacture US pharmaceuticals. It also has a strong indigenous pharmaceutical industry based essentially on generics and indigenous remedies.

But this strength may paradoxically be a weakness in generating novel products: the local industry has strongly opposed the introduction of intellectual property rights in India. Without effective intellectual property protection Indian companies and their investors do not have adequate incentives to develop and commercialize new medicines indigenously. This compares unfavourably with China, which now has a strong intellectual property protection system, albeit with some important loopholes. So far indigenous Indian companies have had only very limited success in the development of novel pharmaceuticals.

Generally companies do not benefit from intellectual property protection until a country has sufficiently developed its scientific and technological infrastructure. Politically it appears particularly difficult for India to progress to this stage whilst vested interests maintain the upper hand in continuing to undermine intellectual property.

Over the last 15 years India became for Western companies a popular site for conducting clinical trials and also for some other aspects of the development process. But scepticism about quality standards of Indian manufacturing and clinical research and of the inadequate regulatory process has led to a recent collapse in trial activity there.

India still lacks a centralized drug regulatory system, with a bifurcated drug regulatory body dividing the regulatory functions between central and state bodies. As a result there is a gross lack of uniformity between states for drug approval processes. Also there is inadequate skilled manpower to ensure effective monitoring and compliance necessary to control the quality of drugs reaching the market.

Whilst there has been an emphasis on training scientists in India, the emphasis has been on chemistry rather than biology. A lack of skills in the latter science is limiting progress in pharmaceuticals.

A further weakness is that no private equity or venture capital fund for R&D exists for pharmaceuticals in India. With all of these adverse factors, it seems most likely that a climate conducive to effective R&D in India is therefore most unlikely to develop in the foreseeable future.

The Charles River Associates report rated India as having a good performance on number of pharmaceutical publications and number of patents filed compared with other 'middle income' countries. (Remember that South Korea was the benchmark for this report.) It was rated only medium for biopharmaceutical R&D expenditure, on conducting clinical trials, employment across pharma R&D and for generating novel medicines. The authors also noted that an Indian National Innovation Plan was drafted in 2008 but was not implemented.

I believe that if Indian companies do become productive in R&D and thereby flourish, it is likely to be from a Western rather an Indian base. This is because the environment in India is still much more in favour of traditional pharmaceutical manufacture and is much less geared to innovative development.

In my view it is unlikely that a climate conducive to effective R&D in India will develop in the foreseeable future. As mentioned above (see p. 160) there appears to have been to some switching of location of their activities by Western companies from India to China.

Brazil

The Brazilian pharmaceutical market was worth $29.9 billion in 2011 and was ranked the tenth biggest in the world. IMS forecast it to rise to fourth biggest by 2016 (IMS 2012c). There have been considerable strides in recent years in making healthcare available to the Brazilian population; public insurance now covers 90 per cent of the population.

The Charles River Associates report rated Brazil as having a good performance compared to other 'middle income' countries on one parameter only: the number of pharmaceutical publications. Brazil rated medium for number of patents filed, biopharmaceutical R&D expenditure (though this has risen dramatically since 2005 from a low base), conducting clinical trials and employment across pharma R&D. On generating novel medicines it was rated as having a poor performance. The effort on pharmaceuticals in Brazil has been much more on manufacturing. There is a focus on state-owned rather than private industry. The Charles River report considered that this was a handicap to successful pharmaceutical R&D, which they considered needed both.

The intellectual property system in Brazil is relatively weak. Of new products that are being developed, it is vaccines rather than new chemical entities that feature. Though the country has high levels of education there is a lack of academic expertise in some areas needed for pharma R&D.

Russia

According to IMS the Russian pharmaceutical market was worth $29.9 billion in 2011 and was ranked eleventh biggest in the world. It is forecast to rise to ninth ranking by 2016 (IMS 2012c). The state healthcare budget has been growing slowly.

The Charles River Associates report gave Russia the lowest ratings of all the BRIC countries. It rated as having a good performance only on employment across pharma R&D. It assessed Russia as having medium performances in biopharmaceutical R&D expenditure, on conducting clinical trials, on publications and on patents.

As with Brazil, Russia was assessed as having a poor performance in generating novel medicines. And like Brazil, in pharmaceuticals the effort in Russia has been much more on manufacturing rather than R&D. There is a preference for local manufacturers; however there has also been weak funding by the government of local pharmaceutical company development. Russia has slow regulatory processes.

Russia and Brazil have never under any system been capable of producing novel pharmaceuticals, though eminent scientists from both have contributed successfully to new product development elsewhere. I believe that both countries are still a long way from being capable of doing so.

Conclusions on Emerging Countries

Whilst each of the above emerging countries has shown strong if not always sustained growth in their national pharmaceutical markets, and this is likely to continue, I consider that none of them are close to making a significant contribution to the number of novel pharmaceutical products the world generates. Acquiring many of the skills needed cannot be done quickly, even if other conditions are conducive to new product development.

Therefore I consider that the idea expressed in Chapter 10, that they could become a threat to the US pharmaceutical industry (see p. 147), is most unlikely. I would in any case expect novel pharmaceuticals from any emerging countries developing them to more often represent a partnering opportunity for big pharma rather than a threat.

Singapore

To end this chapter, I want to point out that there are other sources of new products geographically that have not featured in the past. Singapore is already a developed country with a high standard of living. It has for over 30 years been an important centre for pharmaceutical manufacturing by Western companies.

In 1993 Singapore was the second country to introduce an orphan drugs act, only two years after the US and long before the European Union. From the beginning of this century Singapore instituted a national policy to develop in life sciences. In 2009 as a share of its GDP Singapore spent nearly five times as much on pharmaceutical R&D as the US.

Singapore is seen by Western pharmaceutical companies increasingly as being an attractive base for R&D. It has a well-educated population and a well-developed infrastructure. But it is tiny. This means that the national pharmaceutical market will never become significant globally and so attract big pharma in its own right as is the case with the countries I have discussed earlier in this chapter. That is one drawback as far as building up R&D in Singapore is concerned. It also means that it will never be the source of many patients for clinical trials.

But Singapore has many of the qualities required for successful R&D. And in recent years it has been receiving much investment in R&D from Western pharmaceutical companies. As mentioned in the previous chapter, some of this appears to be at the expense of Japan. But in common with many other countries, currently there is a deficiency in local venture capital support.

More generally, Singapore was ranked top by the World Bank as the country most easy to do business with in each of the three years to 2012. Contrast this with the rankings for BRIC countries: Brazil: 130, Russia: 112, India: 132 and China: 91. Even the unfashionable Japan is ranked no. 24, whilst the United States is near the top at no. 4 (Economy Rankings 2012).

Singapore has most of the capabilities needed to successfully develop novel products with global potential within a few years, albeit on a small scale.

Singapore

13

The United States – By No Means Past Its Peak

The Developed World

I now want to comment briefly on the developed world, particularly as a source of novel products. Most commentators on pharmaceuticals agree that for the time being Europe will continue to show either slow or no pharma market growth or even shrinkage. Its productivity in developing new products has in this century been nowhere near as good as in the second half of the twentieth century. However, its share of all companies globally active in R&D has recently been holding up well. A few European countries, notably Switzerland and the United Kingdom, have a good long-term track record for developing novel products and they are very likely to continue to do so.

But what of the United States? Some misapprehensions have been developing about the biggest country of all in pharmaceuticals, by any score. Perhaps it is past its peak?

US Prospects

In recent years some commentators on the pharmaceutical industry have seen developing countries as the future and have suggested that power is passing from the developed world. I have argued in the last chapter against the developing countries having much of an impact as far as novel products are concerned.

The United States has been seen as losing its power and authority, generally and pharmaceutically. In particular the growth rate of pharmaceuticals in the

US has reached low levels – only 1–2 per cent in 2011. It is difficult to remember that annual growth of the US market was in one year 17 per cent only about a decade ago. Nevertheless the US was far and away the biggest pharmaceutical market in 2011, with sales of $322 billion, nearly three times the size of the second-ranked country, Japan (IMS 2012c).

I believe that the United States will keep its position as the leading country in pharmaceuticals and, most importantly, continue to lead the industry in drug development as well. There is a great deal of evidence to support this, starting from the immediate past and then projecting into the future.

Firstly, the United States accounts for 43.2 per cent of global pharma R&D expenditure. Within the United States, pharmaceuticals account for 23 per cent of all R&D expenditure, equal first with electronic and electrical equipment (The 2012 EU Industrial R&D Scoreboard).

Also, according to a Milken Institute study, US-based firms accounted for 57 per cent of the NCEs produced globally over the 2001–10 period (DeVol, Bedroussian and Yeo 2011). The FDA has recently produced data to show that the United States is beating other countries to the market with new products (FDA 2012).

Until the late 1990s few new products were launched first in the US. But the proportion has been rising since then so that in 2012 it was first country for 75 per cent of all new products launched there.

On progress in cancer specifically, a 2012 report from the Tufts Center for the Study of Drug Development found that between 2000 and 2011, 40 new anticancer drugs were approved in the US but only 30 in Europe. Remarkably, of the 28 new anticancer products approved by both the FDA and EMA, all of them were approved first by the FDA (Tufts CSDD Impact Report, 2012). This is not surprising, since the FDA has been more go-ahead than any other major regulatory authority in expediting approval for products for which there is a high level of unmet need. Cancer is *the* prime area of unmet need.

Turning to clinical trial activity, you may get the impression from the continuing trend towards conducting more of them in developing countries that not many are any longer carried out in the West, including in the US. The lie to this is given by data from the United Nations (UN 2011). Its data showed that in May 2011 the US had 174 clinical trials per million population underway and Europe just 37. Meanwhile Japan had only 15 per million underway.

At registration level, as I explain later (see pp. 191, 194, 199) the era of deterioration in the number of new product approvals by the FDA came to a halt in 2011. This will not have much impact yet on sales but should do so in a few years' time.

Innovation.org, a website of the US manufacturers' association PhRMA, released data in 2012 which showed that since mid-1997 there has been a remarkable increase in the number of compounds in advanced development globally (Innovation.org 2012a). The number of compounds in clinical trials or awaiting approval almost doubled from some 1,600 compounds in 1997 to well over 3,000 in June 2011. However, this report counts per project each region where clinical development is being conducted. And so this growth is partly an expression of the tendency for pharmaceutical development to be conducted in a wider range of countries – including developing countries. Most of the growth in this number has come since 2003, when the number of compounds tallied had reached 2,000.

The upward trend was actually more positive for the US than for Europe, where there was a faltering increase from around 1,200 compounds in 1997 to just over 1,400 in 2011. This is in the face of the trend for more trials to be conducted in developing countries.

The US trend has also been much more positive than for Japan. In the latter country there was actually a slight decline in the total number of compounds, from just over 600 in 1997 to less than 600 in 2011 (see also p. 153). The only area to surpass the United States was the 'All Other' country total, where the number of projects rose even more impressively, from some 500 compounds in 1997 to over 2,400 in 2011 – an expression, as mentioned above, of the trend for big pharma to conduct trials far more broadly geographically.

In 2011 Pharmaprojects® Citeline found that exactly half of all companies active in pharmaceutical R&D were from the US (Pharmaprojects® Citeline 2011a). The next-ranked country was the UK, with a tenth of this share – just 5 per cent! Europe accounted for 26 per cent of all companies active, just over half the US share.

Another indicator of the pharmaceutical lead which the US has appeared in a Jones Lang LaSalle report published in January 2012. It showed that over the 2007–10 period the US increased its global share of inward investment in life sciences significantly compared with the period 2003–06. Whilst China, Brazil and Russia also increased their shares, Europe's fell.

Also on funding, in 2012 a report prepared by Battelle for innovation. org (which is part of PhRMA) found that in 2011 the US accounted for over 80 per cent of worldwide biopharmaceutical-related venture capital funding (innovation.org 2012b). This was a sharp rise over the 60–70 per cent share in the first decade of the twenty-first century.

Thus there is strong evidence at many levels that the US is at least maintaining its lead over other countries and in some respects is increasing its dominance. This suggests a promising pharmaceutical future. I suggest that the US pharmaceutical industry is going to enhance its current leading position in the pharma industry rather than having its position eroded by other countries.

This obviously has important implications for those responsible for investment in pharmaceuticals. I believe that they should certainly be giving as much attention to the US as they have in the past. Whilst there are good long-term reasons for investing in emerging territories too, I believe that increased emphasis on the US is justified by the prospects there. Its sheer size means that it will remain by far the biggest national pharmaceutical market. And I think it is highly likely that it will continue to dominate as the main provider of novel pharmaceutical products in the future.

PART V

Prospects for New Products

No issue is more important to the pharmaceutical industry today than its ability to bring new products to the market. In Part V I first consider in Chapter 14 trends in the number of projects in development and what projections suggest, in terms of numbers of new products reaching the market. Then in Chapter 15 I address the complex issue of trends in attrition rates. As the commercial potential of new products depends on their quality as well as their quantity, I then address this in Chapter 16 before coming to overall conclusions in Chapter 17.

14

Projecting New Product Quantity

New products are the lifeblood of the pharmaceutical industry.

Anon.

Trends in the Number of New Products Launched

The most common slide that presenters at pharma industry conferences show first is the one showing the downturn in the number of new products first launched each year. My version in Figure 14.1 starts in 1970 and finishes in 2011.

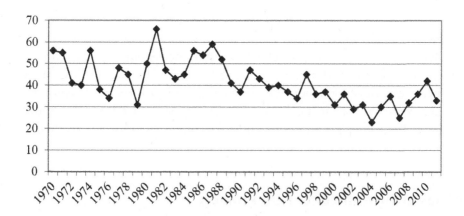

Figure 14.1 **Number of first launches of new products internationally (1970–2011)**

Source: John Ansell Consultancy. Based on data from CMR International (1970–2000), Informa (2001–11)

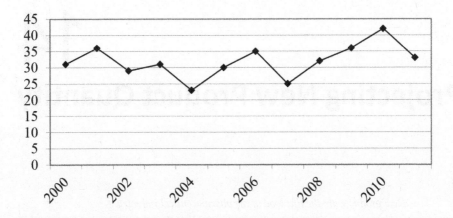

**Figure 14.2   Number of first launches of new products internationally
(2000–11)**

Source: John Ansell Consultancy. Based on data from CMR International (1970–2000),
Informa (2001–11)

Glancing across the whole 41-year trend, it does appear to be a continuing
story of long-term decline. But let's have a look at the trend just for the twenty-
first century (Figure 14.2).

Now we can see that over the 11 years from 2000, the trend in the number
of new products launched each year is at worst stable and at best somewhat
positive. And if we were to just take the period since about 2005, then it looks
rather more positive. Admittedly it is a rather fragile-looking positive trend,
but it certainly can no longer be described as downward. Yet the conventional
wisdom remains what it has been for over 40 years: that the new product
productivity of the pharmaceutical industry continues to show a downward
trend.

Trends in the Number of R&D Projects

I am going to argue below that the recent positive trend is no fluke and is very
likely to continue. To do so I need to explain trends in numbers of projects in
total and at each phase of drug development.

Whilst the number of new products reaching the market has until recent
years been in long-term decline, that certainly has not been the case for the

number of projects in R&D. As pharma R&D expenditure has spiralled, the number of new projects has climbed ever upwards. But this effort has not so far resulted in many more products reaching the market, though as I mentioned above, the trend is now looking more positive than it was only a couple of years ago. But a real understanding of trends requires assessment of long-term trends in numbers of projects by development phase.

Reliable historical data on projects in R&D uniform with current data is available from Informa sources from the year 1993. The data I review comes from its database, Citeline. (Formerly there were two separate databases: Pharmaprojects® and Citeline.) The data I show here is from the published annual reviews by Pharmaprojects® Citeline and from my articles on this topic (Pharmaprojects® Citeline 2011a, 2012; Ansell 2001; Ansell 2011).

TOTAL NUMBER OF PROJECTS

Figure 14.3 shows the total number of compounds in R&D by development phase, from preclinical up to preregistration phase since 1993.

As is plain to see, the total number of projects has more than doubled over this period. Since this has failed to stem the dire decline in the number of new

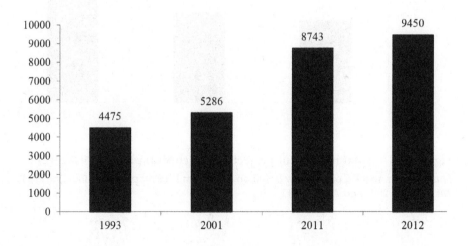

Figure 14.3   Total number of R&D projects up to preregistration phase (1993–2012)

Source: John Ansell Consultancy based on data from Pharmaprojects® Citeline 2011a, 2012; Ansell 2011

products coming onto the market each year, this means that attrition rates have shot up – but how, and where? That is the subject of the next chapter.

Some proportion of the increases in numbers reported below is accounted for by improved tracking of projects by Pharmaprojects® Citeline over time. But the effect of this factor is fairly modest: Pharmaprojects® Citeline considered that it might account for 2–3.5 per cent of all projects (Pharmaprojects ® Citeline 2011a). This factor is likely to be more important for earlier rather than later phase projects, as the latter are less likely to go unnoticed.

PRECLINICAL PHASE PROJECTS

As Figure 14.4 shows, the increase from 2,820 projects in 1993 up to 5,247 in 2012 is also not far short of a doubling in numbers.

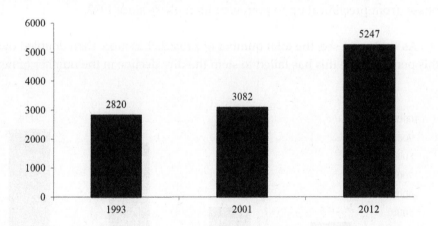

Figure 14.4   Total number of projects in preclinical phase (1993–2012)
Source: John Ansell Consultancy based on data from Pharmaprojects® Citeline 2011a, 2012; Ansell 2001 and Ansell 2011

There did appear to be some tailing off in numbers over the 2009–2011 period when, for the first time, many companies began to cut back their R&D budgets. (Figure 14.5) At the time they tended to focus their resources on advanced projects, notably in the most costly advanced clinical phases

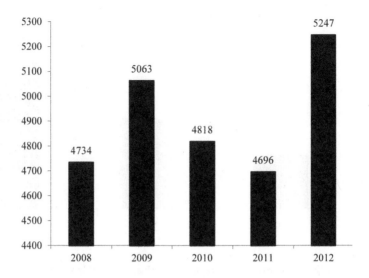

Figure 14.5   Total number of projects in preclinical phase (2008–12)
Source: John Ansell Consultancy based on data from Pharmaprojects® Citeline 2011a, 2012; Ansell 2011

(see p. 18) and cut back particularly on preclinical projects.[1] The apparent recovery in 2012 is surprising. It may just be a fluctuation and not be sustained, given the continuing adverse economic climate and the difficulty start-up companies still face in raising funds.

PHASE I

As Figure 14.6 shows, the number of Phase I projects in 2012 was over three times the number in 1993! There were in 2012 almost 1,500 projects at this phase.

The increase has been steady – but there has been some acceleration in the upward trend since 2010 (Figure 14.7). The pharmaceutical industry certainly does not seem to have problems in generating much larger numbers of Phase I compounds. But that has not at least until recently resulted in more new products reaching the market. We cannot count on the upward trend in in the number of

---

1   According to Pharmaprojects® Citeline (2011) at least the drop in numbers between 2010 and 2011 has more to do with recent reclassification of some preclinical projects into a "no development reported" category – over this period preclinical numbers would otherwise have been steady.

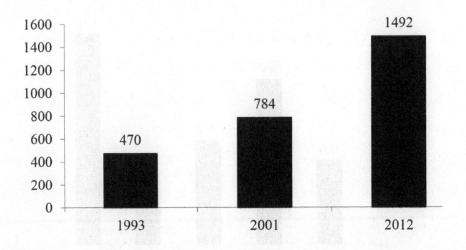

Figure 14.6   Total number of projects at phase I (1993–2012)

Source: John Ansell Consultancy based on data from Pharmaprojects® Citeline 2011a,
2012; Ansell 2001 and Ansell 2011

projects at Phase I continuing, given the adverse economic climate and the recent

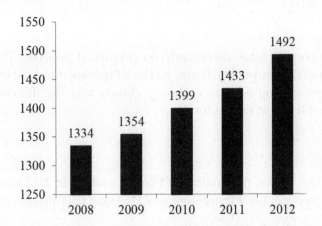

Figure 14.7   Total number of projects at phase I (2008–12)

Source: John Ansell Consultancy based on data from Pharmaprojects® Citeline 2011a,
2012; Ansell 2011

emphasis of pharma companies on late- rather than early-stage research.

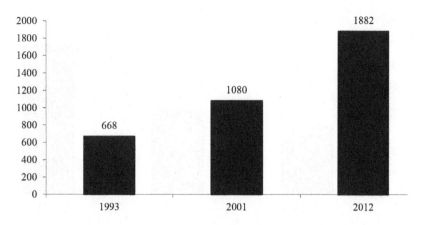

Figure 14.8   Total number of projects at phase II (1993–2012)

Source: John Ansell Consultancy based on data from Pharmaprojects® Citeline 2011a, 2012; Ansell 2001, 2011

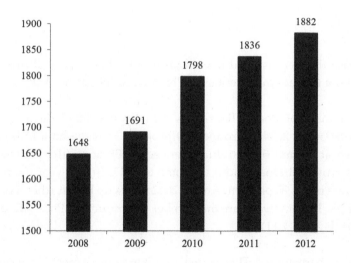

Figure 14.9   Total number of projects at phase II (2008–12)

Source: John Ansell Consultancy based on data from Pharmaprojects® Citeline 2011a, 2012; Ansell 2011

PHASE II

As Figure 14.8 shows, there has been a similar but not quite so strong long-term upward trend as we saw for Phase I. And just as for Phase I, there has been continuing good growth in the number of projects since 2008 (Figure 14.9).

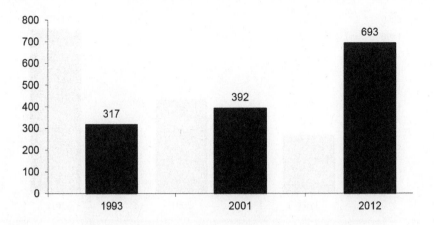

Figure 14.10   Total number of projects at phase III (1993–2012)
Source: John Ansell Consultancy based on data from Pharmaprojects® Citeline 2011a,
2012; Ansell 2001, 2011

PHASE III

With Phase III, there is good overall growth in the number of projects since
1993, but not to the same extent as in Phase I and II (Figure 14.10).

The number of Phase III projects actually plateaued for a long period
between 1995 and 2004 at around 400 projects. It increased a little thereafter
but stayed at around 550 products between 2008 and 2010. However, in no
year was growth dramatic until we come to 2011. In that year the number of
projects was up by 15 per cent. And in 2012 it was up by a further 9 per cent, to
693 projects. Thus in two years the number of products in Phase III jumped by
a quarter! (Figure 14.11).

What is happening? This is just two consecutive positive years, which
we may not see repeated, but it does already put the number of Phase III
projects on a higher plane. In my view the figures reflect at last that the
continual stepping up by the industry of R&D effort, and progress with
enabling technologies, is feeding through for the first time to an improved
number of projects at Phase III. We have seen this progress at each earlier
phase previously and now at last it is feeding through to improved figures
for Phase III too.

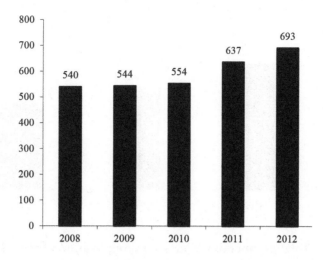

Figure 14.11   Total number of projects at phase III (2008–12)
Source: John Ansell Consultancy based on data from Pharmaprojects® Citeline 2011a, 2012; Ansell 2011

Since we know that the recent trends for those previous phases remain positive, we should expect that this will result in due course in further increases in the number of Phase III projects, though we can expect fluctuations.

It looks as if this is just one more case of things eventually happening in pharmaceuticals (see Chapter 2, pp. 41–52) – but so late that some in the industry have already given up hope and exited pharmaceuticals or cut back their R&D effort.

However, that, for the moment, is as far in development as the positive trends stretch.

PREREGISTRATION PHASE

This is the only phase remaining which still shows a negative trend (Figure 14.12). We can see that there has been a long-term slide in the number of projects in preregistration. But then, it might be expected that it would take time for the fairly recent positive Phase III trend to feed through to the preregistration phase. At least we can see that the negative trend is diminishing (Figure 14.13).

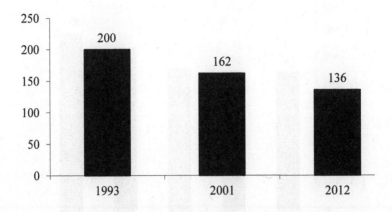

Figure 14.12   Total number of projects at preregistration phase (1993–2012)
Source: John Ansell Consultancy based on data from Pharmaprojects® Citeline 2011a, 2012; Ansell 2001, 2011
This phase ought to benefit further shortly from the recent upward trend in the

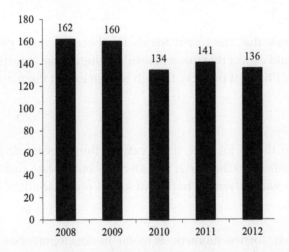

Figure 14.13   Total number of projects at preregistration phase (2008–12)
Source: John Ansell Consultancy based on data from Pharmaprojects® Citeline 2011a, 2012; Ansell 2011

number of Phase III projects.

PROGNOSIS

Both the FDA and the EMA are making projections towards the end of each year, as they have now for several years, that they will be dealing with an increasing number of new product submissions in the following year.

Since there has been recent healthy growth in project numbers for all phases up to Phase III, I would expect this growth in numbers to continue in all clinical phases and beyond, though we should expect fluctuations. In particular, the number of Phase II projects has been growing sufficiently to suggest that the all-important Phase III numbers will rise further.

But this assumes that all other things are equal. And this certainly hasn't been the case over the past quarter-century. We need to examine why the long-term increases in numbers of projects since 1993 did not lead to an improvement in new products reaching the market before we can consider projecting the future.

15

Trends in Attrition Rates

*In my experience, drugs that do not work and drugs that substantially
exceed minimal expectations are easy to spot.*

*Dr Joshua Boger, Founder and Board Director,
Vertex Pharmaceuticals; Boger 2012*

Pharmaceuticals is a high-risk but also potentially high-gain industry. During the lengthy R&D process there are many hurdles to surmount, and very few compounds at the start pass the finishing post.

Data on trends in attrition rates during the development of pharmaceuticals was limited until a decade ago. This is mainly, I believe, because it was not until the early years of this century that it became clear to many of us that attrition rates were increasing. When in 2001 I was writing the series of articles on the quality and quantity of new products I mentioned in the last chapter (Ansell 2001), I found that very little had been published on trends in attrition rates. Because it was not obviously an issue at the time, there was limited reason to analyze attrition.

But fairly quickly in the first decade of this century it became increasingly clear that attrition rates had been rising. Eventually, reports that I shall summarize below suggested that at certain phases attrition had risen. At some phases of development this had been going on well before 2000.

Studies Covering Pre-2000 Attrition

Two reports based on big project databases tend to quite an extent to agree with each other as far as attrition is concerned. (There are other published reports for smaller sets of data which I have excluded.) I report them alongside each other by phase.

The first is an industry presentation by Ian Lloyd of Pharmaprojects® Citeline in 2004. The Pharmaprojects® Citeline database was probably the largest available at the time (Lloyd 2004). This compared success rates for the 10 years to 2001 with those for the 20 years from 1982 to 2001.

In the second analysis, Pammoli, Magazzini and Riccaboni analyzed the Pharmaceutical Industry Database of the IMT Institute for Advanced Studies at Lucca in Italy (2011). This database contained detailed information about R&D projects covering more than 28,000 compounds. The authors tracked trends in attrition rates during five phases: Preclinical, Phase I, Phase II, Phase III and Registration, over the 1990–2004 period. It is disappointing that this recently published report does not cover more recent years.

PRECLINICAL

Both sets of data suggest little evidence of deterioration of attrition rates for the decade up to 2000. If anything, the Pharmaprojects® Citeline data showed some improvement for the 1990s over the 1980s (Pharmaprojects® Citeline 2012).

PHASE I

The Pharmaprojects® Citeline report suggested some limited increase in Phase I attrition rates in the 1990s. The Pammoli et al. survey did not find any worsening at this phase.

PHASE II

Both reports suggested that limited but significant deterioration at Phase II had begun during the 1990s. Evidence from Pammoli et al. suggested that this stretched back to the beginning of the 1990s at least.

PHASE III

The Pharmaprojects® Citeline data indicated that only rather limited deterioration occurred in the 1990s. But the Pammoli et al. data suggested that attrition rates were deteriorating from 1990 at least. Therefore there is no consensus on this phase.

REGISTRATION PHASE

The Pharmaprojects® Citeline data indicated no deterioration in attrition rates at the registration phase during the 1990s. However, the Pammoli et al. data indicated modest deterioration, and right up to 2004. The period they covered predates the Vioxx affair and its consequences, which we consider below (see pp. 190–91).

In conclusion, whilst there are some differences between the two reports, they do show that in the 1990s increases in attrition rates were at no phase a major problem. This was probably the case up to 2004.

Trends in Attrition Rates Since 2000

From 2005 a succession of reports from a variety of sources indicated seriously worsening attrition rates. The time periods differ between reports; some start before 2000. Meanwhile whilst some reports cover all projects in development, others exclude data from smaller pharmaceutical companies and start-up companies. I give more credence to the former.

Because of the diverse nature of these reports, it is often difficult to draw simple conclusions from them. The reports covering the most recent time periods are, for me, the most valuable.

In 2005 the FDA found that the percentage of Phase I compounds ultimately reaching the US market had fallen from 14 per cent to 8 per cent since 1990. This represented a huge, 75 per cent increase in the attrition rate over the period. Additionally, the number of drugs that failed after reaching Phase III had increased from 20 per cent to 50 per cent over a 15-year time span.

John Arrowsmith, scientific director at Thomson Reuters (which incorporates CMR International), reviewed success rates at four different development phases over four two-year periods, the earliest of which was 2002–04 and the latest being 2006–08. Success rates are the inverse of attrition rates. They give the probability of success from a given phase that a product will reach the market. This data came from 14 pharma companies (Arrowsmith 2012). To summarize, he found that from the earliest to the latest period:

- Phase I success rates were halved: from 10 per cent to 5 per cent.

- Phase II success rates fell from 17 per cent to 11 per cent.

- Phase III success rates rose from 51 per cent to 66 per cent.

- For projects submitted for regulatory review, the success rate fell from 95 per cent to 84 per cent.

Thus with the exception with Phase III, there were significant declines in success rates over the 2002 to 2008 period.

CMR data for 2011 included in its Pharmaceutical R&D Factbook covers major pharmaceutical companies that are claimed to account for approximately 80 per cent of the pharmaceutical industry's global R&D expenditure. Two times periods were covered: 2005–07 and 2008–10. CMR International found that the number of new drugs entering Phases I, II and III fell respectively in 2010 by 47 per cent, 53 per cent and 55 per cent (CMR 2012).

CMR also found that attrition rates at Phase III increased substantially. The number of products terminated in Phase III during the 2008–10 period, 55, was more than double the number of terminations during 2005–07.

In February 2011 BIO, the US biotechnology industry association, announced in its BioMedTracker 2011 report results of what it claimed to be the most comprehensive study to date (BIO 2011). This included 4,275 drugs in 7,300 indications in development by pharmaceutical and biotech companies, at any clinical development phase between October 2003 and December 2010. BIO showed that the success rate for compounds from Phase I to achievement of US approval was 9 per cent. This is in line with the FDA figures for 2005 discussed above.

Reasons for Attrition

In a short 2011 review article, Arrowsmith analyzed projects from a group of pharmaceutical companies representing approximately 60 per cent of global R&D expenditure (Arrowsmith 2011b). He found that Phase II success rates had fallen from 28 per cent over the 2006–07 period to 18 per cent for 2008–09.

Of the 108 reported Phase II failures between 2008 and 2010 for new drugs and major new indications for existing drugs:

- 51 per cent were due to insufficient efficacy.

- 29 per cent were for strategic reasons.

- 19 per cent were for clinical or preclinical safety reasons.

According to Arrowsmith, therefore, it is efficacy and commercial reasons rather than safety and early-stage-related issues that have been the main reasons for the discontinuation of projects.

In a previous, uniform review covering later development phases, Arrowsmith found that there were 83 Phase III and regulatory submission failures between 2007 and 2010 (Arrowsmith 2011a). For these failures:

- 67 per cent were due to efficacy issue, of which:

  - *32 per cent were due to no statistically significant improvement versus placebo.*
  - *5 per cent were due to no statistically significant improvement versus active control.*
  - *29 per cent were due to no statistically significant improvement as an add-on therapy.*

- 7 per cent were due to financial and/or commercial reasons.

- 21 per cent were due to safety issues (including risk-benefit).

- 6 per cent were for undisclosed reasons.

Thus just as for Phase II, efficacy and commercial reasons accounted for most of these failures – almost three quarters in total and approaching the figure for Phase II. The overall pattern is similar for both phases.

Attrition at both Phase II and Phase III therefore mainly happens because compounds are either found to be ineffective or are assessed as being insufficiently viable commercially.

Conclusions

Though most evidence exists on attrition rate trends for the clinical phases, what evidence we do have for the preclinical phase suggest that attrition had been much less of a problem at that stage.

For the first two phases, preclinical and Phase I, there was no clear deterioration before the year 2000. But for both Phase II and Phase III the deterioration appears to have been going on at least since 1990. In the clinical phases attrition is much more evident after 2000.

Deterioration of attrition rates at the regulatory phase was modest during the 1990–2004 period but rose sharply thereafter. That increasingly stringent period appears to have come to an end during 2011, at least as far as the United States is concerned. I deal with this recent change in the trend below.

Thus several different factors have been involved in increasing attrition rates, and they have come into play at different times.

The Vioxx Affair

I would regard the most important factor contributing to recent increased attrition rates to be the much more difficult regulatory environment stemming from the Vioxx affair. From 2004 when it became public, Merck & Co, as well as the FDA, were widely considered by the US public to have mishandled the issue of adverse drug reactions to that company's antiarthritis product Vioxx (rofecoxib).

With the consequent strong public disquiet about the regulatory process, which was strongest in the in the US, the FDA was forced to take a much more cautious stance in reviewing New Drug Applications (NDAs). This lasted for some six years, during which the proportion of NDA submissions approved dropped significantly. In 2008 the FDAAA (FDA Amendment Act) was brought into force in response. This included measures to regulate postmarketing studies as well as Risk Evaluation and Mitigations Strategies (REMS). They have since been widely applied to NDAs submitted. The consequence up to 2010 was that though the number of NDA submissions did not change significantly, the number of new products approved was reduced.

The situation began to recover from 2011, and the noticeably more positive attitude of the FDA then was maintained in 2012. The result in both FDA fiscal years is an increase in the number of new products approved, 35 in each year. One consequence is that the US is now first country to approve three quarters of new drugs (see p. 168).

The Impact of Enabling Technologies

Over the past 20 years enabling technologies such as combinatorial chemistry and high-throughput screening (HTS) have contributed very significantly to the increase in the number of compounds generated. But the claimed predictiveness in generating effective compounds through these target-based approaches has often proved disappointing when the compounds so derived have eventually reached the clinic.

HTS, which I discussed earlier (see pp. 47–8), has its defenders who contest its association with increased attrition rates. But certainly another enabling technology, combinatorial chemistry, has turned out not to be as predictive as when first touted in the early 1990s. This is widely considered to have been a significant factor leading to increased levels of compound attrition in clinical phases over the past decade.

In an intriguing review, Swinney and Anthony analyzed new products registered in the United States between 1999 and 2008 (2011). They found that only a modest proportion of small-molecule drugs approved, 23 per cent, resulted from target-based screening approaches. More, 37 per cent, resulted from phenotypic screening, that is, a screen where a compound is tested in a cell- or animal-based assay and the effects are monitored – the conventional type of screening. Thus, the increasing concentration of the pharmaceutical industry on target-based approaches to R&D could, according to the authors, help to explain lower productivity.

The poor-quality compounds generated by enabling technologies in their infancy have been discarded. Also the introduction over the past decade of in vitro pharmacological profiling has been successful in identifying 'off-target' activities early. This rejection of bad compounds and the introduction of better techniques is likely to have been improving the quality of compounds advancing through R&D, and leading to the greater numbers now progressing to advanced phases of R&D (see pp. 178–82).

On the other hand new technologies will undoubtedly keep on emerging, and for each of these there will also have to be a learning curve. Future technological challenges, just as for personalized medicine, for example currently, could well therefore push up attrition rates whilst companies learn how better to apply them.

The Switch to Riskier Areas

With the aim of producing products for areas of greatest unmet need, there has been an increasing tendency of pharmaceutical companies to pursue novel R&D oriented towards more difficult targets. Since the risk levels of uncharted areas will tend to be higher than for the well-trodden ones, this is likely to have contributed to increasing attrition rates.

This is the main conclusion from the article by Pammoli et al. discussed above. The authors pointed to the effect of the changing composition of R&D portfolios on R&D productivity. They found that after 2000 there was an increase in R&D effort in high-risk areas of R&D such as cancer, Alzheimer's disease, obesity, rheumatoid arthritis, Parkinson's disease and diabetes, which are also associated with high attrition rates.

Pammoli et al. went as far as to conclude that cancer was the main culprit: 'Overall, the increase in the number of R&D projects targeting specific cancers is the main driver behind the reorienting of the R&D effort during the past decade.' According to the authors, without the reorienting of R&D effort, R&D productivity would have remained almost constant!

This seems a little implausible. It is clear that deterioration of attrition rates is – as I have shown using Pammoli et al.'s data amongst other sources above – happening at a number of different phases, to differing extents and have come into effect at different times. Whilst it is conceivable that a great, heterogeneous group of indications like cancer has been increasing attrition rates through a multiplicity of effects acting at a variety of levels and times, I cannot see this being anywhere near the whole story behind increased attrition rates. John LaMattina, head of research at Pfizer between 2003 and 2007, considered that this could be a *contributory* factor in the decline of the number of new products produced since the 1990s, as me-toos became less economically viable and a switch into higher risk areas was made (LaMattina 2011). I feel that his degree of emphasis for this factor is closer to the reality: the switch to higher-risk areas is a factor but not the whole explanation. I also think that when the figures are in for the past decade, we may well find that from a regulatory point of view, products for cancer and other areas of strong unmet need will be found to have been *favoured* by regulatory authorities in comparison with other types of therapies. If I am right, this would offset the penalty on attrition rates for these most novel therapy areas found by Pammoli et al. up to 2004.

Greater Commercial Ruthlessness with Projects

Finally, there is a greater awareness of pharmaceutical companies that products which they do succeed in bringing to the market have to make economic sense for those footing the bill. As the Arrowsmith data discussed above show, companies are becoming much more careful to assess before they advance compounds from Phase II to Phase III whether a new product is going to meet reimbursement criteria as well as having clinical advantages.

In future, because cancer is such an intensely competitive R&D area, there are likely to be more and more novel anticancer products which turn out to have only limited benefits. And so as mentioned previously (see p. 35) products capable of being registered will sometimes fall by the wayside because of the more persuasive claims on budgets of stronger new competitors.

Improved Targeting of Drugs

As mentioned in Chapter 2 (see p. 52), in the field of cancer particularly, clinical trials that have targeted a specific genetic population have led to several new products recently reaching the market. This should already be having some impact in reducing attrition rates (Pharmaprojects® Citeline 2011b).

Conclusions

Pharma companies have in recent years already been directing their efforts away from less innovative R&D and towards areas of unmet need, where payer issues will tend to be less problematic. Unfortunately many of those areas are also above-average risk ones, with associated higher attrition rates.

Looking at current company pipelines, I believe many companies are already a good way along this path towards more innovative R&D. *Pharmaceutical Executive*'s 2013 pipeline report found that 'the demand from payers and patients for better evidence of outcomes has imposed new discipline on the R&D process, which is bearing fruit' (Comer 2012b).

I suggest that over the next five years the extent to which they are changing strategy towards higher-risk projects may well not increase much further. Also we see several big pharma companies pulling back recently from the central nervous system area because it is such a high-risk therapeutic area.

Whilst company researchers will gradually gain further experience with existing enabling technologies, dropping useless ones and gaining more experience with the more valuable ones, the beneficial impact on attrition rates could well be tempered by the need to gain experience with further as-yet-undeveloped new technologies as they become available.

On the commercial front, I do not expect companies to need to get even more ruthless in culling advanced-stage clinical projects over the next few years. But that will depend on the quality of the projects in development, which I will address in the next chapter.

The one big ray of hope is that the regulatory climate has recently been improving. The attitude of the FDA has been much more constructive since 2011 and this is already paying off in terms of a greater number of products being approved for marketing. In US regulatory terms, this important contributor to increasing attrition between 2004 and 2010 has therefore performed a *volte face*.

Remember that the number of products registered since 2005 has been approximately stable – the trend can even be interpreted as slightly positive – *despite* a climate of increased attrition rates. Naturally, any improvement in trends in the factors contributing to attrition should be translated into increased R&D productivity.

In aggregate, I believe it is unlikely that the various factors adversely affecting attrition rates to continue with the same force that they have done since 2000; some will head in a positive direction, with a good chance of some modest decrease in overall attrition rates over the coming five years.

16

Trends in New Product Quality

It is all very well tracking trends in *numbers* of new products and projects; what about their quality, at least in terms of commercial potential? Several factors affect this.

Me-Too Products

I mentioned in Chapter 4 (see p. 70), that there has been a noticeable reduction since the mid-1990s in the proportion of all new products accounted for by me-too products. The days when most major pharmaceutical companies consciously decided to develop them are to a large extent past. The cost of developing a new product has become so great that it is unlikely to be profitable unless a runner-up position or perhaps no. 3 look to be guaranteed.

Whilst some room for me-toos therefore still exists, it is more limited than in the past. Only a very few me-toos in each therapeutic market can make a living by undercutting on price. With increasing emphasis on cost effectiveness, this is likely to remain the case for the foreseeable future.

Of course, some companies will unknowingly bring products to the market which they plan to be novel but which turn out to be me-toos. This is always likely to be the case because of the unpredictability of clinical development.

But I believe that the overall quality of new products reaching the market in terms of commercial potential is likely to increase further as the proportion of me-too products continues to further drop away.

Novel Drugs

The obverse of me-too status is novelty. Data published by IMS in 2012 on trends in the number of US drug approvals over the period 2002–11 showed an increase in the number of drugs with new mechanisms of action (IMS 2012c). Numbers of such drugs rose steadily from six products in 2008 to nine in 2011. This came after a period of quite sharp decline between 2003 and 2007.

Pharmaprojects® Citeline found that no less than 11 of the 33 new products first launched globally in 2011 were first in class – that is, they had a mechanism of action not previously approved (Pharmaprojects® Citeline 2011a). A new mechanism of action for a product does not necessarily indicate high commercial potential. Nor is it less likely that it will turn out to be a me-too. But it is probably less likely that this will be the case than for a product in an already known mechanism of action.

Most recently, the FDA considered that of the 35 novel drugs it approved in its fiscal 2012, 15 (43 per cent): 'were particularly notable for their significant contributions to the health and quality of life of patients' (FDA 2012).

We can expect this infusion of an increasing number of new products with novel modes of action to increase overall quality. I would argue on this basis that the quality in terms of commercial potential of new products reaching the market is likely to have been steadily increasing over the half-dozen years up to 2012.

Orphan Drugs

Orphan drugs are by definition for small populations of patients. You might think, therefore, that the revenues they stand to generate will invariably be small. But this is certainly not the case. Several blockbuster drugs were first launched in orphans indications: Epogen/Procrit (epoetin alfa, Amgen), Rituxan/MabThera (rituximab, Roche/Biogen Idec), Remicade (infliximab, Johnson & Johnson) and Botox (botulinum toxin, Allergan).

Also a number of highly successful anticancer products have orphan status in at least some indications. Gleevec/Glivec (imatinib, Novartis) is one striking example. This blockbuster, with 2011 sales of $4.7 billion, has orphan indications amongst the seven it is registered for.

Novartis completely failed to understand the scale of its commercial potential at an early stage in its development. In his prize-winning 2011 book *The Emperor of all Maladies, A Biography of Cancer*, Siddhartha Mukherjee recounts how Novartis nearly gave up developing the product. It was first investigated for activity in chronic myeloid leukaemia, which in the US is suffered by a few thousand patients each year. Despite the publication of highly encouraging preclinical results in 1993, the academic researcher who had developed the product with Novartis had to beg the company to continue to develop it. 'Novartis had a plethora of predictable excuses: "The drug ... would never work, would be too toxic, would never make any money."' Only in 1998 did Novartis relent and allow limited funds for Gleevec's further development. By 2001 it launched the product in first markets.

The majority of sales of another blockbuster, Rituxan/MabThera (rituximab, Roche), have been generated in two orphan indications, chronic lymphatic leukaemia and non-Hodgkin's lymphoma. The total sales of this huge blockbuster reached $6.8 billion in 2012. (Rituxan/MabThera is also indicated in another, nonorphan indication, rheumatoid arthritis.)

Another anticancer product, Temodal/Temodar (temozolomide, Merck & Co) this time for brain cancer, had orphan status for the malignant glioma indication. It briefly achieved blockbuster status shortly before its patents began to expire around 2010, mainly on the strength of sales in this particular type of brain cancer.

Already by 2008 16 orphan products were included in the Top 200 best-selling drug rankings for the US. Since then several other orphan drugs have become commercially successful.

In 2012 a joint Pfizer/Thomson Reuters report by Meekings, Williams and Arrowsmith (2012) showed that the gap between the revenue generated by orphan drugs and nonorphans was narrowing. Moreover the authors suggested that the profitability of orphan drugs was no less than that of nonorphans. They also pointed out that orphan diseases collectively affect 25 million people in the US, or 8 per cent of the total population.

The global orphan drug market is no longer small. Pfizer/Thomson Reuters assessed it to be worth $50 billion. This is 6 per cent of the total global pharmaceutical market. But nevertheless, despite the customary high prices of orphan drugs, the majority of them are likely to achieve below-average levels of revenue and absolute profit as compared with nonorphan products. Thus if the recent recovery in the number of new products of all types launched happened to stem at least partly from an increasing number of new orphan drugs, this might be giving false comfort regarding the capacity of these new products to revive the fortunes of the pharmaceutical industry.

Irena Melnikova, director of strategies and external innovation at Sanofi US, found that in the 1990s 17 per cent of all drugs approved in the United States were orphans (Melnikova 2012). But by the 2005–10 period they accounted for over 35 per cent; a third of orphans approved for this latter period were anticancer products.

Meanwhile, concentrating on the most recent cohort of new products reaching the market, Citeline found that of the 33 new products it found had been launched in first countries in 2011, 7, or 21 per cent, were orphan drugs (Pharmaprojects® Citeline 2011a).

Orphan drugs therefore form a significant though modest proportion of all products and are not much more dominant now than they were in 2007. They should therefore not be having an unduly negative impact on the average commercial potential of the new product cohorts that have reached markets in recent years. Whilst their importance could well increase, I suspect that orphan drugs will have a rather modest effect over the next few years on the average value of products in future annual cohorts.

Conclusions

Taking all the factors I have reviewed above into account, I believe that since the mid-1990s the quality of new products in terms of their average commercial potential is unlikely to have been declining – rather the reverse. The commercial potential of annual cohorts of new products reaching the market is therefore, as far as I can see, rather under-represented by the actual numbers annually launched. I also believe there is little reason to suspect any significant falling off in the average commercial potential of new products reaching the market over the next few years.

I therefore believe it is reasonable in projecting future prospects to take figures for numbers of projects in development at least at their face value. I do this in Chapter 17.

17

Projections and Conclusions

There is still an enormous amount of innovation in the marketplace; it just comes from a more diverse array of sources.
Barbara Ryan of Deutsche Bank, in Dealmaker's Outlook,
Pharmaceutical Executive, June 2012; Looney 2012

In this chapter I will make projections based on the number of projects at different phases as of 2012. I will suggest what they could end up yielding in terms of numbers of new products eventually reaching the market.

Phase III

Let's consider firstly projects at Phase III. On average a project at this phase will reach the market in about three years. In 2009 there were 544 projects at Phase III, according to Pharmaprojects® Citeline.[1] By 2012 there were 693 projects, or 27 per cent more. If the same attrition rates apply over the period 2012–15 as applied over the 2009–12 period, by 2015 we could expect approaching a quarter more products to be reaching the market than in 2012.[2] (I am being just a little conservative here to allow for improved reporting by Citeline of projects over the three-year period to 2012.)

By 2015 I suggest that we could well have just over 40 products per year reaching the market. For comparison, IMS (2012) suggested that 32–7 products

---

1   This figure is from Pharmaprojects® Citeline's Expert Analysis, Annual Review '09, which is no longer available at www.citeline.com.
2   At the time of projecting these figures in December 2012 I did not have full data on the total number of new products launched globally in 2012. However, as previously mentioned (see p. 191), the FDA reported that the number approved in the United States in its fiscal years to October was the same in 2012 as in 2011: 35 products. In January 2013 it was reported that the FDA had approved 39 products in calendar 2012 (Silverman 2013). For the purposes of the extrapolations in this chapter I assumed that the number of new products launched globally in calendar 2012 would be the same as in 2011.

per annum are likely to reach the market over the 2012–16 period, as opposed to an average of 28 per annum over the 2006–10 period (IMS actually gives a range of 160–85 and 140 new products respectively over the two five-year periods). My figures are therefore more optimistic than those from IMS – but not wildly so.

Is this realistic? Remember that the beginning of the 2009–12 period was still in the post-Vioxx period of high regulatory attrition. I think that given the more positive attitude of the FDA in particular, a figure in the low 40s could even be conservative.

I now apply this extrapolation methodology successively to the previous development phases.

Phase II

On average a project at Phase II will take about six years to reach the market. In 2006 there were 1,309 projects at that phase, whereas by 2012 that figure had reached 1,882. This is a 44 per cent increase in the number of Phase II projects. If the same attrition rates apply over the period 2012–18 as did over the 2006–12 period, by around 2018 we could expect at least one-third more products to reach the market than reached it in 2012. (I am being a little more conservative here than in my Phase I extrapolation, to allow for improved reporting by Citeline of projects over the longer, six-year period to 2012.)

In 2018 we could therefore see around 44 products reaching the market. Future attrition rates over this period may well prove to be less fierce than during the 2006–12 period that takes up most of the notorious, post-Vioxx phase.

Phase I

For projections from Phase I, I assume that on average it takes eight years for projects to progress from this phase to the market. If we therefore take the 2004 cohort, in that year there were, according to Citeline data, 756 projects at Phase I.

By 2012 there were 1,492 projects at that phase – not far short of double the number. So that, given the same attrition rates that have applied over the 2004–12 period, and again discounting a little for improved reporting by Citeline, we could see three quarters as many products again reaching the market in 2020 as reached it in 2012. That would be 55–60 products in that year – approaching record levels. Just as for Phase II, future attrition rates may well prove to be less adverse than over the notorious post-Vioxx phase.[3]

Preclinical Phase

Finally, let's look at the projection for the preclinical phase. I assume that products reaching the market in 2012 were on average at preclinical phase a dozen years earlier, in 2000. In that year there were, according to Pharmaprojects, just 3,021 projects at the preclinical phase. By 2012 there were, according to Pharmaprojects® Citeline, 5,247 projects at this phase. This is a 73 per cent increase over the 2000 figure! Even allowing for improved tracking of projects over a much longer period than for the later phases, extrapolation suggests that the number of new products by 2024 could – just as in the Phase I projection above – be about half as many again as reached the market in 2012. This once again, of course, assumes that attrition rates over the next dozen years match those for the dozen years to 2012. That would mean some 50 new products reaching the market in 2021 – slightly less impressive than the Phase I projection but still approaching record levels.

Figure 17.1 summarizes my projections. As with all forecasts, the further they stretch, the more questionable they become. But as Figure 17.1 shows, my projection is simply continuing rather more powerfully to 2024 the upward trend already apparent since 2004.

Since, as I argued in Chapter 16, the commercial potential per new product ought to be at least as much as for new products currently, this is a promising outlook for the pharmaceutical industry. By this score, within a few years the number of new products reaching the market should be sufficient to satisfy the needs of big pharma. By the mid-2020s, the pharmaceutical industry should be out of the abyss and performing again as in the last 20 years of the twentieth century.

---

3   For comparison with the Pharmaprojects® Citeline data on trends in numbers of projects over the clinical phases, in 2012 PhRMA reported that there were currently more than 3,200 projects in clinical trials or at the preregistration phase in the US (PhRMA 2012). This figure was a third higher than the 2,400 projects in development in 2005.

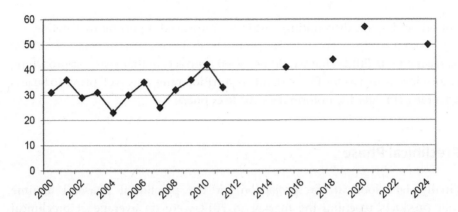

Figure 17.1   Number of first launches of new products projected to 2024
Source: John Ansell Consultancy based on data from Pharmaprojects® Citeline 2011a,
2012; Ansell 2001, 2011

What Could Go Wrong?

In the longer term, many factors which cannot easily be incorporated in
forecasts could come into play. Another Vioxx-type debacle could occur. In
recent years the number of products withdrawn from the market has been
relatively few – on average a couple each year for safety reasons. It would need
such a withdrawal to again be handled hamfistedly for it to turn into another
debacle.

It could well be on the other hand that the pharmaceutical industry will
begin to make much more of enabling technologies than it has to date so that
attrition rates could decline. It could also be that the types of breakthrough
seen in the cancer field flowing now from the enormous efforts that have been
concentrated in this therapeutic area over the past 20 years could start to be
translated more frequently to other therapeutic areas.

My principal conclusion for sceptics is that the actual figures could turn
out to be considerably worse than my projections and still be sufficient for the
pharmaceutical industry to get back to the levels of prosperity it enjoyed until
the late 1990s. But I can by no means rule out a sudden Vioxx-like event ruining
everything for everyone in the industry.

Consequences of a Productivity Upturn

It will take time for long-standing pessimism about the prospects for the pharmaceutical industry to sink in. As late as March 2012 one group (Scannell et al., 2012) considered, 'If someone is optimistic about the prospects for R&D today, they presumably believe that countervailing forces – whatever they are – are starting to abate, or that there has been a sudden and unprecedented acceleration in scientific, technological or managerial processes that will soon become visible in new drug approvals'.

But as Figures 14.3–14.13 showed, things are already on the turn (see pp. 175–82). As I have shown phase by phase, increases in the numbers of projects are at long last working their way through to ever more advanced phases. At long last we have seen a significant upturn in the number of projects at the all-important Phase III. And the numbers of projects at early stage are very substantially up on the numbers which produced the current crop of projects at Phase III. No 'sudden and unprecedented acceleration' in processes of the sort described by Scannell is necessary for a productivity upturn.

You can consider this as the impending culmination of a trend which has been moving at a glacially slow rate over a very long time. The sheer weight of projects progressing through R&D is – phase by phase – overcoming the negative trends in project numbers. The next one to succumb shortly will be the preregistration phase. And since that phase is a short one, a positive impact on numbers of new products reaching the market should follow shortly afterwards.

The Need for Big Pharma to Step Up Efforts

But there is no such thing as a free lunch. Big pharma will need to be more ambitious. It has to realize that the opportunity exists already to step up new product launches. Companies need to go out and acquire rights to a greater number of products if they are to eventually launch more new products. Many big pharma companies think they are sufficiently active in their licensing efforts – which over the past couple of years have faltered. Most need to step up the tempo of their activities. Furthermore, if they do not acquire rights to projects at earlier phases more intensively, then many of those projects will soon wither and die – and the more positive long-term prospects will be undermined.

Also the products that do reach the market will need to be promoted. And they will by no means all be products that can be promoted to small target groups of specialists.

Recent data suggest that though the trend to specialist products is continuing it is by no means overwhelming. Contrary to increasingly received wisdom, small-molecule products are not entirely on the way out.

For example, of the 33 new products that Pharmaprojects® Citeline reported had reached first markets in 2011, 26 (79 per cent) were small molecules (Pharmaprojects® Citeline 2011a). Some of these were for specialists – such as anticancer products. But the figures suggest that detailing of small-molecule products to GPs is far from dead. Roughly half of this cohort of products appear to be GP-oriented rather than specialist-oriented products. This means that there are opportunities for companies ready and willing to gear themselves up again for mass detailing to GPs as well as to specialists. But even with an upturn in productivity it will be several years before there is likely to be a need for most big pharma companies to increase sales force strengths.

With hindsight we can now see how damaging the Vioxx affair was to the pharmaceutical industry. I would rank it as the worst event to befall the pharmaceutical industry since thalidomide. If Vioxx had been handled more competently by its manufacturer, the FDA would not have been under fire to make the regulatory process more stringent. You can argue that eventually another Vioxx-type affair would have happened. But if Vioxx had been handled more professionally, the impact of the emerging cardiovascular side-effects need not have caused so much bad publicity. It did not happen with any other recent product withdrawal. It has taken a good half-dozen years for the pharmaceutical industry to recover the situation.

Now there are measures which regulatory authorities have put in place that should help to prevent a similar *cause celebre* arising. With hindsight, it would have been better for the pharmaceutical industry – if to an extent irksome – if they had been in force before 2004.

That may appear to be the end of the story as far as gauging future prospects of new products is concerned. But there is one final factor that needs review in Part VI.

PART VI
Getting a True Fix on Prospects

In Part VI I look retrospectively at how sales forecasts by pundits and companies for new products have tended to underestimate commercial potential. I suggest that today's forecasts are likely to be underestimating potential in the same way. I then look at studies on profitability and suggest that they have also underestimated the proportion of products which turn out to be profitable.

18

Underestimating Potential – A Common Feature of Pharmaceutical Forecasting

One of the most difficult things to do in the pharmaceutical industry is to predict peak sales of a drug.

LaMattina 2012

Introduction

Whilst the realization is beginning to dawn that we can expect an upturn in the number of new products reaching the market shortly, this does not mean that according to some predictions that future sales will match the upturn in numbers. The purpose of this chapter is to show that, much more often than not, past forecasts have underestimated the prospects for new products. We should bear this in mind, therefore, with current forecasts for emerging new products.

Both commentators and the pharmaceutical industry itself have a woeful record of underforecasting new product sales. This is not widely understood, and for this reason I am devoting a whole chapter to underforecasting.

The pharmaceutical industry does tend to be pessimistic about its prospects in a more general way. The late lamented monthly *Scrip Magazine*, which existed between 1994 and 2005, published an annual review edition, the leading article of which was regularly full of forebodings. Here is a sample:[1]

---

1   I include as the first example the bleak leading article title for the year before *Scrip Magazine's* inception, from a one-off *Review* magazine, the parent journal *Scrip* published just prior to setting up *Scrip Magazine*.

1992   Annus Horribilis

1993   A Year to Retrench, Restructure, Rethink

1994   An End or a Beginning?

1999   Will R&D Provide Jam Tomorrow?

2000   Exciting Times or Just an Ongoing Slog?

2002   Looking Back at an Uncertain Future

2003   The Old Order Comes to an End.

2004   Misery Loves Company.

You would not imagine from the above litany that this whole period of a dozen years was a golden era of pharmaceutical industry performance.

There does seem to be a strong streak of foreboding stretching to pessimism amongst those working in and commenting upon the pharmaceutical industry. I suggest below some of the psychology behind this. I go on to propose that the industry needs to take a much more objective view of its prospects. If it does not, then it will reject or abandon options that could help secure its future.

Underestimating the Commercial Potential of New Products

I do not pretend that new product potential is never overestimated. So let's just start with a massive overestimation of a product's commercial potential. Before it was launched in 2006, Pfizer forecast that its inhalable insulin product, Exubera, could become a blockbuster, reaching sales of $2 billion dollars by 2010. By 2007 Exubera sales amounted to just $12 million.

Several factors led to this disastrous downfall. The device for Exubera that Pfizer had licensed from Nektar Therapeutics and developed with that company was unwieldy; there were some safety issues, with reports of reduced lung function, as well as some consumer marketing problems. But perhaps the most important factor was the lack of payer coverage. Rather than specifically trying to convince payers, Pfizer relied on demand from the consumer and doctor to persuade payers to grant coverage, a strategy it had used successfully with previous products. If payers had acceded as far as Exubera was concerned, this would have increased their costs for insulins by about fivefold. Exubera was described on blogs as one of the most stunning failures in the history of the pharmaceutical industry.

Exubera is indeed an extreme example. Usually failures when they do occur are less dramatic. Also companies often sense that their prospects are not that good when they launch them, particularly when the product profile is unexciting or flawed. But failures are much less common than some commentators would lead you to believe. For example, there are now fewer failures of 'me-too' products because as I have already mentioned (see p. 195) most companies grew to understand that there is limited room for such products, and they don't get involved as readily in developing them as they did prior to about 30 years ago.

A more competent top management than was running Pfizer in the Exubera era would have discontinued the product way before launch, based on the unfavourable market research findings it had been receiving but taking insufficiently seriously.

Misleading Initial Sales

It is not uncommon for sales of a new product to build up steadily rather than spectacularly. Analysts are sometimes misled by this and jump to the conclusion that a new product is going to be a flop. Eli Lilly's antiplatelet agent Effient (prasugrel), which was first launched in 2009, had disturbingly modest sales in its first couple of years on the market – $27 million in 2009 and $115 million in 2010. This gave rise to negative comments from analysts. However, by 2011 sales had reached $302.5 million and during 2012 they grew strongly to reach $457 million. Effient now looks well set to become a blockbuster.

Denosumab is another example. This is an anti-RANKL monoclonal antibody developed by Amgen which, as Prolia, is indicated in osteoporosis and under another brand name, Xgeva, for bone cancer. In some quarters it was expected to be the most valuable upcoming product just before it was launched. It was first launched by Amgen in 2010, and for a couple of years sales failed to live up to expectations, some commentators assuming that it would no longer become a big success. However, by 2012, sales of Prolia and

Xgeva had reached $472 million and $748 million respectively. In aggregate, therefore, the two brands had surpassed the $1 billion blockbuster threshold.

This tendency of some commentators to write off products too quickly may reflect a lack of understanding that it takes time for new products to reach a peak – on average a dozen years, as I have earlier explained (see pp. 20–21, 243–6).

I first noticed the common tendency to underestimate sales of new products when I was researching an article covering this phenomenon (Ansell 2006). I have now revisited the examples I cited in that article of leading successful products whose sales had been underestimated and I've added below more recent examples. The psychology behind forecasting is also interesting, and so I will then consider why there should be this tendency to underforecast.

Underforecasting Products Which Became Blockbusters

CLARITIN

In its 1988 annual report, the then Schering Corporation considered the prospects for its nonsedating antihistamine Claritin (loratidine): 'One of the Company's most exciting new products is CLARITIN, approved in 17 overseas markets with US approval expected soon. When fully established, the product is projected to generate sales of $200-to-$300 million annually' (Schering Corporation 1989).

Schering's enthusiasm was certainly more than borne out. Their expectations were out by a factor of 10–15, depending on whether you take the upper or lower bounds of the company's expectations. For Claritin eventually achieved peak sales in 2001 of $3.159 billion dollars, and a ranking of fifth best-selling product in that year.

GLAXO'S 1990S-ERA PRODUCTS

In the early 1990s Glaxo was in the advanced stages of developing a promising crop of new products, all of which became blockbusters. In May 1990, Kleinwort Benson Securities gave global forecasts for these products (*Scrip* 1990).

The first product, Imigran/Imitrex (sumatriptan), was forecast by Kleinwort Benson to reach sales of £850 million in 1999/2000.[2] The product actually achieved sales in 2000 of £705 million, somewhat less than forecast. However, it did go on to achieve sales of £798 million in 2002, just 7 per cent less than Kleinwort Benson's forecast.

For the second Glaxo product, Serevent (salmeterol), Kleinwort Benson was even more accurate. This product achieved peak sales in 2000 of £622 million – just 3 per cent more than the £600 million it had projected.

However, for the third product, Zofran (ondansetron), Kleinwort Benson's forecast was far too low. It projected sales of £150 million for 1999/2000, whereas Glaxo had already achieved sales of £327 million in 2000. And this was far from the end of the story. For Zofran went on to reach a sales peak of £846 million in 2006.

Finally, Kleinwort Benson gave forecasts for two fluticasone products, Flixotide/Flovent and Flonase/Flixonase. Its forecast of £250 million for 1999/2000 was under a fifth of the aggregate fluticasone sales of £1.288 billion achieved in 2000 by Glaxo. The sales of one of the two fluticasone products, Flonase/Flixonase, went on to reach £656 million in 2005.

We can draw several conclusions from this case. Firstly, long-range forecasting is a very difficult exercise, and it is to Kleinwort Benson's credit that its forecasts were reasonably accurate for 1999/2000 for Imigran/Imitrex, and remarkably accurate for Serevent. But in the case of two other products its underestimations were huge. One of these was a specialist product, and the first member of its pharmacological class, Zofran. Perhaps this cautioned Kleinwort Benson against proposing a large forecast.

Also, sales of three of these Glaxo products went on to reach greater heights. Kleinwort Benson's forecasts, being for 1999/2000, were generally too short term to fully reflect the potential of the Glaxo pipeline. This is despite the fact that Kleinwort Benson's timespan was by no means short in comparison with those used by other forecasters made at the time – often five or even only three years. As I illustrate throughout this book, underestimation of longevity is a common reason for underestimating a new product's sales.

---

2   Glaxo's financial year ran till the end of June until 1995; thereafter it followed the calendar year.

More recently a fixed combination of fluticasone and salmeterol from GlaxoSmithKline, Advair/Seretide, has also beaten analysts' forecasts. At the time the product was launched in the United States in April 2001, *Scrip* reported: 'Analysts see huge potential for Advair/Seretide in the US, particularly in light of its successful start elsewhere ... By 2003, global sales predictions for the combination product are in the region of £1–1.5 billion' (*Scrip* 2001).

This accorded more or less with expectations within the company – Glaxo expected Advair/Seretide to reach sales levels of between £1 billion and £2 billion per annum.

Whilst the sentiments were correct, the scale of these projections were not. The product reached sales of £1.631 billion in 2002, comfortably exceeding the range suggested. By 2012 they had reached £5.046 billion. Advair/Seretide was second best-selling product globally in 2006. Again, projections that were too short term led to gross underestimation of the eventual sales of the product.

OTHER EXAMPLES

Nexium (esomeprazole, AstraZeneca), the successor product to Prilosec/Losec (omeprazole) was a rather similar case. SG Securities issued forecasts for this product when its UK launch was imminent in August 2000: 'We would expect Nexium to achieve rapidly (and within two years) a 20 per cent+ share of the Losec franchise with corresponding sales of more than $1 billion' (*Scrip* 2000). In fact Nexium sales in 2002 reached very nearly double this: $1.978 billion. They went on thereafter by leaps and bounds to reach a peak of $5.216 billion in 2007. Nexium reached no. 4 ranking for globally best-selling products in 2006.

There are many other celebrated cases. In October 1996, when the antipsychotic Zyprexa (olanzapine, Eli Lilly) was launched in its first market, the United States, Hambrecht & Quist was quoted as believing that it could have sales of $1 billion 'in four or five years' time' (*Scrip* 1996). In fact its sales had already passed $1 billion by 1998, reached $2.366 billion in 2000, $3.087 billion in 2001, and went on eventually to reach peak sales of $5.026 billion in 2010. This was more than five times the sales level envisaged by Hambrecht & Quist.

At the beginning of 2003, the year in which another antipsychotic Abilify (aripiprazole, Bristol-Myers Squibb, Otsuka) was first launched by Bristol-Myers Squibb, JP Morgan's opinion was that 'Abilify has a solid shot at success, but our $1.4 billion projection by 2007 is insufficient to move Bristol-Myers Squibb's underlying revenue growth in any given year beyond 2003' (ICIS 2003). As it turned out, Abilify had exceeded $1.4 billion globally by the year after its first launch, 2004 ($1.488 billion sales in that year), and reached sales of $4.991 billion by 2011. It had become a major product, with a global sales ranking of fifteenth.

Merck & Co's leukotriene antagonist for asthma, Singulair (montelukast) was first launched in 1997. At the time it was launched in the US the following year, ABN-AMRO were quoted as believing that it would end up as the leading product in its class, beating two earlier entrants, and that its annual sales could reach 'over $500 million within a few years' (*The Pharma Letter* 1998a). Singulair sales actually reached $502 million the following year, 1999! But more importantly, its eventual sales were over 10 times this level: $5.479 billion in 2011 just before patents began to expire. At this point it was Merck's biggest product by far, rather than being the half-blockbuster anticipated by ABN-AMRO.

In an article in April 1998 on the first launch of the antiplatelet drug Plavix (clopidogrel; Sanofi, Bristol-Myers Squibb), in the US, *The Pharma Letter* reported: 'Analysts feel that clopidogrel has the potential to become a blockbuster product, breaking the $500 million mark, but only if clear superiority over aspirin can be shown.' The sales of Plavix peaked at approaching 20 times this figure: $9.624 billion in 2009, when it was the second-ranked product by global sales after Lipitor. It was still second best-selling product globally in 2011 shortly before generic erosion set in (*The Pharma Letter* 1998b).

Turning to more recent examples, let's start with the anticancer product Avastin (bevacizumab, Roche). ICIS reported a variety of forecasts in March 2004 when it was first approved, in the US. The most optimistic of these was from Morgan Stanley, which forecast that sales would reach $1.452 billion in 2008 (ICIS 2004). This did take into account projected additional indications, which Avastin went on to obtain. In fact sales reached well over three times that level, at $4.991 billion in that year, and peaked in 2010 at over $7.291 billion.

Aricept (donepezil; Pfizer, Eisai) was the first successful drug launched for Alzheimer's disease, in 1996. *The Pharma Letter* reported that Ken Nover of A.G. Edwards, an enthusiast for the product, considered that: 'Aricept should be a major product for both Eisai and Pfizer ...' 'Mr Nover said that Aricept could easily make sales in excess of $500 million a year.' As it turned out, global sales of Aricept peaked at well over eight times this level, at $4.386 billion in 2009 (*The Pharma Letter* 1996).

And last but by no means least we have the biggest product of them all, Lipitor. At the London *Economist* Pharma Summit meeting in 2011, Freda Lewis-Hall of Pfizer said that the 'first peak-sale estimates of $500 million were off by a factor of 25' (Grogan 2012). And as a coda, the product taking over now from Lipitor as the biggest-selling statin, Crestor, was estimated variously at launch to reach sales in a range of $2–5 billion (*The Pharma Letter* 2003). By 2012 its sales had already exceeded $7 billion.

It is important to note that in none of the cases above were forecasters expecting products to fail. But very commonly ideas of what products could achieve fell well short of the mark, as some of the examples above indicate, even when forecast by enthusiasts for the products.

The standard of forecasting has not improved since I first looked at this issue in 2006. If anything, it has fallen. The more recent successful products I have subsequently analyzed provide some of the most spectacular examples of underforecasting.

The Psychology Behind Underforecasting

Why should there be this widespread practice of underforecasting for successful products? I believe there are numerous reasons which encourage it.

WHY PUT FORWARD AN ULTRAHIGH FORECAST WHEN ONE THAT IS ALREADY HIGH WILL BE IMPRESSIVE ENOUGH?

In my experience this mentality exists both within pharmaceutical companies and financial institutions. In the early 1980s the proton pump inhibitor omeprazole emerged as an interesting agent which could have advantages over the highly successful H2-antagonists for treating ulcers and other gastrointestinal disorders. The company I was working for at the time was interested in acquiring regional rights to market the product from the company developing it, Astra. A page-and-a-half review which a clinical colleague passed to me led me to identify four potential advantages for omeprazole over H-2 antagonists.

I therefore submitted to my director for the board's consideration a high forecast, which he considered embarrassingly so. I went through the assumptions I had made in the forecast and asked him which figure was too high. He was unable to select any of them. However, we agreed a compromise: I would reduce all the forecasts to a quarter of what I had proposed. Armed with those figures he felt comfortable presenting them to the board. They were in turn happy enough with the figures, and a meeting was agreed with Astra.

However, my company did not succeed in acquiring the regional rights in question from Astra (but then, no company did). After stuttering further development, omeprazole was launched some five years later in its first market as Losec. Within a few years its global sales had passed the sales of all other products. Losec was no. 1 globally best-selling product between 1998 and 2000. Of course, even the original forecasts I had submitted were far exceeded, though I cannot now remember sufficiently to know by how much. As a consultant I have subsequently quite frequently encountered this reluctance to submit a high forecast.

IT IS PREFERABLE TO BE CONSERVATIVE IN MAKING FORECASTS

Sometimes companies prefer to be conservative. The danger is that they miss out on opportunities that fall below the cut-off level for acceptance.

Other companies prefer middle-of-the-road forecasts. They feel comfortable because that way the chances of being wrong are minimized. Opportunities can also be missed with middle-of-the-road forecasts, when good opportunities are thereby underestimated.

In my view, the *most likely* forecast is the one which should be aimed at and encouraged by senior management.

LACK OF IMAGINATION FROM THE FORECASTER

There is commonly a lack of imagination – or thinking of future prospects too much in today's terms, with a lack of long-term perspective:

- The first billion-dollar products, Tagamet and Zantac, reached that level in 1986.

- The first product to reach $5 billion in sales was Prilosec/Losec, 13 years later in 1999.

- The first product to reach $10 million was Lipitor, five years later in 2004 – with its sales peaking at $13.833 billion in 2006.

No product has surpassed Lipitor's peak, or is likely to do so for a few more years yet. But it will happen before very long, and I suspect that we will see the first $20 billion product before too long.

A few years ago I submitted a forecast for a product to a client which peaked at around $20 billion. This caused a similar state of consternation as I had experienced in the case of Losec above. This time I argued my corner more strongly and the forecast was endorsed as it was.

Today's forecasters may feel uncomfortable sticking out their necks in suggesting figures of $20 billion or more – but that is likely to be the reality with today's bigger opportunities now in development.

LACK OF AWARENESS OF ALL POTENTIAL INDICATIONS

There can be a lack of awareness of the future therapeutic scope for a product, or a reluctance to forecast for all but the most immediate indications.

By launch of the first indication, most companies will have a programme of further approvals projected for additional claims, presentations and new indications. But quite commonly further applications for a new product only emerge after a product has reached the market for its first indication. Failure to forecast for these can hardly be blamed on the forecaster. But some imagination perhaps needs to be applied in some circumstances: for example, the product may have several potentially small additional indications and a couple of larger ones. To be too conservative about getting a range of indications approved could risk killing the product when a more comprehensive forecast covering a range of indications will show that it is capable of eventually achieving much more than this.

THE LIFESPAN OF PRODUCTS AND ACCOUNTABILITY

Rarely will a forecaster be called upon to account for a long-term projection – because with normal staff movement and turnover, the timespan is just too long. Forecasters – whether analysts in banks or in pharmaceutical companies – may be less mindful of being in error and pay less attention to the forecasts they make because of this. The majority of banks I cite above in this section no longer exist, at least as the same entity.

UNFAMILIARITY WITH INDICATION OR DISEASE AREA

Unfamiliarity with or lack of information about an indication or disease area can be responsible for underforecasting. Viagra is an example of a product whose great success was largely unanticipated outside Pfizer because there had been no previous successful prescription product for male erectile dysfunction.

Three years before Viagra was launched I was asked by a Japanese company to assess the market for another antihypertensive in male erectile dysfunction. My calculations showed that there was indeed sufficient commercial potential to merit further development. However, the company did not advance the project, I suspect because of its unfamiliarity with this indication.

OVERESTIMATION OF MARKET SATISFACTION/SATURATION

When there is a breakthrough it is sometimes difficult to imagine a better product succeeding it – particularly within the company which developed it! I saw this at first hand at Glaxo in the 1980s when I was working in the antiulcerant market. Prilosec/Losec (omeprazole, Astra) surpassed the sales peak reached by Zantac (ranitidine, Glaxo), which had itself massively exceeded the sales of the then supposedly ultimate gastrointestinal product in its field, Tagamet (cimetidine, Smith, Kline & French). Glaxo could have licensed in a competing proton pump inhibitor but seriously underestimated the threat from Losec. Also at that time Glaxo found it difficult to accept that a product invented outside the company could be superior to one it developed in-house. Christensen (see p. 95), has found that this reaction is common when a disruptive technology such as this emerges.

There were many sceptics about the commercial potential of the antihypertensive Rasilez/Tekturna (aliskiren, Novartis) in what was supposed to be a rather well satisfied market with many good alternative therapies available. This product was first launched in 2007. Despite these concerns, its sales exceeded $600 million in 2011. However, its promotion by Novartis was then unfortunately suspended because of emerging side-effect problems. The point had at least been made that there was room for a novel antihypertensive despite the level of satisfaction in the market apparently being high.

INSUFFICIENT NUMBER OF YEARS PROJECTED

I gave several examples above of underforecasts which were at least partly inaccurate because the forecasters made their projections for an insufficient number of years. This is often a reason for serious underestimation of commercial potential. The traditional horizons assumed by many pharmaceutical forecasters of six, five, or even three years are completely outdated. Around a dozen years is much more realistic time for the average successful product to take to reach its peak sales level (see pp. 20–21, 243–6). And this is just an average – some forecasts should be projecting for much longer than this.

UNDERESTIMATION OF FUTURE PRICE LEVELS

Specialist products tend to be priced considerably higher than office-based practitioner (GP)-oriented products. As specialist products come to account for a greater share of all blockbusters, this factor is becoming increasingly important in assessing the contribution of new products to the future growth of the pharmaceutical industry.

Sometimes there is a feeling that with the price sensitivity of payers increasing, no prices will be approvable that are more than a few per cent higher than the prices of existing products in the market. Inspection of prices of recently launched products shows that this can indeed apply to some new products in highly competitive markets. But frequently, new products are today still being launched at a substantial premium. Reference to the prices of recently introduced and existing products in a particular therapeutic market will soon give some indication of what is possible for a new product.

UNDERESTIMATION WHEN FACTORING UP COMMERCIAL POTENTIAL

Forecasters sometimes fail to adequately consider what level of turnover will result when factoring up the commercial potential of a product in an apparently esoteric indication – for example a less common cancer indication such as a brain cancer. I mentioned the example of Temodal/Temodar (temozolomide, Merck & Co) in my review of orphan drugs (see p. 197) and it is worth mentioning further some of the background.

This product was licensed by Cancer Research Campaign Technology to Schering-Plough in 1993. Schering-Plough later became part of Merck & Co.

The consensus amongst the pharmaceutical licensing fraternity at the time was that the product, as a pro-drug of an existing anticancer product, dacarbazine, was a modest innovation. It was therefore widely adjudged to be a modest commercial proposition – and certainly not a potential blockbuster. However, Schering-Plough had the confidence in the product's prospects to take it on.

As mentioned previously (see p. 197), Temodal/Temodar gained orphan drug status for malignant glioma. The product was eventually approved for two different types of brain cancer: glioblastoma and astrocytoma. Launched in 1999, sales built no more than steadily, but continued growing to reach a peak of $1.073 billion in 2009 – just over the blockbuster threshold. Meanwhile Cancer Research UK, as it now is, has earned much more substantial royalties than it probably ever imagined it would receive, and has been able to plough these back into research.

MISCONCEPTIONS OVER ORPHAN DRUG POTENTIAL

I discussed earlier (see pp. 196–8) that although orphan drugs can have modest commercial potential, there are now quite a number that have become big commercial successes. Orphan drugs are often allowed very high prices, since the impact on drug budgets can be limited when there are so few patients. Specialist drugs that obtain orphan drug status can acquire an unjustified association with limited commercial potential which evidence I cited earlier shows is no longer justified.

GAUGING TIMING OF TAKE-OFF FOR A NEW CONCEPT

As mentioned in Chapter 2 (see pp. 41–52) it is often very difficult to gauge exactly when a new concept is going to take off. In pharmaceuticals lengthy phases of slow progress are unfortunately common. My impression over the past few years is that forecasters are finding it more difficult now to predict exactly when sales are going to take-off. More often than not, industry forecasters or publishers of industry reports tend to pessimism when in doubt.

Several companies provide consensus forecasts calculated from individual forecasts made by bank analysts. These may well be of value in assessing short-term prospects of products already on the market. But my findings above show that they should certainly not be used for long-term forecasting as they will more often than not underestimate the commercial potential of new products in development. They are the pharmaceutical equivalent of financial derivatives.

As a consensus of several forecasts, the assumptions on which they are based are rendered opaque, and probing their basis becomes difficult.

TALLYING UP THE PROS AND CONS

This is a considerable list – 12 factors in all tending to underforecasting. Set against this, how many reasons are there to overforecast?

To impress investors is a not uncommon one. But overforecasting risks criticism and loss of credibility, and so a good defence has to be in place ready to counter criticism. In practice I find that this acts as a deterrent to overforecasting and tends to encourage the reverse.

I believe that the psychology behind forecasting will not change much in future – and the factors behind underforecasting of products are therefore likely to persist. Companies are likely to go on underforecasting and thereby undervaluing their intellectual property. That does present opportunities to companies with greater vision who can pick up products like Temodal/ Temodar.

Financial Prospects Then and Now

In June 2012 an interesting extrapolation by Berggren et al. from McKinsey & Company was published. This calculated the commercial prospects of new products launched in recent years and compared them with those to be launched in future. The report came out with rather positive conclusions.

The McKinsey group used Pharmaprojects® Citeline data for pipeline products and proprietary consensus forecasts. They compared projections for the values of the pipelines over two snapshots, 2006 and 2011. The value of the 2006 snapshot for products to be launched over the 2007–11 period was $40 billion. Meanwhile the value of the 2011 snapshot for products to be launched over the 2012–16 period was $58 billion: 45 per cent greater. This is an impressive jump in commercial potential, which was calculated to represent a compound annual growth of just over 7.7 per cent per annum.

Now this work was based on those notorious consensus forecasts I found so feeble in predicting the full potential of new products of the past. Of course, it may be that the current forecasters are a much more expert bunch than their predecessors or are more inclined to go out on a limb about the prospects of new products than their predecessors a decade ago. But I doubt it. I suspect that these forecasts will, just as in the past, prove to be underestimates of the reality. Which means that prospects could well be considerably brighter than even the McKinsey forecasts suggest.

Personalized Medicine – A Further Area of Underestimation

The advent of genomics was seized upon by the blockbuster-is-dead lobby around 2003 as support for the idea that the age of the blockbuster product was passing. This view was based on the assumption that the commercial potential of each disease would be divided according to the genetic subtypes of that disease. These would then be treated by a series of specifically tailored new products. With the development of biomarkers – cellular or molecular indicators of disease or susceptibility of disease – the era of personalized medicine would have arrived. The new products resulting would, through their specificity and hence greater effectiveness, replace the much less specific blockbusters.

Even the medically qualified (and usually astute) business consultant Clay Christensen followed this line as late as 2009 in his aforementioned coauthored book *The Innovator's Prescription* (see p. 96), although he preferred to use the term *precision* rather than *personalized*: 'The advent of "precision medicine" heralds product-line fragmentation in pharmaceuticals. Volumes per therapeutic compound will drop significantly, as the number of therapeutic compounds expands. Blockbuster drugs will become rare.'

Christensen and his coauthors envisaged this to create serious problems for major pharmaceutical companies – because of their dependence on new blockbusters as their lifeblood. But this outcome has so far has proven misleadingly simplistic and was quickly confounded. I have already mentioned the multibillion-dollar example Gleevec/Glivec (see pp. 42, 196–7).

The very first pharmacogenomic products, Herceptin (trastuzumab, Roche), which was launched in 1998, passed the $1 billion mark in 2004 and had reached $5.9 billion in sales by 2011. Yet Genentech nearly gave up the product at one point, according to Siddhartha Mukherjee. In his book which I have already cited, *The Emperor of All Maladies*, he recounts the story that Genentech was worried about pouring money into the development of Herceptin and crippling the company's finances. Genentech wanted to concentrate on simpler and what it perceived to be more profitable products. Fortunately these reservations were overcome by a small, committed group of scientists and clinicians outside the company who had been working on the product.

Here, therefore, are two products, Gleevec/Glivec and Herceptin, which are not just run-of-the-mill blockbusters but enormous products, both ranking in the Top 20 best-selling products.

Now this is not to say that there will be products used only for a modest number of patients, whose commercial potential will indeed also be modest. But these spectacular successes suggest that other fruits of personalized medicine could become clear commercial successes – up to and beyond blockbuster level.

Conclusions

Whilst as the example of Exubera shows, forecasts for new products can sometimes wildly overestimate potential, underestimation is far more common. Big pharma companies should therefore not fall into the trap of taking literally the published projections of new product potential. If they are as accurate as in the past, today's forecasts are in danger of underestimating the potential of new products.

In the next chapter I put profitability estimations under the microscope.

19
Probing Profitability Estimates

How accurate is received wisdom on the profitability of pharmaceutical products? Not a great deal of work has been done on this in recent years and therefore the industry tends to fall back on rather dated estimations – about which I have considerable misgivings.

A much-quoted report published in 2002 by Henry Grabowski of Duke University and Joseph DiMasi of Tufts University Center for the Study of Drug Development concluded that the top 10 per cent of products by sales generate half of total profits. It also concluded that only 30 per cent of new products from the 1990s covered their costs. This was the latest in a series of such studies on the US market that the Tufts Center has been conducting every decade since the 1970s. Although another decade has passed since the most recent report, this remains the most recent full survey and is still the most widely quoted source on the profitability of products.

However, one further article in 2010 with two coauthors in common with the 2002 study suggested that more realistic assumptions on the cost of capital by that time would reduce the percentage of this cohort of new products which it then found profitable down to only 20 per cent (Vernon, Golec and Dimasi 2010).

I have long been sceptical about the pessimistic findings from such analyses, which do not seem to me to ring true. I have therefore tried to assess profitability with a quite different approach using global product sales. It is not reasonable to expect pharmaceutical companies to readily divulge information on profitability, which they for understandable reasons rarely becomes public. My approach to this problem had to be quite different.

Assessing Profitability

How high do sales of a product have to be for it to be profitable? How much below blockbuster level do you have to fall before a product is unprofitable? This will depend on the nature of the product, in particular how much it costs to manufacture and sell it. Monoclonal antibodies are much more expensive to manufacture than small-molecule products. But on the other hand they will commonly be much less expensive to market because the target prescribers who need to be reached consist of one or a few relatively small specialist groups.

In Table 19.1 I show the number of products first approved in each year between 2002 and 2008 which made it into the Top 500 global best-selling product rankings for 2010 (PharmaLive 2011).

Table 19.1   Number of products first approved in each year between 2002 and 2008 attaining top 500 global best-selling product ranking

	2008	2007	2006	2005	2004	2003	2002
Total number of products appearing	13	19	27	22	23	20	28
Net of non-NCEs*	13	19	26	21	18	19	26
No. blockbusters ($1 billion sales)	0	1	4	2	10	6	10
No. products reaching $0.5 billion	0	5	9	9	11	9	14
No. products reaching $0.333 billion	2	10	14	11	14	13	20
Total no. new products first launched	32	25	35	30	23	31	29

* Products excluded from Net of NCEs row:
- drug delivery device range extensions
- chiral forms of already marketed products
- combination products whose components have previously been marketed.

Source: John Ansell Consultancy based on rankings from PharmaLive 2011

Though PharmaLive includes approval dates for each product, I know from my experience of using its ranking data over the years that sometimes it has failed to include first territories to launch. However, for the more recently launched products in its rankings, the data tends to be more complete on this point. This slight deficiency in the data does, however, mean that a few of the products included in a given annual cohort of products approved should actually belong to an earlier annual cohort. And so my calculations are a little rough and ready because of this.

A few of the products appearing in the PharmaLive Top 500 product rankings are not new chemical activities or active substances. There are combination products whose components are already on the market as plain products. Also there are chiral forms of products that have already been successful as racemates. An example is Clarinex, containing desloratidine, the chiral form of the nonsedating antihistamine loratidine from Schering-Plough, marketed earlier as Claritin. There are also novel presentations of existing products which are range extensions, for example Venlafaxine XR (Teva). I have excluded all such products from row 2 onwards of Table 19.1.

The total number of new products first launched in the years 2002 to 2008 shown in the last row of Table 19.1 ranges between 23 and 32. We can see that only a few of these are blockbusters. The number tends to increase over time as you might expect. From two of the earliest annual cohorts of first approvals in Table 19.1, 2002 and 2004, 10 blockbusters resulted.

I think that most people in the industry would agree that a half-blockbuster – a product featuring in the rankings with sales of at least $0.5 billion, is very likely to be a profitable product, if we consider that on average a successful product will generate revenues over about a dozen years (see pp. 20–21, 243–6). After all, many of these products will go on to greater heights. Table 19.1 shows that after a few years on the market, each annual cohort of new products was generating around 10 half-blockbusters:

- 9 products from four years earlier in 2006;

- another 9 from the 2005 cohort of new product launches;

- 11 from the 2004 cohort;

- 9 from the 2003 cohort;

- 14 from the 2002 cohort.

The number of new products launched each year between 2002 and 2008 fluctuates. But we can see that about a quarter of new products are becoming half-blockbusters after four years and that after eight years this has risen to nearly half. And as I have explained (see p. 22) the average product reaches its peak some four years later at around a dozen years after launch.

How low in sales level can you go and still be profitable? Products with sales below half a billion dollars are sometimes considered to be niche products. Certainly some of these products are marketed profitably. I would suggest that the level lies somewhere between a half and a third of a billion dollars. (Remember again, that some of these third of a billion dollar products we see here at a snapshot in time will go on to higher sales levels.)

I think it is reasonable to assume that some but not all products represented here at the third of a billion dollar level will more than cover their costs during their life on the market. What proportion of products reaching this level make the rankings? It works out that in most years back from 2007, the percentage of products reaching a third of a billion dollars is around 40 per cent of the total launched, with the earliest 2002 cohort much above this at almost 70 per cent. On average, of course, products will not reach their peak for another four years, so that this percentage can be expected to rise further.

Whilst I would not expect all products registered in Table 19.1 as reaching a third of a billion dollars to turn out to eventually be profitable, I suggest that approaching half of all products *at least* are likely to become profitable. This is much greater than the 30 per cent estimated by Tufts in 2002 and very much greater than its more recent downgrading to 20 per cent.

Issues of the Distribution of Profitability

The Tufts report also had some important findings on the distribution of profitability which I too find dubious. The Tufts methodology for calculating profitability depends on a great number of different inputs, is of necessity complex and relies on numerous assumptions. The majority of these do appear reasonable to me. I discussed them in detail in a 2005 article (Ansell 2005).

The authors constructed worldwide sales profiles over the life cycle of each drug. In the 2002 survey this was for the 1990s cohort of launches in the US. They projected an in my opinion realistic 20 years of sales in the market. The mean number of years to peak sales was 10 years – somewhat less than my data on average longevity suggests is reasonable, but not seriously so. This might explain some of the discrepancy because it does not give quite long enough on average for registering sales.

But the Tufts assumptions on promotional expenditure were, I found, too conservative:

- In Year 1 on the market, promotional expenditure = sales. I think most marketing management would find this very unusual. Launches are normally into the second or third year before this is the case, even with successful products. Typically in my experience, the equivalent of 150–225 per cent of Year 1 sales is spent on promotion for an office-based, practitioner-oriented product.

- In Year 2 promotion is equal to 50 per cent of sales in that year.

- In Year 3 promotion is equal to 25 per cent of sales in that year.

I consider it likely that the last two assumptions are underestimates but I would not quibble with them.

But after Year 3, Grabowski et al. made absolutely no allocation for promotional expenditure. They retained this assumption from their earlier analyses because 'interviews with industry participants indicated that the initial post-launch years continue to be the focus of marketing and promotion activities'.

However, as I showed in my 2005 article, the reality is that leading products are being strongly promoted on average for *at least five years* post-launch. I believe this still to be the case. I showed that in quite a number of cases promotion continued at a very high level for very much longer than this. For example Lipitor (atorvastatin, Pfizer), which was first launched in the US in 1996, was still being strongly promoted there right up to the end of 2011 shortly before its patents expired. Indeed in 2011 Lipitor still topped all products in its expenditure on one promotional medium, direct-to-consumer promotion. Another leading product, Advair (salmeterol + fluticasone, GlaxoSmithKline), which was first launched in 2001 was still being strongly promoted 10 years later (*Med Ad News* 2012a). Thus Grabowski et al.'s assumptions on promotional expenditure are far from reflecting reality.

As promotion is a major area of cost (see p. 12) this must mean that margins and profitability are considerably overstated in Grabowski et al.'s study. Yet in their conclusions the authors calculated that the 1990s cohort of products generated only a modest NPV. Indeed a reduction of 3 per cent in margin would have wiped this out.

Remember also that in the 2010 Tufts follow-up report the profit situation was even more adverse, with only 20 per cent of products covering their R&D costs. Allowing for a more realistic duration of promotional expenditure, that is, not restricting promotion to the first three years on the market, would probably be enough to drag most products into loss – which again is far from the reality.

What was the reality on profitability in the 1990s and early years of this century over which period Grabowski et al. did their first calculations in 2002? It was a time when the pharmaceutical industry was doing rather well. Go back to 2000 and you find that nearly all big pharma companies had margins above 25 per cent, most in the 25 per cent to 35 per cent range and a few above this (Ansell 2001).

In their 2002 report, Grabowski et al. concluded – just as in a previous survey they conducted covering 1980s drugs – that the top 10 per cent of products by sales generated half of total profits from the 1990s cohort. Now those most successful products will be the ones that stand to be promoted the longest and at a much more substantial level than the rest. And so in failing to allow for any promotional expenditure after the first three years on the market, those bigger products are thereafter getting a 'free ride' in terms of their profitability. Thus Grabowski et al.'s apportionment of profitability across bigger and smaller products is highly suspect.

The unfortunate consequence is that those companies who have taken Grabowski et al.'s findings to heart may well have been dissuaded to an excessive extent from developing products of less than impressive size. Financial analysts' and potential investors' expectations of the industry will similarly have been deflated.

Returning to the results of my own estimations above, if we assume that at least half of all products launched eventually become profitable rather than the 20 or 30 per cent calculated by the Tufts group, that has enormous implications for what size products companies should be developing.

As I explained in Chapter 1 (see pp. 31–2) the pharmaceutical industry has a long 'tail' of medium-sized pharmaceutical products. This means that there is far greater scope for developing profitable products than current received wisdom reflecting the Tufts calculations of a decade ago suggests.

Sizing Up Profitable Products

My recommendation is therefore that in considering which drug projects to proceed with, companies should not be dissuaded from developing all but potential blockbusters – or even less than half-blockbusters. The balance of total profitability is not as heavily weighted against non-blockbusters as Grabowski et al. have suggested. I therefore believe that companies ought to take seriously some products whose forecast potential is below a half a billion dollars per annum.

There are signs that some big pharma companies such as GlaxoSmithKline now appreciate that apparently smaller or esoteric indications can reap much bigger rewards than the conventional wisdom often suggests. At Sanofi's annual press conference in February 2012, its head of R&D, Elias Zerhouni, was reported as stating that 'we are no longer in the race to find the next blockbuster'. Rather, the focus of Sanofi is on developing drugs with 'genuine medical value' and 'translational feasibility' (*Pharma Times* 2012).

Companies which take the trouble to explore less obvious therapeutic areas and indications – of which there are many – should be able to unearth profitable prospects. They will also for a time face less strong competition in those areas.

Unfortunately many companies find it difficult to deal with unfamiliar areas, and they tend to feel the need for caution when considering them. Exploring esoteric areas takes more effort. There are often no off-the-peg reports available to provide initial guidance. This approach also often involves above-average risk. But I believe strongly that this is an approach that more big pharma companies should be investigating.

PART VII

Conclusions and Summary

20

Assessing the Transformative Powers of Strategies

I don't think we can save our way out of the enormous challenge we face.
The best course is to maintain our focus on advancing our pipeline.
John Leichleiter, Chief Executive Officer, Eli Lilly & Co,
April 2012; Armstrong 2012

The Future Shape of the Pharmaceutical Industry

I have argued in several places in this book that the diversity of the pharmaceutical industry is a strength – which should if possible be maintained. Over the past 25 years to my knowledge at least, there have been expectations that its future shape would become simpler. But this never actually happens. You can see examples of this today, in particular, with the search for one elusive new business model for the industry.

There are also those who believe that the pharmaceutical industry will end up divided into two camps at opposite extremes. The views of Severin Schwan, CEO of Roche, on this were described at a 2012 industry conference as follows: 'He sees the drugs industry becoming polarized, with only companies that are truly innovative or extremely efficient makers of generic medicines being able to survive' (Hirschler and Burger 2011). Roche, of course, belongs to the former category.

The industry veteran Roy Vagelos has a rather different vision for the future, but again divides the industry into two camps: 'Looking ahead, Vagelos sees an epic battle between two contrasting visions of the industry. One is built around a model of diversification, where the big bets will no longer be placed on discovering new drugs, while in-house commitments to R&D shrink in favor of building closer ties to external players, including academia and small biotech licensees. The second is to retain a strong internal focus on drug innovation through continued emphasis on R&D as a key strategic function, with scientists at the top of the food chain' (Looney 2011).

The second camp of Vagelos is the same as Schwan's first category. But their other categories differ.

I do not see the industry dividing into two camps in either of these ways. And I believe that it will retain its current level of diversity. As I have explained in this book, big pharma is diverse in the products it markets. This is likely to continue because, as I have shown, diversity is also a feature of big pharma companies' current R&D pipelines. Companies should build on their own particular core competences. They should not adopt bland, off-the-peg strategies or attempt to imitate each other.

The Long Timescales of Pharma

As I have shown throughout this book, the sheer timescale of a pharmaceutical product's life demands strategies and planning quite different to those which may work well in other industries.

There is still a widespread lack of appreciation within the pharmaceutical industry of the sheer time that developments take to reach fruition. Over the past decade or so, there has been understandable disappointment with the returns from enabling technologies, sometimes to the point where companies have pulled out of what later turned out to be productive technologies.

Of course, some technologies will inevitably be found wanting and need to be abandoned. But there needs to be more understanding within pharma that things usually take much longer than originally expected before they start generating a return. If big pharma companies cannot tolerate this state of affairs, then they should perhaps be considering diversification into lower-risk industries, which might well, of course, also bring them lower returns. There are some signs that the recent vogue for diversification is already beginning to show – as in the past – that the grass is not often greener on the other side.

Which Strategies Make Most Sense for the Future?

In this book I have considered a full range of alternative strategies that a big pharma company can take. Some companies – GlaxoSmithKline most notably – have over recent years been exploring practically the whole range of these strategies. Perhaps this is an imaginative approach, but it could also be described as a scattergun policy. Since 2007, when Sir Andrew Witty was appointed CEO, GlaxoSmithKline has:

- reduced the scale of research to much smaller units with the aim of improving new product productivity;

- increased its efforts in R&D in new therapeutic areas and indications whilst dropping others the company has considered less likely to be productive, notably within CNS;

- increased its presence in developing territories;

- bought into generics – particularly in developing countries;

- acquired rights to some additional OTC brands whilst divesting others;

- acquired a variety of different types of small- or medium-sized pharmaceutical companies;

- formed new alliances (including multicompany alliances) with other companies in the pharmaceutical industry as well as with outsiders;

- strengthened its venture capital arm.

As one of the largest pharmaceutical companies, GlaxoSmithKline has the luxury of being able to try out such a wide range of different strategies. Not all big pharma companies can afford such a wide range of experimentation. There is also the danger of giving insufficient attention to the most promising strategies. As I show below, there are ominous signs that this is already happening as far as effort on R&D is concerned.

New Product Trends

Sometimes it is difficult when working within an industry to discern long-term trends. I have argued in this book that there is good evidence of a recovery in new product productivity which is working its way through now to the most advanced stages of development. I believe that this trend is sufficiently powerful by itself to transform big pharma and is the most obvious route for big pharma to do so. I have also argued that new products are likely on average to be of better quality than in the past – that is, in terms of their commercial potential. But big pharma companies will need to recognize this quickly and start to take advantage of the increasing scale of future opportunities whilst they exist. They will need to shift the balance of their support back to earlier stage development rather than just focussing on the late stage projects. If they do not, the currently healthy numbers of pre-clinical and early-stage clinical projects will soon start to dwindle.

Declining Big Pharma Pipelines

According to Pharmaprojects® Citeline, in 2012 seven of the Top 10 companies had fewer projects in their R&D pipelines than in 2011 (Pharmaprojects® Citeline 2012). The 1,880 projects that these companies were developing in 2012 accounted for 18.0 per cent of all projects in development. This represented a decline from the 20.3 per cent they accounted for in the previous year.

Obviously if big pharma companies are to take advantage of the increasing productivity of biotech and smaller pharmaceutical companies, then they have to ensure that they have rights to a good share of the intellectual property in development. This disconcerting drop in their pipeline share suggests that a number of big pharma companies no longer have their eyes on the main chance.

Big pharma is still currently more interested in pursuing other, diversionary strategies and in short-term economies – including in R&D. This dangerous trend is underlined by data showing that in 2012, whilst the total R&D expenditure of the pharmaceutical industry grew by 4.5 per cent over the previous year, Top 10 pharma company R&D expenditure grew by only 1.6 per cent (Cacciotti 2012). Not all big pharma companies have followed this trend: Roche, for example, is committed to a stable R&D budget.

Not surprisingly given the variety of the other strategies it is pursuing, GlaxoSmithKline has been slightly deemphasizing R&D over the past few years. The number of products in its R&D pipeline fell from 289 in 2010, to 269 in 2011 and 257 in 2012 (Pharmaprojects® Citeline 2011a, 2012). I contend that this does not make sense in an era when an increasing number of products are in development – and rights to an increasing number are becoming available.

I see it as vital that big pharma steps up its interest in acquiring rights to intellectual property from start-up companies and other sources. This has faltered over the past couple of years. With other lines of financial support, particularly venture capital, being severely constrained in recent years, many of the products in early development will sooner rather than later need financial support. If they do not get it from big pharma or elsewhere, promising products will founder. They will not have the chance of further development and never emerge from the drug development 'Valley of Death'.

By 2012 some 20 pharmaceutical companies had set up their own venture funds – far more than only a few years ago and one encouraging sign that the pharmaceutical industry does realize the increasing importance of adequate funding of earlier-stage projects.

To put a more aggressive slant on the situation, because of the healthy number of projects which are going to be available from start-up companies, and the likely strong need of many of their developers for partners to progress them, there is nothing to stop a big pharma company from consciously deciding to grab more than its 'fair share'.

This will naturally require yet more licensing effort. Big pharma companies may balk at stepping up an activity that most think they have been expanding sufficiently over the past couple of decades. But stepping up licensing further would be a relatively inexpensive measure.

However, because the vast majority of intellectual property acquired will by no means be in ready-to-market form, this also means that big pharma will have to cater for the additional, advanced-stage R&D involved in developing greater numbers of projects. This will involve substantial additional expenditure. No doubt big pharma companies will need to reconsider some of the more peripheral activities they have got involved with over the past few years if they are to afford this. And inevitably there will be a gap before the resulting new products start to make a substantial impact on the sales and profits of companies.

How would this fit with other strategies?

Developing Countries

New products don't tend to get early or wide distribution in developing countries. So expansion there may not be particularly helpful in exploiting them. Whilst it is sensible for big pharma companies to continue to develop their presence in developing countries to benefit from the growth of these markets, margins are often much lower than in developed countries. This strategy can make some significant contribution to total corporate profits of a big pharma company but it cannot be expected to do more than that.

Developing countries themselves are, as I have argued, likely to develop only a very modest number of novel products with global potential. But when they succeed, this is more often likely to represent an opportunity than a threat, since the developers will commonly need a big pharma company partner to fully exploit such products.

Diversification Strategies

My main conclusion on the wide variety of diversification strategies is that rather too many of them are blind alleys, and at worst snakes rather than ladders. Also, many types of diversification do not individually represent big enough opportunities to make a substantial impact on the bottom line of a big pharma company. Even a range of diversifications may not add up to much in this respect.

Diversifications can make particular sense if they add to a particular area of expertise the company already has. Thus Roche exerts enormous efforts to build up diagnostics, through alliances and a very active acquisition strategy, because it has therapeutic products, particularly for cancer, which require complementary diagnostics if they are to succeed.

But most attempts at diversification do not have such obvious synergies. And once a company starts to diversify away from pharmaceuticals it is straying into areas where profit margins are often substantially lower than in pharmaceuticals. Moreover, a great deal of management time is likely to be diverted away from the mainstream pharmaceutical business.

Megamergers

There has been no megamerger mania for several years now. The consensus has formed that they do not work. The idea – once widely advanced – that they promote R&D productivity is not far short of risible. However, if two companies deficient in new products and with a dwindling range of marketed products do decide to merge purely as consolidation, then that might still make good sense. It may provide some temporary solution to a lack of new products.

Generics

I fear for companies which have embarked on the latest round of diversification into generics. Remember the 1990s experience! And now the situation is about to get worse. For we have far more companies competing in generics than at that time. This means more competition, lower prices and lower profit margins. Also, the end of the patent cliff is nigh, so that any company now in generics will be competing for a decreasing number of products as they come off patent. No wonder that several leading generics companies are stepping up their efforts in novel drug R&D.

Other Strategies within Pharma

Other strategies closer to home are of mixed relevance to big pharma companies. Biosimilars are probably too small an opportunity except perhaps in the very long term. Orphan drugs could make more sense, and there is probably room for a few more big pharma companies to enter this area.

The Longer Term

What of the longer term? Some commentators consider that as more and more drugs reach the market, the scope for improving therapy has become less and that eventually there will be little scope left for new drugs. I believe this is fallacious. Whilst it is true that some indications such as hypertension and ulcers are now well provided for, there is still vast scope in many for improving therapy. I am not alone in believing this.

John LaMattina recently considered that 'there are still major medical needs that exist for problems like cancer, Alzheimer's, atherosclerosis, diabetes and resistant infections. There are also a host of other needs in orphan diseases, diseases of the emerging world, and even for areas, like depression and pain, where drugs already exist but where improvements are needed' (LaMattina 2012).

Later in 2012, the US President's Council of Advisors on Science and Technology (PCAST) issued a report which also put this issue in perspective: 'Despite major breakthroughs for some diseases, many of the most common human diseases are not effectively treated by existing therapies' (PCAST 2011).

PCAST members went on to cite a whole range of inadequately treated diseases. They pointed out that many common types of cancer, including lung, colon, breast and prostate cancer, are incurable once they have metastasized. Also, heart disease and stroke remain leading causes of mortality despite advances in treatment. Infectious diseases remain an important challenge with the emergence of antibiotic-resistant bacteria and multi-drug-resistant tuberculosis, and new viral pandemics may cause widespread mortality. Also psychiatric diseases remain a tremendous burden on society, with existing treatments having limited efficacy, particularly for Alzheimer's disease.

According to the PCAST report, 96 per cent of orphan diseases lack effective therapies. There are approximately 8,000 recognized orphan diseases, and as I have already mentioned, some 250 new orphan diseases are being identified each year.

The PCAST report recommended aiming at *doubling* over the next decade the rate of invention of innovative new medicines for patients, whilst at the same time increasing drug safety. It did not say how many drugs currently being successfully developed it considers are innovative and thereby further quantify this. But this is a refreshingly challenging target that may help to lift the sights of the pharmaceutical industry.

The Transformation of Big Pharma

To transform a company is no easy task. It involves changing its culture as well as adopting new strategies. Perhaps three-quarters of all attempts are failures.

However, the opportunity which exists now to transform big pharma does not actually involve disruption or radical transformation. It requires instead a stepping up of emphasis on new product acquisition and development. This means that the chances of this transformation being successful should be much higher than with more radical ones.

Naturally the world has been changing. As PwC has recently succinctly put it: 'The commercial environment is getting harsher. Healthcare payers are imposing new cost constraints on providers and are scrutinizing the value of medicines more carefully. They want new therapies that are clinically and economically better than the existing alternatives, together with hard, real-world outcomes data to back any claims about a medicine's superiority' (PwC 2012b).

Along the same lines, Ben Comer of *Pharmaceutical Executive* has recently come to the following conclusions: 'The irony is that, even with the resolution of the so-called crisis in R&D and a return to a more productive pipeline, the industry must still confront a gradual but irrevocable erosion of control over access and pricing for these "next generation" products' (Comer 2012b).

No one would suggest that new products will be accepted as easily in the future as they have been in the past. Companies have to be more astute in the types of products they bring to the market and how they market them. But I believe this is already happening. And so the more big pharma companies strive to acquire rights to a good share of these upcoming new products, the better their chances will be of transforming themselves into companies that will survive and prosper.

Transforming Big Pharma in a Nutshell

The pharmaceutical industry differs strikingly from other industries. This has a major impact on the strategies which work in pharmaceuticals and those which do not. Long development timescales in particular have a broad-ranging impact.

The distinctive characteristics of the pharmaceutical industry mean that management concepts from outside the industry are applicable to varying extents. Occasionally they are more applicable than they are to other industries.

But often pharma companies would do better to concentrate on analysing the factors involved in an issue in depth rather than relying on management concepts.

After decades of focussing down on pharmaceuticals and the divesting of other activities, there has been a new trend for several years now for big pharma to diversify. This is only infrequently likely to be any more successful than it was when attempted in the past.

Megamergers have generally been unsuccessful, and their role should be a limited one. Smaller mergers can make more sense, particularly in acquiring products or enabling technologies.

Big pharma has been right to increase its presence in emerging countries. However, companies in these countries are unlikely to be the source of many novel products with global potential. The US is well set to increase its presence further in pharmaceuticals, in particular as a source of new products.

The number of new products reaching the market in future will continue its recent rise, albeit with fluctuations. Factors that have contributed to increased attrition rates, particularly over the past decade, are likely to stabilize. Also the serious increase in attrition rates at the preregistration phase in the US has gone into reverse. This will help to boost the number of new products reaching the market. Meanwhile, the average quality of new products looks to be improving, and this should benefit their commercial potential.

The industry needs to heed that forecasting methodologies still in use have in the past often tended to grossly underestimate eventual sales. Also standard figures cited on profitability considerably underestimate the proportion of products that turn out to be profitable. Both sources of underestimation unjustly undermine the confidence of big pharma and investors in the future prospects of the industry and the extent to which they are prepared to invest in it.

The surest route to transforming the prospects of big pharma companies is to step up activity in acquiring and developing new products. This is now realistic because the amount of intellectual property available is much greater than it was a decade ago. No other strategies have sufficient transformative powers, though they may be useful as a stopgap pending the maturation of forthcoming new product sales.

Appendix:
Measuring Global Longevity

I have applied in this book a methodology to calculate average product longevity (that is time to peak global sales) which I developed and then used to calculate global product longevity in a series of publications (Ansell 2000, 2002, 2004, 2008). With this methodology I use only data available at the time to measure longevity and do not consider any data in subsequent years.

For example, sales of the lipid-altering product Zetia (ezetimibe, formerly Schering-Plough; now Merck & Co) first peaked after five years on the market in 2007. Therefore despite the fact that Zetia resumed growth and has overtaken this peak and sales were still rising in 2011, for the 2007 Top 50 products I continued to consider that it peaked in that year in any later consideration of the 2007 cohort. Measuring longevity in this way ensures consistency in comparing cohorts of top 50 products from different years, though it does lead to slight underestimation of true longevity.

The source of sales rankings for this report is annual editions of giving top product rankings. I have analyzed the annual sales and rankings produced by this magazine since 1993. These rankings have included each year the global sales of at least the top 100 products and in some years as many as 500. Since 2001 only the top 200 products have been ranked. My calculations now cover the top 50 products for every year between 1994 and 2011. In assessing whether and when products have peaked, in the few situations where this has been unclear, I considered data from additional sources, opting whenever possible for data provided by the company marketing the product in question. Also, when sales peak and remain at the same level in the following year, I take the first year as the peak year.

All sales data by *Med Ad News* are expressed in dollars. After a long period of relative stability, the US dollar weakened against other major currencies in the early years of this century but is now approximately back to where it was 10–15 years ago. As sales are quoted in dollars, when this currency was relatively weaker against others, this could for some products in some cases extend longevities of products when this would not have been the case if calculations had been made at constant exchange rates. I believe that this factor has had a very modest impact on my calculations. Principally this is because around 60 per cent of global sales of products are in the US. For example, for leading products in 2011 the percentages were: Lipitor 62 per cent, Advair 53 per cent, Plavix 73 per cent, Crestor 55 per cent, Nexium 79 per cent.

I concentrate on brands rather than active compounds. Thus, EPO (epoetin alfa) was represented both by Amgen's Epogen and by Johnson & Johnson's Procrit in the 2006 global top 50 product rankings. With the dwindling in the popularity of co-marketing deals, this has gradually reduced in importance as a factor in analysing Top 50 cohorts.

Although I consider a product's launch year to be its first year in its first country of launch, there have been a very few exceptions. For example, metformin was marketed outside the United States by its originator, Merck KGaA, from the late 1950s. In the 1990s it become a success again in the United States as Bristol-Myers Squibb's Glucophage. Because the originator's brand had not had major sales for many years, I considered that Glucophage's life began with its US launch in 1995 rather than 40 years earlier. There have been no similar examples like this in recent years.

Calculating Average Global Longevity

The methodology used for the Top 50 product cohorts is illustrated by the calculations for the 2011 cohort. The 18 products in Tables A.1 and A.2 that had already peaked have a longevity ranging between five and 22 years – a difference of greater than a factor of four. The average number of years that these products took to peak was 10.7 years. ('+' in Tables A.1 and A.2 indicates that a product has yet to peak.)

A further step is necessary to calculate a more realistic average time to peak sales. I therefore then consider those products in the top 50 cohort whose sales have not yet peaked. In the case of my calculation for 2011, the longevities of 12 other products that have already exceeded the 10.7 years average of the peaked products in the cohort. When I added in these 12 products, conservatively incorporating into the calculation the number of years they have been growing so far, I arrived at an average longevity for 2011 of 12.7 years.

Table A.1 Longevity of the top 25 global best-selling products (2011)

Current Ranking	Main Product Names	Generic Name	Main Companies Marketing	Year of 1st Launch	Year of Peak Sales	Years to Peak Sales
1	Lipitor	atorvastatin	Pfizer, Astellas	1997	2006	9
2	Plavix, Iscover	clopidogrel	Bristol-Myers Squibb, Sanofi–Aventis	1998	not reached	13+
3	Remicade	infliximab	Johnson & Johnson	1998	not reached	13+
4	Humira	adalimumab	Abbott	2003	not reached	7+
5	Advair, Seretide	fluticasone + salmeterol	GlaxoSmithKline	1999	2010	11
6	Enbrel	etanercept	Amgen, Pfizer	1998	not reached	13+
7	Crestor	rosuvastatin	AstraZeneca, Shionogi	2003	not reached	8+
8	Rituxan/MabThera	rituximab	Roche, Biogen Idec	1997	not reached	13
9	Seroquel	quetiapine	AstraZeneca, Astellas	1997	not reached	14+
10	Avastin	bevacizumab	Roche	2004	2010	6
11	Herceptin	trastuzumab	Roche	1998	2010	12
12	Diovan range, Co-Diovan	valsartan	Novartis	1996	2010	14
13	Singulair	montelukast	Merck & Co	1997	not reached	14+
14	Lantus	insulin glargine	Sanofi Aventis	2000	not reached	11+
15	Abilify	aripiprazole	Otsuka, Bristol-Myers Squibb	2002	2009	9+
16	Gleevec, Gleevec	imatinib	Novartis	2001	not reached	10+
17	Zyprexa	olanzapine	Lilly	1996	2010	14
18	Nexium	esomeprazole	AstraZeneca	2000	2007	7
19	Spiriva	tiotropium	Boehringer Ingelheim	2002	not reached	9+
20	Cymbalta	duloxetine	Eli Lilly	2004	not reached	7+
21	Copaxone	glatiramer	Teva, Sanofi Aventis	1997	not reached	14+
22	Prevnar	pneumococcal vaccine	Pfizer	2000	not reached	11+
23	Atacand/Blopress	candesartan	AstraZeneca, Takeda	1997	2008	11
24	Neulasta	pegfilgrastim	Amgen	2002	not reached	9+
25	Lucentis	ranibizumab	Roche, Novartis	2006	not reached	5+

Source: John Ansell Consultancy, based on *Med Ad News* data (*Med Ad News* 1994–2011), company data and other sources

Table A.2   Longevity of the global best-selling products (2011), ranked nos 26–50

Current Ranking	Main Product Names	Generic Name	Main Companies Marketing	Year of 1st Launch	Year of Peak Sales	Years to Peak Sales
26 Lyrica		pregabalin	Pfizer	2004	not reached	6+
27 Januvia		sitagliptin	Novartis	2006	not reached	5+
28 Actos		pioglitazone	Takeda	1999	2008	9
29 Symbicort		budesonide, formoterol	AstraZeneca, Astellas	2000	not reached	11+
30 Micardis		telmisartan	Boehringer Ingelheim, Astellas	1999	not reached	12+
31 Lexapro, Cipralex		escitalopram	Forest, Lundbeck	2002	2010	8
32 Atripla		efavirenz, emtricitabine	Gilead	2006	not reached	5+
33 Revlimid		lenalidomide	Celgene	2006	not reached	5+
34 Benicar/Olmetec, Benicar HCT		olmesartan	Daiichi Sankyo	2002	not reached	9+
35 Oxycontin		oxycodone	Purdue, Mundipharma, Shionogi	1996	2010	14
36 Avapro, Aprovel, Avalide		irbesartan	Sanofi Aventis, Bristol-Myers Squibb	1997	2010	13
37 Lovenox, Clexane		enoxaparin	Sanofi Aventis	1987	2009	22
38 Celebrex		celecoxib	Pfizer	1999	not reached	12+
39 Truvada		tenofovir, emtricitabine	Gilead	2004	not reached	7+
40 Avonex		interferon beta-1a	Biogen Idec	1996	1996	15+
41 Zetia		ezetimibe	Merck & Co, Schering-Plough	2002	2007	9+
42 AcipHex, Pariet		rabeprazole	Eisai, Johnson & Johnson	1998	2007	9
43 Alimta		pemetrexed	Eli Lilly	2004	not reached	7+
44 NovoLog/Novo Rapid		insulin aspart	Novo Nordisk	1999	not reached	12+
45 Humalog		insulin lispro	Eli Lilly	1996	not reached	15+
46 Rebif		interferon beta-1a	Merck Serono	1997	not reached	14+
47 Aranesp		darbepoetin alfa	Amgen	2001	2006	5
48 Lupron/Leuplide		leuprolide	Takeda, Abbott	1984	not reached	27+
49 Aricept		donepezil	Eisai, Pfizer	1997	2009	12
50 Epogen		epoetin alfa	Amgen	1988	2004	16

Source: John Ansell Consultancy, based on *Med Ad News* data (*Med Ad News* 1994–2011), company data and other sources

References

Ansell, J. 1988. Dispelling the Myth of the Product Life Cycle. *Pharmaceutical Executive*, 8(3), 38–42.

Ansell, J. 1996. Mega-Mergers Reconsidered: Critical Consequences of Becoming too Big. In *Spectrum – Pharmaceutical Industry Dynamics*. Waltham, MA: Decision Resources, Inc.

Ansell, J. 2000. More Mileage Than Meets the Eye: Revealing True Product Potential and Its Impact. In *Spectrum – Pharmaceutical Industry Dynamics*. Waltham, MA: Decision Resources, Inc.

Ansell, J. 2001. Taking the Real Measure of Pharma's Prospects. *Scrip Magazine*, 101, 21–3; 102, 27–31; 103, 11–13.

Ansell, J. 2002. Getting to Grips with Declining Product Life Span. In *Spectrum – Pharmaceutical Industry Dynamics*. Waltham, MA: Decision Resources, Inc.

Ansell, J. 2004. Determining Pharmaceutical Products' Staying Power. In *Spectrum – Pharmaceutical Industry Dynamics*. Waltham, MA: Decision Resources, Inc.

Ansell, J. 2005. Putting Promotion in Perspective In *Spectrum Pharmaceutical Industry Dynamics,* Waltham, MA: Decision Resources, Inc.

Ansell, J. 2006. Blockbusters Are Alive and Well: Why Their Numbers Continue to Rise. In *Spectrum – Pharmaceutical Industry Dynamics*. Waltham, MA: Decision Resources, Inc.

Ansell, J. 2008. Product Life Spans: Trends in the Quality and Staying Power of New Products. In *Spectrum – Pharmaceutical Industry Dynamics*. Waltham, MA: Decision Resources, Inc.

Ansell, J. 2009. Trends in the Therapeutic Area Focus of Leading Pharmaceutical Companies: A New Survey. *Business Development & Licensing Journal*, 8, 7–13.

Ansell, J. 2011. Product Pipeline Trends Bring New Optimism. *Business Development & Licensing Journal*, 16, 24–7.

Ansell, J. and Minter, B. 2002. Product Crowding in the Cancer Market. *Scrip Magazine*, 110 (March), 6–9.

Apothecurry. 2012. 1 August. Available at: http://apothecurry.wordpress.com/2012/08/01/5-takeaways-from-quintiles-media-round-table-on-biosimilars/ [accessed: 14 December 2012].

Armstrong, D. 2012. Eli Lilly CEO Says Cost Cutting Won't Solve Drug Sales Loss. *Bloomberg* April 12. Available at: http://www.bloomberg.com/news/2012-04-12/eli-lilly-ceo-says-cost-cutting-won-t-solve-drug-revenue-losses.html [accessed: 20 December 2012].

Arrowsmith, J. 2011a. Trial Watch: Phase III and Submission Failures: 2007–2010. *Nature Reviews Drug Discovery*, 10, 87. Available at: http://www.nature.com/nrd/journal/v10/n2/full/nrd3375.html [accessed: 24 December 2012].

Arrowsmith. J. 2011b. Trial Watch: Phase II Failures: 2008–2010. *Nature Reviews Drug Discovery*, 10, 328–29. Available at: http://www.nature.com/nrd/journal/v10/n5/full/nrd3439.html [accessed: 16 December 2012].

Arrowsmith. J. 2012. From the Analyst's Couch. A Decade of Change. *Nature Reviews Drug Discovery*, 10, 328–9. Available at: http://www.nature.com/nrd/journal/v11/n1/full/nrd3630.html [accessed: 24 December 2012].

Berggren, R., Møller, M., Moss, R., Poda, P. and Smietana, K. 2012. Outlook for the Next 5 Years in Drug Innovation. *Nature Reviews Drug Discovery* 11, 435–6.

BIO. 2011. *BIO / BioMedTracker Clinical Trial Success Rates Study, BIO CEO & Investor Conference*. New York: Bio Biotechnology Industry Organization. Available at: http://www.biotech–now.org/wp–content/uploads/2011/02/bio–ceo–biomedtracker–bio–study–handout–final–2–15–2011.pdf [accessed: 14 December 2012].

Boger, J. 2012. To Boost R&D, Stop Flying Blind and Start Observing. In *Beyond Borders, Global Biotechnology Report*. Ernst & Young, 22–23. Available at: http://www.ey.com/Publication/vwLUAssets/Beyond_borders_2012/$FILE/Beyond_borders_2012.pdf [accessed: 14 December 2012].

Cacciotti, J. and Clinton, P. 2012. *Pharm Exec 50: Growth from the Bottom Up*, May. Available at: http://www.pharmexec.com/pharmexec/article/articleDetail.jsp?id=773562 [accessed: 16 December 2012].

Castellani, J. 2012. John J. Castellani National Press Club Remarks. 20 September. Available at: http://phrma.org/news-media/speeches/john-j-castellani-national-press-club-remarks [accessed: 16 December 2012].

Chatterjee, B. and Kwan, C. 2012. Doing Business in China – Considerations for Effectively Leveraging Emerging Markets. *Pharmaceutical Processing*. Available at: http://www.pharmpro.com/articles/2012/08/newsletter-Doing-Business-in-China/ [accessed: 20 December 2012].

Christensen, C., Grossman, J.H. and Hwang, J. 2009. *The Innovator's Prescription*. New York: McGraw-Hill.

CIM 2012. Chartered Institute of Marketing. Available at: http://www.cim.co.uk/marketingplanningtool/intro.asp [accessed: 1 January 2013].

CMR. 2012. The CMR International Pharmaceutical R&D Factbook 2011. *CMR International*. Available at: http://thomsonreuters.com/products_services/science/science_products/a–z/cmr_factbook/ [accessed: 14 December 2012].

CMR International. 1970–2000. Annual Assessments of New Product First Launches from a Variety of CMR Reports.

Comer, B. 2012a. Clayton Christensen on the Future of Pharma. *Pharmaceutical Executive*. Available at: http://blog.pharmexec.com/2012/05/11/clayton-christensen-on-the-future-of-pharma/ [accessed: 16 November 2012].

Comer, B. 2012b. *Pharm Exec's 2013 Pipeline Report*. Available at: http://www.pharmexec.com/pharmexec/article/articleDetail.jsp?id=796504 [accessed: 2 January 2013].

Cooper, R. 2011. GlaxoSmithKline chief Andrew Witty an 'Extreme Bull' on Emerging Markets. *The Daily Telegraph*, 27 October. Available at: http://www.telegraph.co.uk/finance/newsbysector/pharmaceuticalsand chemicals/8851599/GlaxoSmithKline-chief-Andrew-Witty-an-extreme-bull-on-emerging-markets.html [accessed: 14 December 2012].

CSDD. 2011a. *Number of Monoclonal Antibody Products in Development Continues to Increase*. Available at: http://csdd.tufts.edu/news/complete_story/pr_ir_nov–dec_2011 [accessed: 20 December 2012].

CSDD. 2011b. *Lack of Clinically Useful Diagnostics Hinder Growth in Personalized Medicines*. Available at: http://csdd.tufts.edu/news/complete_story/pr_ir_jul–aug_2011 [accessed: 20 December 2012].

Danzon, P., Nicholson, S. and Sousa Pereira, N. 2003. Productivity in Pharmaceutical-Biotechnology R&D: The Role of Experience and Alliances. *NBER Working Papers*, 9615.

Denyer, S. 2012. India's Manufacturing Hits Brick Wall as Economy Slows. *Washington Post*, 31 May. Available at: http://www.washingtonpost.com/world/asia_pacific/indias-manufacturing-hits-brick-wall-as-economy-slows/2012/05/31/gJQAlYar4U_story.html [accessed: 20 December 2012].

DeVol, R.C., Bedroussian, A. and Yeo, B. 2011. The Global Biomedical Industry: Preserving U.S. Leadership. *Milken Institute*. Available at http://www.milkeninstitute.org/pdf/CASMIFullReport.pdf [accessed: 14 December 2012].

Diaceutics. 2011. *Pharma Readiness for Personalized Medicine*. Available at: http://www.diaceutics.com/ [accessed: 20 December 2012].

Diamond, J. 1997. *Guns, Germs and Steel: A Short History of Everybody for the Last 17,000 Years*. London: Jonathan Cape.

Diamond, J. 2012. What Makes Countries Rich or Poor. *New York Review of Books*, 26 May.

DiMasi, J. A. and Faden, L. B. 2011. Competitiveness in Follow-on Drug R&D: A Race or Imitation? *Nature Reviews Drug Discovery*, 10(1), 23–7.

Economy Rankings. 2012. *The World Bank*. Available at: http://www. doingbusiness.org/rankings [accessed: 14 December 2012].

EphMRA. 2011. Anatomical Classification Guidelines V2012, © EphMRA. Availableat:http://www.ephmra.org/classification/anatomical-classification. aspx [accessed: 24 December 2012].

Ernst & Young. 2012. *Beyond Borders, Global Biotechnology Report 2012*. Available at: http://www.ey.com/GL/en/Industries/Life-Sciences/Beyond-borders--- global-biotechnology-report-2012 [accessed: 20 December 2012].

EvaluatePharma World Preview 2018. 2012 Available at: http://www. evaluatepharma.com/worldpreview2018.aspx [accessed: 14 December 2012].

FDA. 2005. *Critical Path Initiative: History, Objectives, Approach*. Available at: http://www.fda.gov/oc/criticalpath/presentations [accessed: 16 December 2012].

FDA. 2012. *FY 2012 Innovative Drug Approvals. Bringing Life-Saving Drugs to Patients Quickly and Efficiently*. Available at: http://www.fda.gov/ downloads/aboutfda/reportsmanualsforms/reports/ucm330859.pdf [accessed: 20 December 2012].

Fenby, J., 2012. *Tiger Head, Snake Tails*. London: Simon & Shuster.

Frontline. 2006. The Age of AIDS, Interview Margaret Heckler. *Frontline*. 30 May. Available at: http://www.pbs.org/wgbh/pages/frontline/aids/interviews/ heckler.html [accessed: 28 December 2012].

Grabowski, H, Vernon, J. and DiMasi, J. 2002. Returns on Research and Development for 1990s New Drug Introductions. *Pharmacoeconomics*, Supplement 3, 11–29.

Grabowski, H. and Kyle, M. 2012. Mergers, Acquisitions, and Alliances. In *The Oxford Handbook of the Economics of the Biopharmaceutical Industry*, ed. Danzon, P. and Nicholson, S. Oxford: Oxford University Press.

Grogan, K. 2011a. Beware Hype over Biomarkers, Says Daiichi Sankyo Cancer Boss. *Pharma Times*. 17 October. Available at: http://www.pharmatimes.com/ article/11-10-17/Beware_hype_over_biomarkers_says_Daiichi_Sankyo_ cancer_boss.aspx [accessed: 31 December 2012].

Grogan, K. 2011B. Tough 2012 for Pharma but Industry Still Rated Highly. *Pharma Times*. 15 December. Available at: http://www.pharmatimes.com/ article/11-12-15/Tough_2012_for_pharma_but_industry_still_rated_highly. aspx [accessed: 2 January 2013].

Grogan, K. 2012. The Spirit of Discovery. *Pharmaceutical Times*, 4, 23–5.

Harrill, S. 2011. Lilly's Decentralized Global Launch Strategy. *PharmExecBlog*. Available at: http://blog.pharmexec.com/2011/12/07/lillys-decentralized- global-launch-strategy/ [accessed: 20 December 2012].

Hassan, F. 2013. *reinvent. A Leaders Playbook for Serial Success*. Hoboken, NJ: Jossey-Bass. Available at: http://www.josseybass.com.

Hindle, T. 2008. *Guide to Management Ideas and Gurus*. London: *The Economist* in association with Profile Books Ltd.

Hirschler, B. and Burger, L. 2011. Big Pharma Gets a Driving Lesson from Carmakers. *Reuters*. Available at: http://in.reuters.com/article/2011/12/14/pharmaceuticals-autos-idINDEE7BD0AI20111214 [accessed: 30 December 2012].

Hoffman, D. 2011. Downsizing Trend Leaves Pharma Without the Kinds of Employees It Needs. *Pharmalot.com*. Available at: http://www.pharmalot.com/2011/09/op-ed-pharma-layoffs-small-minded-survivors/ [accessed: 16 December 2012].

ICD-10. 2010. *International Classification of Diseases*. Available at: http://apps.who.int/classifications/icd10/browse/2010/en [accessed: 16 December 2012].

ICIS. 2003. *US Pharmaceuticals May See Revival in 2003*. Available at: http://www.icis.com/Articles/2003/01/03/187433/us-pharmaceuticals-may-see-revival-in-2003.html [accessed: 2 January 2013].

ICIS. 2004. *FDA Approves the First Angiogenesis Inhibitor for the Cancer*. Available at: http://www.icis.com/Articles/2004/03/04/562583/fda-approves-the-first-angiogenesis-inhibitor-for-the-cancer.html [accessed: 16 December 2012].

IMS. 2012a. *The Use of Medicines in the United States: Review of 2011*. Available at: http://www.imshealth.com/ims/Global/Content/Insights/IMS%20Institute%20for%20Healthcare%20Informatics/IHII_Medicines_in_U.S_Report_2011.pdf.

IMS. 2012b. *Total US Promotional Spend by Type, 2011*. Available at: http://www.imshealth.com/deployedfiles/ims/Global/Content/Corporate/Press%20Room/Top-Line%20Market%20Data%20&%20Trends/2011%20Top-line%20Market%20 Data/Global_Pharma_Market_by_Spending_2003-2011.pdf [accessed: 16 December 2012].

IMS. 2012c. The Global Use of Medicines: Outlook Through 2016, IMS Market Prognosis, *IMS Institute for Healthcare Informatics*. Available at: http://www.imshealth.com/deployedfiles/ims/Global/Content/Insights/IMS%20Institute%20for%20Healthcare%20Informatics/Global%20Use%20of%20Meds%202011/Medicines_Outlook_Through_2016_Report.pdf [accessed: 14 December 2012].

IMS. 2012d. *Total Unaudited and Audited Global Pharmaceutical Market, 2003 – 2011*. Available at: http://www.imshealth.com/deployedfiles/ims/Global/Content/Corporate/Press%20Room/Top-Line%20Market%20Data%20&%20Trends/2011%20Top-line%20Market%20Data/Global_Pharma_Market_by_Spending_2003-2011.pdf [accessed: 24 December 2012].

IMS Health. 2012. *Top Line Market Data, Top 20 Global Products, 2011*. Available at: http://www.imshealth.com/deployedfiles/ims/Global/Content/Corporate/Press%20Room/Top-Line%20Market%20Data%20&%20Trends/Top_20_Global_Products.pdf [accessed: 14 December 2012].

In Vivo. 1997. 15(11), 26–36. Windhover Information Inc.

Informa. 2001–2011. Annual assessments of new products by various Informa publications over the period, including *Scrip Magazine, Scrip*, Citeline and Pharmaprojects®.

innovation.org. 2012a. *Medical Research in the U.S. Outpaces the Rest of the World*. Available at: http://www.innovation.org/index.cfm/search [accessed: 24 December 2012].

innovation.org 2012b. *The Biopharmaceutical Research and Development Enterprise: Growth Platforms for Economies Around the World*. Available at: http://www.innovation.org/index.cfm/newscenter/FeaturedStudies?Year=2012&NID=82 [accessed: 16 December 2012].

Interbrand. 2011. Best Global Brands. Available at: http://www.interbrand.com/en/best-global-brands/best-global-brands-2008/best-global-brands-2011.aspx [accessed: 16 October 2011].

James, B. 2003. Big Pharma: The Beginning of the End or the End of the Beginning? In *Spectrum, Pharmaceutical Industry Dynamics*. Waltham, MA: Decision Resources, Inc.

Jones Lang LaSalle 2012. *Life Sciences Cluster Report. Global. 2011*. Available at: http://www.joneslanglasalle.co.uk/ResearchLevel1/Global_Life%20Sciences%20Cluster%20Report_2011_gb.pdf [accessed: 20 December 2012].

Kay, J. 2007. Leaders Should Say Goodbye to Their Haloes. *Financial Times*, 8 May. Available at: http://www.johnkay.com/2007/05/08/leaders-should-say-goodbye-to-their-haloes [accessed: 14 December 2012].

LaMattina, J. 2011. The Impact of Mergers on Pharmaceutical R&D. *Nature Reviews Drug Discovery*, 10, 559–60.

LaMattina, J. 2012. There Never Has Really Been 'Low Hanging Fruit' in Pharma R&D. *Forbes Pharma & Healthcare*, 2 March. Available at: http://www.forbes.com/sites/johnlamattina/2012/03/02/there-has-never-really-been-low-hanging-fruit-in-pharma-rd/ [accessed: 16 December 2012].

Lemos, G. 2012. *The End of the Chinese Dream: Why Chinese People Fear the Future*. Princeton, NJ: Yale University Press.

Liebowitz, J. 2006. *Strategic Intelligence*. Boca Raton, New York: Auerbach Publications.

Lloyd, I. 2004. *R&D Timelines*. Business day, IBC Drug Discovery Technology Conference, London.

Looney, W. 2011. P. Roy Vagelos: Getting to No. 1 – and Staying There, *Pharmaceutical Executive*, 10(31), 50. Available at: http://www.pharmexec. com/pharmexec/P-Roy-Vagelos-Getting-to-No-1mdashand-Staying-Ther/ ArticleStandard/Article/detail/744335 [accessed: 16 December 2012].

Macarron, M. et al. 2011. Impact of High-Throughput Screening in Biomedical Research. *Nature Reviews Drug Discovery* 10, 188–95.

McKeown, M. 2012. *The Strategy Book*. Harlow: Pearson Education Limited.

Med Ad News. 1994–2011. Top Medicine Highlights. Annual reports.

Med Ad News. 2012a. May. Available at: http://www.pharmalive.com/ subscriptions/magazine.cfm?m=MN&issueDate=07%2F2012&from=%2F magazines%2Fmedad%2Fview.cfm%3FarticleID%3D11392 [accessed: 14 December 2012].

Med Ad News. 2012b. July. Available at: http://www.pharmalive.com/ subscriptions/magazine.cfm?m=MN&issueDate=07%2F2012&from=%2F magazines%2Fmedad%2Fview.cfm%3FarticleID%3D11392 [accessed: 14 December 2012].

Meekings, K.N., Williams C.S. and Arrowsmith J.E. 2012. Orphan Drug Development: An Economically Viable Strategy for Biopharma R&D. *Drug Discovery Today*, 17(July), 13–14. Available at: http://www.drugdiscovery today.com [accessed: 23 December 2012].

Melnikova, I. 2012. Rare Diseases and Orphan Drugs. *Nature Reviews Drug Discovery*, 11, 267–8.

Mestre-Ferrandiz, J., Sussex, J. and Towse, A. 2012. *The R&D Cost of a New Medicine*. London: Office of Health Economics.

Mukherjee, S. 2011. *The Emperor of all Maladies, A Biography of Cancer*. London: Fourth Estate.

Pammolli, P. Fabio, Magazzini, L. and Riccaboni, M. 2011. The Productivity Crisis in Pharmaceutical R&D. *Nature Reviews Drug Discovery*, 10, 428–38.

Pascheles, P. and Bogan, C. 2012. The Ultimate Business Model: Planning That Thousand Year Future. *Pharmaceutical Executive*, 32–7. Available at http://www.pharmexec.com/pharmexec/article/articleDetail.jsp?id=784899 [accessed: 14 December 2012].

Paul, S.M., Mytelka, D.S., Dunwiddie, C.T., Persinger, C.C., Munos, B.H., Lindborg, S.R. and A.L. Schacht. 2010. How to Improve R&D Productivity: The Pharmaceutical Industry's Grand Challenge. *Nature Reviews Drug Discovery*, 3, 203–14.

PCAST. 2011. *Report to the President on Propelling Innovation in Drug Discovery, U.S. Intellectual Property Enforcement Coordinator Annual Report on Intellectual Property Enforcement*. US President's Council of Advisors on Science and Technology. Available at: http://www.whitehouse.gov/sites/default/files/ microsites/ostp/pcast-fda-final.pdf [accessed: 16 December 2012].

Perrior, T. 2010. Overcoming Bottlenecks in Drug Discovery. *DDW* (Fall). Available at: http://www.ddw-online.com/drug-discovery/p146720-over coming-bottlenecks-in-drug-discoveryfall-10.html [accessed: 28 December 2012].

The Pharma Letter. 1996. *First Approval Of Eisai's Aricept For Alzheimer's*. Available at: http://www.thepharmaletter.com/file/17371/first-approval-of-eisais-aricept-for-alzheimers.html [accessed: 16 December 2012].

The Pharma Letter. 1998a. Merck's Singulair Cleared in USA for Asthma. Available at: http://www.thepharmaletter.com/file/87264/mercks-singulair-cleared-in-usa-for-asthma.html [accessed: 29 December 2012].

The Pharma Letter. 1998b. *Sanofi/B-MS Launch Plavix In First Market, USA*. Available at: http://www.thepharmaletter.com/file/9479/sanofib-ms-launch-plavix-in-first-market-usa.html [accessed: 16 December 2012].

The Pharma Letter. 2003. *First Launch, in Canada, for AstraZeneca's Superstatin Crestor*. Available at: http://www.thepharmaletter.com/file/77861/first-launch-in-canada-for-astrazenecas-superstatin-crestor.html [accessed: 2 January 2013].

Pharma Live. 2011. *Top 500 Prescription Medicines, A Special Report*. Available at: http://www.pharmalive.com/special_reports/sample.cfm?reportID=361 [accessed: 21 December 2012].

Pharma Times. 2012. *Sanofi's Smarter R&D Taps into Explosion of External Innovation*. Available at: http://www.pharmatimes.com/article/12-02-21/Sanofi_s_smarter_R_D_taps_into_explosion_of_external_innovation.aspx [accessed: 21 December 2012].

Pharmaprojects® Citeline. 2011a. *Pharma R&D Annual Review for 2011*. Available at: http://www.citeline.com/resource-center/whitepapers/ [accessed: 16 December 2012].

Pharmaprojects® Citeline. 2011b. *Peering into the Crystal Ball – A Year in Clinical Trial Outcomes*. Available at: http://www.citeline.com/thought-leadership/ [accessed: 18 December 2012].

Pharmaprojects® Citeline. 2012. *Pharmaceutical R&D Annual Review for 2012*. Available at: http://www.citeline.com/resource-center/whitepapers/ [accessed: 16 December 2012].

PhRMA. 2012. *PhRMA Member Companies Invested $49.5 Billion In Research and Development in 2011*. Pharmaceutical Research and Manufacturers of America. Available at: http://www.phrma.org/media/releases/phrma-member-companies-invested-49-5-billion-research-development-2011 [accessed: 16 December 2012].

Prahalad, C.K. and Hamel, G. 1990. The Core Competence of the Corporation. *Harvard Business Review*, May–June, 79–91.

PwC. 2012a. *Pharmaceutical and Life Sciences Industry Insights, PwC 15th Annual Global CEO Survey.* Available at: http://www.pwc.com/ceosurvey [accessed: 18 December 2012].

PwC. 2012b. *From Vision to Decision. Pharma 2020.* Available at: http://www.pwc.com/en_GX/gx/pharma-life-sciences/pharma2020/assets/pwc-pharma-success-strategies.pdf [accessed: 2 January 2013].

Scannell, J., Blanckley A., Boldon, H. and Warrington, B. 2012. Diagnosing the Decline in Pharmaceutical R&D Efficiency. *Nature Reviews Drug Discovery,* 11, 191–200.

Schering Corporation. 1989. 1988 Annual Report.

Scrip. 1990. Glaxo's Four Blockbusters. *Scrip World Pharmaceutical News,* 2 May, 1510, 15.

Scrip. 1996. Zyprexa Launched in USA. *Scrip World Pharmaceutical News,* 8 October, 2170, 19.

Scrip. 2000. AstraZeneca Announces Nexium Price. *Scrip World Pharmaceutical News,* 16 August, 2566, 20.

Scrip & Scrip Magazine. 1991–2003. Scrip's *Annual Review* issues.

Scrip Magazine. 2002. *Scrip's Review of 2001,* 2, 45.

Scrip World Pharmaceutical News. 1993. *Review of 1992.*

Sharma, R. 2012. Breakout Nations. In *Pursuit of New Economic Miracles.* New York: W.W. Norton.

Silverman, E. 2013. FDA Approved How Many New Drugs in 2012? *Pharmalot.* Available at: http://www.pharmalot.com/2013/01/fda-approved-how-many-new-drugs-in-2012/ [accessed: 3 January 2013].

Smith, B. 2011. *The Future of Pharma, Evolutionary Threats and Opportunities.* Basingstoke: Gower Publishing.

Stovall, S. 2011 Glaxo Scientists Brush Up on Sales Pitches. *Wall Street Journal,* 11 October. Available at: http://online.wsj.com/article/SB10001424052970203 499704576622423810621248.html [accessed: 20 December 2012].

Superbrands (UK) Ltd. 2012. Supplement to *The Guardian,* 3 March.

Swinney, D. and Anthony, J. 2011. How Were New Medicines Discovered? *Nature Reviews Drug Discovery,* 10, 507–19.

Royal Society. 2005. *Personalised Medicines: Hopes and Realities.* Available at: http://royalsociety.org/policy/publications/2005/personalised-medicines/ [accessed: 15 December 2012].

Timmerman, L. 2011. Eli Lilly CEO John Lechleiter on Tackling the Pharmaceutical R&D Crisis (Part 2) *BioBeat.* Available at: http://www.xconomy.com/national/2011/11/22/eli-lilly-ceo-john-lechleiter-on-tackling-the-pharmaceutical-rd-crisis-part-2/ [accessed: 16 December 2012].

Tufts CSDD. 2011. *Management Implications of the Global Regulatory Environment*. Tufts Center for the Study of Drug Development. Available at: http://csdd. tufts.edu/news/complete_story/rd_pr_august_2011/ [accessed: 28 December 2012].

Tufts CSDD Impact Report. 2012. *U.S. Offers Patients Faster, Greater Access to Cancer Drugs than Europe*. Available at: http://csdd.tufts.edu/files/uploads/ jul-aug_2012_ir_summary.pdf [accessed: 1 January 2013].

The 2012 EU Industrial R&D Investment Scoreboard. 2012. European Commission, JRC/DG Research & Innovation. Available at: http://ec.europa. eu/dgs/jrc/index.cfm?id=1410&dt_code=NWS&obj_id=15810&ori=RSS [accessed: 20 February 2013].

UN. 2011. Population Estimates and Projections Section. United Nations, Department of Economic and Social Affairs, Population Division, as quoted in DeVol, Bedroussian and Yeo, The Global Biomedical Industry: Preserving U.S. Leadership. *Milken Institute*. Available at http://www.milkeninstitute. org/pdf/CASMIFullReport.pdf [accessed: 14 December 2012].

Vernon, J.A., Golec, J.H. and Dimasi, J.A. 2010. Drug Development Costs When Financial Risk Is Measured Using the Fama-French Three-Factor Model, *Health Economics*, 19(8), 1002–5.

Wilsdon, T., Attridge, J., Fiz, E. and Ginoza, S. 2012. Policies That Encourage Innovation in Middle-Income Countries. *Charles River Associates*. Available at: http://www.ifpma.org/fileadmin/content/Publication/2012/CRA_Policies_ that_encourage_innovation_in_middle-income_countries_Web.pdf [accessed: 16 December 2012].

Withers & Rogers. 2012. Research Shows Gap in Patent Filing Activity for Biological Drugs and Small Molecules Is Widening. Available at: http:// www.withersrogers.com/news/242/113.

Young, A., Chaudhry H.J., Rhyne, J. and Dugan, M. 2011. A Census of Actively Licensed Physicians in the United States. *Journal of Medical Regulation*, 96(4), 10.

Index